Concepts in Communication

Concepts in Communication

Jimmie D. Trent

Miami University of Ohio

Judith S. Trent

University of Dayton

Daniel J. O'Neill

Youngstown State University

Allyn and Bacon, Inc.   Boston

Acknowledgements

"Rhetoric: Its Functions and Scope" by Donald C. Bryant, from *Quarterly Journal of Speech,* xxxix (December, 1953), 401–424. Reprinted by permission of the author and publisher.

"Toward a Meaning-Centered Philosophy of Communication" by Dean C. Barnlund, from *Journal of Communication,* v. 12, no. 4, 197–211. Reprinted by permission of the author and publisher.

"A Fresh Attitude Toward Rationalism" by Robert L. Scott, from *The Speech Teacher,* xvii (March, 1968), 134–139. Reprinted by permission of the author and publisher.

"The Substance of Rhetoric" by Karl R. Wallace, from *Quarterly Journal of Speech,* xlix (October, 1963), 239–249. Reprinted by permission of the author and publisher.

"The Problem of Style in Presidential Discourse" by Ronald H. Carpenter; printed by permission of the author.

"A Summary of Research on Order Effects in Communication" by Loren Anderson; printed by permission of the author.

"The Concept of Ethos and the Structure of Persuasion" by Paul I. Rosenthal, from *Speech Monographs,* xxxiii (June, 1966), 114–126. Reprinted by permission of the author and publisher.

"The Impact of Evidence on Decision-Making" by William R. Dresser, from *Journal of the American Forensic Association,* iii (May, 1966), 43–47. Reprinted by permission of the author and the publisher.

"A Summary of Experimental Research on the Effects of Evidence in Persuasive Communication" by James C. McCrosky, from *Quarterly Journal of Speech,* lv (April, 1969), 169–176. Reprinted by permission of the author and publisher.

"Evaluative and Formulative Functions in Speech Criticism" by Jon M. Ericson, from *Western Speech,* (summer, 1968), 173–176. Reprinted by permission of the author and publisher.

"Speech Criticism and American Culture" by Anthony Hillbruner, from Western Speech, (summer, 1968), 162–167. Reprinted by permission of the author and publisher.

"The Experimentalist as Critic" by Henry E. McGuckin, Jr., from *Western Speech,* (summer, 1968), 167–172. Reprinted by permission of the author and publisher.

"A Case Study in Speech Criticism: The Nixon-Truman Analog" by L. W. Rosenfield, from *Speech Monographs,* xxxv (November, 1968), 435–450. Reprinted by permission of the author and publisher.

"The Rhetoric of Protest: Song, Speech, and Attitude Change" by Stephen Kosokoff and Carl W. Carmichael, from *Southern Speech Journal,* xxxv (summer, 1970), 295–302. Reprinted by permission of the authors and the publisher.

"Solidarity Forever" (quoted in Kosokoff/Carmichael), in *Songs of the Workers: The Little Red Song Book* by Ruth Chaplin, (Chicago: Industrial Workers of the World,) 1956, p. 10. Reprinted by permission of Industrial Workers of the World, 2440 North Lincoln Avenue, Chicago, Illinois.

"I've Got Sixpence" (quoted in Kosokoff/Carmichael); reprinted by permission of E. Y. Harburg.

"Last Night I Had the Strangest Dream" (quoted in Kosokoff/Carmichael), see p. 241.

"An Interpersonal Ethic for Communication" by Paul W. Keller and Charles T. Brown, from *The Journal of Communication,* xviii (March, 1968), 73–81. Reprinted by permission of the authors and the publisher.

"Empathic Listening" by Charles M. Kelley, from *Small Group Communication: A Reader* (Dubuque, Iowa, 1970); reprinted by permission of the author.

"Defensive Communication" by Jack R. Gibb, from *The Journal of Communication,* 11 (September, 1971), 141–148. Reprinted by permission of the author and publisher.

"Interpersonal Trust in Small Group Communication" by Kim Giffin, from *Quarterly Journal of Speech,* liii (October, 1967), 224–234. Reprinted by permission of the author and publisher.

"When Angry, Look Again!" by Irving J. Lee, from *How to Talk with People,* (New York: Harper & Row 1952) 113–120. Copyright 1952 by Harper & Row, Publishers, Inc.; reprinted by permission of the publishers.

"A Man of Class" by Rev. Philip Jerome Cleveland (quoted in I. J. Lee), from Coronet, 1947, p. 45. Reprinted by permission of Esquire, Inc.; © 1947 by Esquire, Inc.

"The Black Bag" by John W. Keltner. This brief resume of a series of events that took place in the classroom of Dr. Charles S. Goetzinger at Oregon State University in the spring of 1967 is reprinted with permission of the publisher from *Interpersonal Speech-Communication* by John W. Keltner. © 1970 by Wadsworth Publishing Company, Inc., Belmont, California.

Contents

Concepts of Communication Criticism **183**

Part

3.

Preface

As the title suggests, this is a book about some major concepts in speech communication. It is not a book of rules to follow in a communication project; rather, it is a collection of ideas and information, gathered from various sources, which should aid students in formulating their own methods of improving communication.

This book should thus be viewed as an introduction to the academic field of speech communication. Each reading reprinted here first appeared in a journal or book written or edited by a scholar in speech communication. The five original essays were written by persons currently active in teaching students of speech communication.

Some of the readings are based upon research methods which are traditional in the field of speech. The concepts stated in the traditionally-oriented readings are derived primarily from critical studies of speakers and their messages in an historical context. Wallace's essay on good reasons and Scott's on rationalism are examples of emphasis on message construction.

Other readings are based on empirical studies of the effects of varying communication attempts. The primary emphasis is on audience or listener behavior, and the concepts represent conclusions about conditions which affect the understanding or acceptance of messages. McCroskey's work on evidence and Kelly's conclusions about listening are examples of the communication approach.

The derivation of concepts from both the traditional and the communication approaches reflects the editors' belief that students should understand both in order to become purposeful and effective communicators. It is important to gain a better understanding of the communication and interaction process, and of listeners, in order to become a better communicator.

An introduction precedes each of the four major sections. The introductions survey the concepts in the appropriate sections and show the relationships between the concepts and the process of becoming a skilled, responsible communicator.

For those who wish to do further reading, references are suggested at the end of each article. A summary of key concepts of communication is included following the final major section.

The editors wish to thank Dr. Loren Anderson and Dr. Ronald Carpenter for preparing original articles for publication in this volume. We are also grateful to those credited on the "acknowledgements" page for permission to reprint articles and readings.

Finally, the editors wish to thank Allen K. Workman and Frank Ruggirello of Allyn and Bacon, Inc. Their suggestions have been invaluable.

Jimmie D. Trent
Judith S. Trent
Daniel J. O'Neill

Part 1.

Concepts
Of
Communication

1.

Introduction (by Jimmie D. Trent). If you are beginning the study of speech-communication, you may possibly have some preconceived ideas about the content of the course. You may have either taken or heard about high school speech courses such as debate, oratory, extemporaneous speaking, or interpretative reading. You perhaps know that many speech courses help students gain confidence before groups, improve delivery in speaking, and learn speech preparation.

Your previous speech courses may have taken a narrow, simplified, rule-following approach to developing better speakers or readers. Many speech textbooks have been called "cookbooks" because the rules for successful speaking are presented as if they were recipes (if you follow these steps, you will become a skilled speaker).

Rules have been stipulated for the speaker in such areas as delivery ("It should be extemporaneous and conversational"), voice control ("It should be resonant, contain variety, and articulation should be clean"), and bodily movement ("Movement should have meaning and appear natural"). Rules have often been stipulated for the development of the message: (It is to be organized according to prescribed forms, follow the rules of logic, contain appropriate types of support material and visual aids, and utilize stylistic devices).

It is not surprising that the rule book approach has formed the image for the study of speech, since so many people who have studied public speaking have never gotten beyond the "rules." In the past, most high school courses and a great many basic college courses have been devoted to this approach. If a student were to get beyond rules, he had to become a speech major in college or, in many cases, take graduate courses. The great body of theory and research underlying the traditional approach to speech has been concealed from elementary students as they learned the rules. Adaptation to the audience was considered important but skills prescribed by rules absorbed most of the time.

Speech has traditionally been considered a liberal art, with historical roots in classical rhetoric and with scholarship devoted to intensive study of the practices of successful public speakers. The findings of such research have formed the basis for rule formulation. Even the most basic speech texts give evidence of this background in the form of excerpts from Aristotle's *Rhetoric* and from such famous speakers as Daniel Webster or John F. Kennedy. Some rhetorical principles were derived from the findings of psychological research but the core of knowledge used by traditionalists has been derived from historically-oriented research.

Traditionally, the study of speech concentrated on public speaking, with the speaker and his message receiving primary emphasis. When traditional speech scholars did concern themselves with interpersonal relations, they usually did so in the context of discussion. John Dewey's reflective thinking pattern was, for many years, the only accepted means of progression in decision-making. That argumentation formed a major portion of discussion textbooks is indicative of the emphasis which was placed upon message formulation.

Thus the field of speech was devoted almost exclusively to public speaking, rules of behavior for speakers, and techniques for developing messages. Audiences in general and individual listeners in particular, while not totally ignored, did not receive emphasis proportional to speakers and messages from traditional speech theorists. While the field has moved from this emphasis, many of these traditional concerns are still basic issues that need attention.

One of the best statements of the traditional approach to speech is Donald C. Bryant's 1953 article, "Rhetoric: Its Functions and Its Scope." Professor Bryant's article gives a better understanding of the nature and scope of the traditional approach to speech than is generally available in basic speech courses. A reading of his article will show his reliance upon the theoretical formulations of Aristotle and other rhetoricians since classical times. His description and definition of rhetoric reflects the speaker-message orientation of the traditional approach. Bryant's emphasis is primarily upon persuasion, and his statement of ethics justifies the study of methods for influencing the attitudes and actions of others. The relationship of rhetoric to other fields of study or activity is discussed. And while the traditional principles of rhetoric are derived primarily from historical study of theories and men, Bryant reflects the ever-present concern of most traditionalists with applying knowledge from other academic fields, particularly psychology.

In the decade of the 1960's, a school of thought which emphasized empirical study of the communication process gained prominence in the speech field. By 1970, the influence of the communication scholars had become so great that the name of the national organization of speech scholars was changed from the Speech Association of America to the Speech Communication Association. To a large extent, the communication approach represents a natural progression away from traditional theorizing *about* speech, and toward a concern for applying principles of behavior derived from the social sciences. The modern specialist in speech communication is a social scientist whose concentration of interest is on communication between people.

Scholars in speech communication concentrate their research on studying audiences and individual listeners. It is not that speakers and messages are considered to be unimportant; they are considered as variables which affect audience attitudes, understanding, and behavior.

Concepts of speech communication today are derived from empirical measurements of listener behavior under conditions where speaker-message variables can be precisely described, if not controlled or manipulated, by a researcher or experimenter.

Where the emphasis of traditional speech scholars has been primarily in the context of public speaking, the study of speech communication scholars has extended to the context of two-way communication events such as small group discussions, interviews, negotiations, and interactions within organizations.

Speech communication specialists have become less concerned with rules for constructing and delivering messages, and more with how people affect people and how meanings are derived from messages. They have emphasized the multitude of variables which have not been traditionally taught as a part of the "art of speaking."

The second article in Part One contains a proposal for revising the field of speech into a broadly based field of speech communication. Dean C. Barnlund in "Toward a Meaning-Centered Philosophy of Communication," criticizes teachers in the field of speech who assume a "superficial, or narrow, or opportunistic concept of communication." He objects to the listener being regarded as a passive object while emphasis is placed on speakers and messages. Barnlund's meaning-centered philosophy of communication "admits that meaning in the sender, and the words of the message are important, but regards as most critical the state of mind, the assumptive world and the needs of the listener or observer."

After objecting that (as of the writing of his paper in 1961) "there is little in the traditional view of speech that is helpful in the analysis of conversation, interviewing, conflict negotiations, or in the diagnosis of the whole span of communication disorders and breakdowns that are receiving so much attention currently," Barnlund outlines five broad guidelines for approaching the study of communication.

Barnlund approaches the ethics of communication from the viewpoint of invading the private world of the listener. He calls for communication that "is entirely consistent with the protection and improvement of man's symbolic experience."

While the views stated by Barnlund have gained wide acceptance among speech communication scholars, others still emphasize communication which is intended to gain belief or change attitudes. And many curriculum offerings still place primary emphasis on the teaching of public speaking.

Nevertheless, the influence of communication theorists and scholars is great throughout the field. Public speaking is still taught but, beginning with Raymond S. Ross's *Speech Communication* (first published in 1965), the models and principles of communication theory have appeared in an increasingly large percentage of public speaking textbooks. And while some message-centered courses such as argumentation are still offered at most institutions, other courses (e.g., discussion) have reduced or eliminated message orientation as empirically derived findings gained prominence. Meanwhile, the curricula of many speech departments in the 1960's and early 1970's introduced new courses in interpersonal communication.

Central to the new approaches to teaching speech communication is an understanding of the complex process of communication between human beings. In the third article in Part One, Jimmie D. Trent and Judith S. Trent present a verbal-pictorial model of the process of human communication. While their model can only suggest the complexity of the communication process, it does emphasize that speakers formulate ideas and listeners reformulate ideas. And while the multitude of variables which affect the formulation and reformulation of ideas can not be exhaustively treated here, enough are presented to give you an overview of the process sufficient to begin your study of communication.

Does the change in the speech-communication field mean that the rules are no longer of any value to you? While some communication scholars would argue against the learning of rules, this book's material does not particularly lead to that conclusion. The material here will certainly show that the rules can be overemphasized. It will also show that knowledge of the rules alone or acquisition of the traditionally taught skills alone is not enough to prepare you for the communication situations which you are likely to encounter. It will particularly point to an obligation to place primary emphasis on your listener when you prepare a communication attempt. But you will still find there is value in developing skills of delivery, organization, support, and language usage. After you understand your listener and the process involved in his reformulation of ideas, you will have to select the type and form of signal you will send to represent your idea. As you develop skills, you increase the range of signals from which you can choose. While increasing your range of skills, you must still understand the full communication context if you are to maximize your chances of success.

Rhetoric: Its Functions and Its Scope

Donald C. Bryant

When a certain not always ingenuous radio spokesman for one of our large industrial concerns some years ago sought to reassure his audience on the troublesome matter of propaganda, his comfort ran thus: Propaganda, after all, is only a word for anything one says for or against anything. Either everything, therefore, is propaganda, or nothing is propaganda; so why worry?

The more seriously I take this assignment from the Editor to reexplore for the *Quarterly Journal of Speech* (1953), the ground surveyed by Hudson and Wichelns thirty years ago, and since crossed and recrossed by many another, including myself,[1] the nearer I come to a position like our friend's conclusion on propaganda. When I remember Quintilian's *Institutes* at one extreme of time, and lose myself in Kenneth Burke's "new rhetoric" at the other, I am almost forced to the position that whatever we do or say or write, or even think, in explanation of anything, or in support, or in extenuation, or in despite of anything, evinces rhetorical symptoms. Hence, either everything worth mentioning is rhetorical, or nothing is; so let's talk about something encompassable—say logic, or

Note: [In December, 1953, when this article appeared,] Mr. Bryant (Ph.D., Cornell, 1937) [was] Professor of English and Speech at Washington University, St. Louis. As Associate Editor of *QJS*, he made many scholarly contributions to literary and rhetorical criticism, including notably *Edmund Burke and His Literary Friends* (Washington University Studies—New Series Language and Literature—No. 9, December, 1939).

[1] Hoyt H. Hudson, "The Field of Rhetoric," *QJSE,* IX (April 1923), 167–180; Herbert A. Wichelns, "The Literary Criticism of Oratory," *Studies in Rhetoric and Public Speaking in Honor of James Albert Winans* (New York, 1925), pp. 181–216; Donald C. Bryant, "Some Problems of Scope and Method in Rhetorical Scholarship," *QJS*, XXIII (April 1937), 182–188, and "Aspects of the Rhetorical Tradition," *QJS*, XXXVI (April and October 1950), 169–176, 316–332.

semantics, or persuasion, or linguistics, or scientific method, or poetics, or social psychology, or advertising, or salesmanship, or public relations, or pedagogy, or politics, or psychiatry, or symbolics—or propaganda.

But that is not the assignment. Others have dealt with those subjects, and have given us such illuminating definitive essays as "Speech as a Science" by Clarence Simon,[2] "The Spoken Word and the Great Unsaid" by Wendell Johnson,[3] "General Semantics[1955]" by Irving Lee,[4] and many other interpretive essays and *apologiae* for the various branches of our curricula and for the multiform captions in our departmental catalogues and organization charts. Among these, "Rhetoric and Public Address" can hardly be thought neglected over the years, at least in the *QJS* and *SM*. But perhaps we have assumed too quickly that rhetoric is now at last well understood. On the other hand, Hudson's "The Field of Rhetoric" may be inaccessible or out of date, and Burke's "new rhetoric" too cumbersome or recondite in statement, even after Marie Hochmuth's admirable exposition of it.[5] Even if all this be true, however, one can hardly hope to clarify here what may remain obscure in the work of thirty years—or twenty centuries; but in proper humility, no doubt one can try. At least, common practice seems to presume a restatement of most complex ideas about once in a generation.

I shall not undertake to summarize Hudson's or Wichelns' pioneer essays, relevant as they are to the central problem. They and certain others like Hunt's "Plato and Aristotle on Rhetoric"[6] are by now woven into the fabric of our scholarship. Nor shall I try to duplicate the coverage of my two papers on "Aspects of the Rhetorical Tradition." They can be easily reread by anyone interested.

One further limitation upon the scope of this essay seems necessary: I shall not try to present a digest of rhetoric or even an explanation of the main principles of rhetorical method. Those are also easily available, from Aristotle's *Rhetoric* to the newest textbook in persuasion. Furthermore, I intend to discuss no particular system of rhetoric, but the functions and scope which any system will embrace.

[2] *QJS*, XXXVII (October 1951), 281–298.

[3] *Ibid.* (December 1951), 419–429.

[4] *QJS*, XXXVIII (February 1952), 1–12.

[5] *Ibid.* (April 1952), 133–144.

[6] *Studies . . . in Honor of James Albert Winans*, pp. 3–60.

CONFUSION IN MEANING OF "RHETORIC"

problems in defining
rhetoric

Very bothersome problems arise as soon as one attempts to define rhetoric, problems that lead so quickly to hair-splitting on the one hand or cosmic inclusiveness on the other, and to ethical or moral controversy, that the attempt usually ends in trifling with logomachies, gloss on Aristotle, or flat frustration. *Rhetoric* is a word in common parlance, as well as in technical use in the SAA and the Chicago school of literary critics. Hence we may presume it to have meanings which must be reckoned with, however vague, various, and disparate; for a word means what responsible users make it mean. Various as the meanings are, however, one occasionally encounters uses which seem little short of perverse, in persons who ought to know better. Not long since, a doctoral candidate in the classics, who had written as his dissertation a "rhetorical" analysis of one of St. Paul's sermons, was asked how Aristotle had defined rhetoric. Though the question, it would appear, was relevant, the candidate was unable to answer satisfactorily. Whereupon the questioner was taken firmly to task by one of his fellow examiners and was told that after all rhetoric could be adequately defined as a *way of saying something.* Now of course rhetoric may be so defined, as poetic may be defined as a way of making something; but there is little intellectual profit in either definition.

restricted
interpretations
of rhetoric

Rhetoric also enjoys several other meanings which, though more common and less perverse, serve to make analysis of it difficult. In general these are the same meanings which Hudson reviewed thirty years ago: bombast; high-sounding words without content; oratorical falsification to hide meaning; sophistry; ornamentation and the study of figures of speech; most commonly among academic folk, Freshman English; and finally, least commonly of all, the whole art of spoken discourse, especially persuasive discourse. This last meaning has gained somewhat in currency in thirty years, especially among scholars in speech and renaissance literature.[7] During the same period the use of the term *rhetoric* (or the combinations *composition and rhetoric* and *grammar and rhetoric*) to label courses and textbooks in Freshman English has somewhat

[7] In his *The Ethics of Rhetoric* (Chicago: Henry Regnery, 1953), which has appeared since this article has been in proof, Richard M. Weaver of the College at the University of Chicago makes an interesting and useful effort to restore rhetoric to a central and respectable position among the arts of language and to assign it the function of giving effectiveness to truth.

declined, and simultaneously the "rhetorical" content of them has declined also. The tendency now is to prefer just *Composition* or *English Composition,* or to resort to such loaded names as *Basic Writing, Effective Writing, Problems in Writing, Writing with a Purpose,* or *Communication and Analysis.*

In one of his early speeches, President Eisenhower declared that we want action from the Russians, not rhetoric, as evidence of their desire for peaceful settlement. Here is the common use of *rhetoric* to mean empty language, or language used to deceive, without honest intention behind it. Without question this use is in harmony with the current climate of meaning where what our opponents say is rhetoric, and what we say is something else. Hence our attempt to define rhetoric leads almost at once into questions of morals and ethics.

Rhetoric as figures of speech or artificial elegance of language is also a healthy perennial, nurtured in literary scholarship and criticism as well as lay comment. Hence the second of the two meanings of *rhetorical* in *Webster's New Collegiate Dictionary* is "emphasizing style, often at the expense of thought." Here we encounter a second obscuring or limiting factor in our attempt at definition. We are to describe rhetoric in terms of those elements of a verbal composition for which it is to be held responsible. This mode of procedure has always been attractive. It can produce interesting and plausible conclusions, and it can be defended as schematically satisfying and pedagogically convenient. Thus it proved in the *trivium* of the middle ages and renaissance. If grammar has charge of the correctness of discourse, and if logic has charge of the intellectual content, then it is natural to assign to rhetoric the management of the language of discourse (or the *elocutio*), and if we do not include poetic in our system, the imaginative and emotional content also.

Another definition in the *New Collegiate Dictionary* points to the identification of rhetoric not with the elements of verbal composition but with the *forms* or *genres:* "The art of expressive speech or of discourse, orig. of oratory, now esp. of literary composition; esp., the art of writing well in prose, as disting. from versification and elocution." This approach is promising and on the whole the most popular through the ages. "Originally of oratory, now especially the art of writing well in prose—" this phrase does well enough as a general description of the scope of rhetoric in ancient Greece, as Baldwin has pointed out, when prose itself was virtually defined as oratory and history, and when even history was composed largely in the spirit of oratory. That is, rhetoric could be the art of prose when prose was predominantly concerned with the intentional, directional energizing of truth, of finding in any given situation all the available means of persuasion, and of using as many of them as good sense dictated.

Even then, however, the weakness of genres as the basis for constructing theories or writing handbooks was evident. What is the art of Plato's dialogues, which are in prose? or of Sappho's compositions, which are poems? Neither poetic nor rhetoric is adequate to either. The difficulty multiplies as variety in the kinds of compositions increases in Roman, renaissance, and modern times, and as print supplements—and often supplants—speech as the medium of verbal communication. As *poetic,* the art of imitation in language, became crystallized in Roman and renaissance learning as the theory and practice of the drama (especially tragedy) and the epic, so *rhetoric,* in Quintilian's and Cicero's theory the whole operative philosophy of civil leadership, showed in practice as the art of making winning speeches in the law courts, or later in public exhibitions. The very doctrine in rhetoric of the epideictic or ceremonial speech, as I shall show later, is excellent evidence of the weakness of the types or *genres* as the basis for definition.

All these meanings of rhetoric, in spite of their limitations, contribute something to the exposition of our subject, and the pursuit of each has yielded lucrative insights into the subject, or at least into the problem. Some of them, especially rhetoric as bombast, as excessive ornamentation, and as deceit, are evidence of the falling off of rhetoricians from time to time from the broad philosophy of the art which they inherited from the founders. For a redefinition, therefore, I know no better way of beginning than to return to that broad philosophy.

WORKING DEFINITION OF RHETORIC

rhetoric: the rationale
of informative and
suasory discourse

First of all and primarily, therefore, I take rhetoric to be the *rationale* of *informative and suasory discourse.* All its other meanings are partial or morally-colored derivatives from that primary meaning. This rhetoric has been, at least since Aristotle; and at least since Aristotle there has existed a comprehensive, fundamental codification of its principles. It would be idolatrous to suggest that Aristotle uttered the first and last authentic words on rhetoric, or that his system is still adequate, or that it was completely satisfactory even for the Greeks of his day. Like his poetic theory, however, it enjoys unequalled scientific eminence in its field though it has sustained many additions and modifications through the centuries. Its limitations are historical rather than philosophical. Like the limitations of his poetic, the limitations of his rhetoric derive mainly from his failure to consider phenomena which had not yet occurred and to make use of learnings which had not yet been developed.

Now as then, therefore, what Aristotle said of the nature and principles of public address, of the discovery of all the available means of persuasion in any given case, must stand as the broad background for any sensible rhetorical system. Much of Aristotle's formulation, even in detail, survives ungainsaid and can only be rearranged and paraphrased by subsequent writers. Again to cite a parallel with his poetic: though the relative importance of plot in drama has shifted radically since Aristotle, when good plots are made their excellences will still be best discovered by the application of Aristotle's criteria. Similarly, though modern psychology is very different from that of the Greeks, and doubtless more scientific, modern enlightenment has produced no new method of analyzing an audience which can replace Aristotle's.

Aristotle's work as background for sensible rhetorical systems

Aristotle, however, identified rhetoric with persuasion. His chief interests lay in the speaking to popular audiences in the law court and in the legislative assembly, and his system of classification and analysis obviously was framed with those types of speaking as its principal object. Some means of persuasion, however, in spite of Aristotle's comprehensive definition, are not within the scope of rhetoric. Gold and guns, for example, are certainly persuasive, and the basic motives which make them persuasive, profit and self-preservation, may enter the field of rhetoric; but applied directly to the persons to be persuaded, guns and gold belong to commerce or coercion, not to rhetoric.

No more shall we admit the persuasive use of all symbols as belonging to rhetoric. Undoubtedly the persuasive force of pictures, colors, designs, non-language sounds such as fog horns and fire alarms, and all such devices of symbolic significance is great and useful. Traffic lights, however, are not normally agents of rhetorical influence. No more, in themselves, are elephants, donkeys, lions, illuminated bottles of whiskey, or animated packs of cigarettes. Their use has a kinship to rhetoric, and when they are organized in a matrix of verbal discourse, they become what Aristotle called the extrinsic or non-artistic means of persuasion. They are instru-

definition of rhetoric limited to discourse

ments of the wielder of public opinion, and they are staples of two techniques which must be recognized as strongly rhetorical—advertising and propaganda. Unless we are to claim practically all interhuman activity as the field of rhetoric, however, some limits must be admitted, even within the field of persuasion. True, in the "new rhetoric" of Kenneth Burke, where the utmost extension rather than practical limit-setting is the aim, any manifestation of "identification," conscious or unconscious, is within rhetoric. Though the classic limitations of rhetoric are too narrow, others are too broad. Therefore I am assuming the traditional limitation to discourse.

Aristotle included exposition as well as persuasion

Let us look now at Aristotle's apparent failure to include exposition as well as persuasion within rhetoric. Ancillary to persuasion, of course, exposition is clearly included. The idea of *demonstration,* the characteristic result of the logical mode, implies the most perfect exposition for audiences susceptible of reasoned instruction. Furthermore, another aspect of Aristotle's system admits exposition to independent status. At the expense of a slight venture into heresy (though I believe only a benign heresy) I suggest that any systematic construction of human phenomena, even Aristotle's, will either leave out something important and significant, or will include a category, however named, which is, in effect, "miscellaneous." That I think Aristotle did in discussing the rhetoric of the ceremonial or epideictic speech. The success of his categories, even so, is remarkable. The extension and effective application to the ceremonial speech in general of the principles of the persuasive speech whose end is active decision, provide very plausible coverage of that somewhat anomalous form. The threefold, tripartite classification of speeches was too nearly perfect to abandon:

Forensic (time, past; ends, justice and injustice; means, accusation and defense.)

Epideictic (time, present; ends, honor and dishonor; means, praise and blame.)

Deliberative (time, future; ends, the expedient and inexpedient; means, exhortation and dehortation.)

When the problems of what to do with time-present in the system, and with Pericles' funeral oration among the observed phenomena had to be solved, the coincidence was too attractive to be resisted. It provided for a piece of practical realism which no system should be allowed to defeat. Through that adjustment Aristotle admitted within the scope of rhetoric the predominantly literary performance on the one hand and gave an opening on the other for the primarily informative and instructional as well as the demonstrative and exhibitionistic. Through this third category rhetoric embraces, in a persuasion-centered system, the *docere* and *delectare,* the teach and delight, of the Roman and renaissance rhetoric-poetic and permits them an independent status outside their strictly ancillary or instrumental functions in persuasion.

Aristotle's system, therefore, and his rationale of effective speaking comprehend with very little violence the art of the good man skilled in speaking of Cicero and Quintilian, or Baldwin's equation of rhetoric to the art of prose whose end is giving effectiveness to truth[8]—effectiveness considered in terms of what happens to an audience, usually a popular or lay audience as distinguished from the specialized or technical audience of the scientific or dialectical demonstration. This distinction, strictly speaking, is a practical rather than a logical limitation, a limitation of degree rather than kind. No matter what the audience, when the speaker evinces skill in getting into their minds, he evinces rhetorical skill.

If the breadth of scope which I have assigned to rhetoric is implicit in Aristotle's system, the basic delimitation of that scope finds early and explicit statement there. Rhetoric is not confined in application to any specific subjects which are exclusively its own. Rhetoric is method, not subject. But if it has no special subjects, neither are all subjects within its province. In its suasory phase, at least, rhetoric is concerned, said Aristotle, only with those questions about which men dispute, that is, with the contingent—that which is dependent in part upon factors which cannot be known for certain, that which can be otherwise. Men do not dispute about what is known or certainly knowable by them. Hence the characteristic concern of rhetoric is broadly with questions of justice and injustice, of the expedient and the inexpedient (of the desirable and undesirable, of the good and the bad), of praise and blame, or honor and dishonor.

rhetoric is method, not subject

To questions such as these and their almost infinite subsidiary questions, vital and perennial as they are in the practical operation of human society, the best answers can never be certain but only more or less probable. In reasoning about them, men at best must usually proceed from probable premise to probable conclusion, seldom from universal to universal.

[8] *Ancient Rhetoric and Poetic* (New York, 1924), p. 5.

Hence Aristotle described the basic instrument of rhetoric, the enthymeme, as a kind of syllogism based on probabilities and signs.

rhetoric concerns
human affairs, not
scientific certainties

Rhetoric, therefore, is distinguished from the other instrumental studies in its preoccupation with informed opinion rather than with scientific demonstration. It is the counterpart, said Aristotle, of dialectic. Strictly speaking, dialectic also may be said to attain only probability, not scientific certainty, like physics (and, perhaps, theology). The methodology, however, is the methodology of formal logic and it deals in universals. Hence it arrives at a very high degree of probability, for it admits the debatable only in the assumption of its premises. Rhetoric, however, because it normally deals with matters of uncertainty for the benefit of popular audiences, must admit probability not only in its premises but in its method also. This is the ground upon which Plato first, and hundreds of critics since, have attacked rhetoric—that it deals with opinion rather than knowledge. This is the ground also from which certain scholars have argued,[9] after some of the mediaeval fathers, that rhetoric really deals, characteristically, not with genuine probability but only with adumbration and suggestion. It is, they say, distinguished from dialectic in *degree* of probability—dialectic very high, and rhetoric very low.

The epistemological question is interesting, and in a world of philosophers where only certain knowledge was ever called upon to decide questions of human behavior, it would be the central question. Rhetoric exists, however, because a world of certainty is not the world of human affairs. It exists because the world of human affairs is a world where there must be an alternative to certain knowledge on the one hand and pure chance or whimsey on the other. The alternative is informed opinion, the nearest approach to knowledge which the circumstances of decision in any given case will permit. The art, or science, or method whose realm this is, is rhetoric. Rhetoric, therefore, is the method, the strategy, the organon of the principles for deciding best the undecidable questions, for arriving at solutions of the unsolvable problems, for instituting method in those vital phases of human activity where no method is inherent in the total subject-matter of decision. The resolving of such problems is the province of the "Good man skilled in speaking." It always has been, and it is still. Of that

[9] For example, Craig La Drière, "Rhetoric as 'Merely Verbal' Art," *English Institute Essays—1948,* ed. by D. A. Robertson, Jr. (New York, 1949), pp. 123–152.

there can be little question. And the comprehensive rationale of the functioning of that good man so far as he is skilled in speaking, so far as he is a wielder of public opinion, is rhetoric.

THE PROBLEMS OF VOCABULARY IN THIS ESSAY

Traditionally *rhetoric* and *oratory* have been the standard terms for the theory and the product. The *rhetor* was the speaker, the addresser of the public, or the teacher of speaking; the *rhetorician,* the teacher of rhetoric or the formulator of the principles of rhetoric. Hence the special bias of the terms as I use them has been and probably still is oral. That is a practical bias and is not carelessly to be thrown away. From the beginning of publication in writing, however, essentially rhetorical performances, whether already spoken or to be spoken, have been committed to paper and circulated to be read rather than heard—from Isocrates' *Panathenaicus* or Christ's *Sermon on the Mount* to Eisenhower's message on the state of the nation. Furthermore, for centuries now, especially since the invention and cheapening of the art of printing, the agitator, the teacher, the preacher, the wielder of public opinion has used the press quite independently of the platform. Hence, obviously, rhetoric must be understood to be the rationale of informative and suasory discourse both spoken and written: of Milton's *Aeropagitica* as well as Cromwell's Address to the Rump Parliament; of John Wilkes' *North Briton* as well as Chatham's speech on the repeal of the Stamp Act; of Tom Paine's *Common Sense* as much as Patrick Henry's Address to the Virginia Assembly; of Swift's pamphlet on the *Conduct of the Allies* as well as Dr. Sacheverell's sermon on Passive Obedience; of George Sokolsky's syndicated columns in the press equally with Edward R. Murrow's radio commentaries or Kenneth McFarland's appearances before conventions of the Chambers of Commerce. I will use *rhetoric* and *rhetorical* with that breadth of scope.

> rhetoric: includes both spoken and written discourse

Furthermore, the terms *orator* and *oratory* have taken on, like *rhetoric* itself, rather limited or distorted meanings, not entirely undeserved perhaps, which make them no longer suitable for the designation of even the normal *oral* rhetorical performance. *Practitioner of public address,* or some such hyphenated monstrosity as *speaker-writer,* might be used as a generic term for the product of rhetoric, but the disadvantages of such manipulations of vocabulary are obvious. I am using the terms *speech* and *speaker* for both written and oral performance and written and oral performer, unless the particular circumstances obviously imply one or the other. Likewise, in place of such a formula as *listener-reader,* I shall use *audience,* a usage not uncommon anyway.

One must face still another problem of vocabulary, that of the term *rhetoric* in the three distinguishable senses in which I use it: (1) as the rationale of informative and suasory discourse, a body of principle and precept for the creation and analysis of speeches; (2) as a quality which characterizes that kind of discourse and distinguishes it from other kinds; (3) as a study of the phenomenon of informative and suasory discourse in the social context. Similarly, I fear, the term *rhetorician* will sometimes mean the formulator and philosopher of rhetorical theory; sometimes the teacher of the technique of discourse; sometimes the speaker with rhetorical intention; and finally the student or scholar whose concern is the literary or social or behavioral study of rhetoric. I have been tempted to invent terms to avoid certain of these ambiguities, such as *logology,* or even *rhetoristic* (parallel with *sophistic*), but the game would probably not be worth the candle.

In summary, rhetoric is the rationale of informative and suasory discourse, it operates chiefly in the areas of the contingent, its aim is the attainment of maximum probability as a basis for public decision, it is the organizing and animating principle of all subject-matters which have a relevant bearing on that decision. Now let us turn to the question of the subject-matters in which rhetoric most characteristically functions and of the relations it bears to special subject-matters.

SUBJECTS OF RHETORICAL DISCOURSE

rhetorical discourse
includes virtually all
subjects

Wrote Aristotle, "The most important subjects of general deliberation . . . are practically five, viz. finance, war and peace, the defense of the country, imports and exports, and legislation." This is still the basic list, though legislation now would be far more generally inclusive than it was to the Athenian assembly. In addition, within the scope of rhetorical discourse fall the subjects of forensic address—crime and its punishment and all the concerns of justice and injustice. Furthermore, the concerns of teaching, preaching—moral, intellectual, practical, and spiritual instruction and exhortation—and commercial exploitation, wherever the problems of adaptation of idea and information to the group mind are concerned, depend upon rhetorical skill for their fruition. Thus we are brought again to the position that the rhetorical factor is pervasive in the operative aspects of society.

Does this mean that the speaker must be a specialist in all subjects, as well as in rhetorical method? Cicero seemed willing to carry the demands thus far, at least in establishing his ideal orator; and this implication has been ridiculed from Plato onwards for the purpose of discrediting first the claims of the sophists and then all men "skilled in speaking." Plainly, in practice and in plausible human situations, the suggestion is absurd. Does the public speaker or the columnist or the agitator have to be a military specialist in order rightly to urge peace or war? Does the citizen have to be a dentist and a chemist and a pathologist intelligently to advocate the use of fluorine in the municipal water supply? He does not become a specialist in these fields, of course, any more than the head of an industrial plant is the technical master of the specialties of all the men who serve under him. "He attempts to learn the authorities and sources of information in each, and to develop a method which he can apply to specific problems as they arise. He learns, in any given situation, what questions to ask and to answer. The peculiar contribution of the rhetorician is the discovery and use, to the common good, of those things which move men to [understanding and] action."[10] Looked at another way, the relation of rhetoric to the subject-matters of economics, or public health, or theology, or chemistry, or agriculture is like the relation of hydraulic engineering to water, under the specific circumstances in which the engineer is to construct his dam or his pumping station or his sewage system, and in view of the specific results he is to obtain. He develops a method for determining what questions to ask and answer from all that which can be known about water. If he is a good hydraulics engineer, he will see to it that his relevant knowledge is sound, as the good speaker will see to it that his relevant knowledge of hydraulic engineering is the best obtainable if he is to urge or oppose the building of a dam in the St. Lawrence River. If either is ignorant, or careless, or dishonest, he is culpable as a man and as a rhetorician or hydraulics engineer.

It was not the scientific chronologist, the astronomer Lord Macclesfield, who secured the adoption in England of the Gregorian calendar, thoroughly as he understood the subject in all its mathematical, astronomical, and chronometrical as-

a speaker, although not a specialist, must be informed

rhetorician develops methods to find relevant and reliable knowledge

---

[10] Hudson, "Field of Rhetoric," *QJSE,* IX (April 1923), 177.

pects. It was the Earl of Chesterfield, learning from the chronologist all that was essential to the particular situation, and knowing rhetoric and the British Parliament, who was able to impress upon his fellows not necessarily the validity of the calculations but the desirability and the feasibility of making a change. If the truth of scientific knowledge had been left to its own inherent force with Parliament, we would doubtless be many more days out of phase with the sun than England was in 1751. As Aristotle observed in his brief and basic justification of rhetoric, truth itself has a tendency to prevail over error; but in competition with error, where skillful men have an interest in making error prevail, truth needs the help of as attractive and revealing a setting as possible. In the Kingdom of Heaven, truth may be its own sole advocate, but it needs mighty help if it is to survive in health among the nations on earth. As Fielding wrote of prudence in *Tom Jones:* "It is not enough that your designs, nay, that your actions, are intrinsically good; you must take care that they shall appear so. If your inside be never so beautiful, you must preserve a fair outside also. This must be constantly looked to."[11]

rhetoric: concerned with making appearance match reality

In this sense even honest rhetoric is fundamentally concerned with appearances, not to the disregard of realities as Plato and his successors have industriously charged, but to the enforcement of realities. Rhetoric at the command of honest men strives that what is desirable shall appear desirable, that what is vicious shall appear vicious. It intends that the true or probably true shall seem so, that the false or doubtful shall be vividly realized for what it is. A bridge or an automobile or a clothes-line must not only *be* strong but must *appear* to be so. This fact has been an obstacle to the use of many new structural materials. Accustomed to an older kind, we have been reluctant to accept the adequacy of a new, more fragile-seeming substance. Hence one important reason for surrounding steel columns with stone pillars is the necessity of making them seem as strong as their predecessors. Appearances, then, must be the concern of the wielder of public opinion, the rhetorician. Through ignorance or malice, to be sure, skill in establishing appearances may be applied to deceive. This is a grave peril which must be the concern of all men of good will. Knowledge of the devices of sophistry will always be acquired by those whose purposes are bad; ignorance of them will provide no defense for the rest. No great force can be used without hazard, or ignored without hazard.

---

[11] Book III, Chapter 7, Modern Library Edn., p. 97.

The force understood, rather than the force not understood, is likely to be the force controlled. That understanding is provided by rhetoric, the technique of discourse addressed to the enlightenment and persuasion of the generality of mankind— the basic instrument for the creation of informed public opinion and the consequent expedient public action.

OCCASIONS OF RHETORICAL DISCOURSE

Whether we will or no, we cannot escape rhetoric, either the doing or the being done to. We require it. As Edmund Burke wrote, "Men want reasons to reconcile their minds to what is done, as well as motives originally to act right."[12] Whether we seek advice or give it, the nature of our talk, as being "addressed," and of the talk of which we are the audience, as being addressed to us, necessitates speaking the language of the audience or we had as well not speak at all. That process is the core of rhetoric. It goes on as genuinely, and is often managed as skillfully, over the frozen-meats counter of the local supermarket as in the halls of Congress; on the benches in front of the Boone County Court House on Saturday afternoon before election as below the benches of the Supreme Court the next Wednesday morning; around the table where a new labor contract is being negotiated as in the pulpit of Sainte-Marie de Chaillot where Bossuet is pronouncing the funeral oration upon Henriette d'Angleterre; in the Petition from Yorkshire to King George III for redress of grievances as in the Communist Manifesto or the Declaration of Independence.

rhetoric has many uses

  As we are teachers, and as we are taught, we are involved with rhetoric. The success of the venture depends on a deliberate or instinctive adjustment of idea-through-speaker-to-audience-in-a-particular-situation. Pedagogy is the rhetoric of teaching, whether formally in the classroom or the book, or informally in the many incidental situations of our days and nights. The pscyhological principle, for example, that we learn through association becomes a rhetorical principle when we use it to connect one day's lesson with what has gone before. It is the same principle by which Burke attempted to establish in the minds of the House of Commons the rights of American colonists when he identified the colonists with Englishmen, whose rights were known.

[12] *Correspondence* (1844), I, 217.

As we are readers of newspapers and magazines and all such information-giving and opinion-forming publications, and as we write for them, we are receiving or initiating rhetorical discourse, bad or good, effective or ineffective. The obligations of the journalist as investigator of the facts, as thinker about the facts, as discoverer of ideas and analyst and critic of ideas, are fundamental. They demand all the knowledge and skill that the political, scientific, and technical studies can provide. The journalist's distinctive job, however, is writing for his audience the highest grade of informative and suasory discourse that the conditions of his medium will permit. Whether editorial writer, commentator, or plain news-writer, reaching into his audience's mind is his problem. If the people who buy the paper miss the import, the paper might as well not be published. Call it *journalism* if you choose; it is the rhetoric of the press: "it is always public opinion that the press seeks to change, one way or another, directly or indirectly."[13] Seldom can the journalist wait for the solution of a problem before getting into the fray, whether the question be a more efficient way of handling municipal finances or independence for India. He must know the right questions to ask and the bases for answering them with greatest probability for his audience now. That is his rhetorical knowledge.

The same is true of the radio and television news reporter, news analyst, and commentator. He must have rhetorical skill to survive in his occupation, and he must have knowledge and integrity if his effect is to be beneficial rather than destructive to informed public opinion. His staple, also, whether good or bad, is rhetoric. His efforts are aimed at the public mind and are significant only as they affect the public mind. If he is an honest rhetorician, he does not imply of most things, "It is so because," but only "I believe so because"; or "I recommend so because it seems probable where I cannot be sure." If he is tempted into exploiting the force of extravagant and authoritative assertion, his morals rather than his rhetoric have gone awry. Whether the use be honest or dishonest, the instrument is rhetoric.

It is obvious and commonplace that the agitator, the political speaker, the pamphleteer, the advocate, the preacher, the polemicist and apologist, the adviser of kings and princes, the teacher of statesmen, the reformer and counter-reformer, the fanatic in religion, diet, or economics, the mountebank and messiah, have enhanced the stature of a noble discourse or

[13] *The Press and Society: A Book of Readings,* ed. by George L. Bird and Frederic E. Merwin (New York, 1951), preface, p. iv.

have exploited a degraded, shallow, and dishonest discourse. It matters not that we resort to exalted names for the one—eloquence, genius, philosophy, logic, discourse of reason; and for the other, labels of reproach and contempt—sophistry, glibness, demagoguery, chicanery, "rhetoric." That naming process itself is one of the most familiar techniques of rhetoric. The fact is that in their characteristic preoccupation with manipulating the public mind, they are one. They must not all be approved or emulated, but they must all be studied as highly significant social phenomena, lest we be ignorant of them, and hence powerless before them, for good or for ill.

all users of rhetoric worth studying

Similarly, though perhaps not so easily acceptable into rhetoric, we must recognize most of what we know as advertising, salesmanship, propaganda, "public relations," and commercial, political, and national "information" services. I shall have some special consideration to give to these later. At present I merely cite them as great users of rhetoric. In this day of press, radio, and television perhaps their rhetoric is that most continuously and ubiquitously at work on the public.

RELATIONS OF RHETORIC TO OTHER LEARNINGS

These, then, are fundamental rhetorical situations. In them human beings are so organizing language as to effect a change in the knowledge, the understanding, the ideas, the attitudes, or the behavior of other human beings. Furthermore, they are so organizing that language as to make the change as agreeable, as easy, as active, and as secure as possible—as the Roman rhetoric had it, to teach, to delight, and to move (or to bend). What makes a situation rhetorical is the focus upon accomplishing something predetermined and directional with an audience. To that end many knowledges and sciences, concerning both what is external to audiences and what applies to audiences themselves, may be involved, many of which I have discussed in a previous essay.[14] These knowledges, however, have to be organized, managed, given places in strategy and tactics, set into coordinated and harmonious movement towards the listener as the end, towards what happens to him and in him. In short, they have to be *put to use,* for, as Bacon said, studies themselves "teach not their own use; but that is a wisdom without them, and above them, won

"rhetorical situations"

[14] "Aspects of the Rhetorical Tradition" (1950), see above, note 1,

by observation." "Studies themselves do give forth directions too much at large, except they be bounded in by experience."[15] Rhetoric teaches their use towards a particular end. It is that "observation," that "experience" codified, given a rationale. Other learnings are chiefly concerned with the discovery of ideas and phenomena and of their relations to each other within more or less homogeneous and closed systems. Rhetoric is primarily concerned with the relations of ideas to the thoughts, feelings, motives, and behavior of men. Rhetoric as distinct from the learnings which it uses is dynamic; it is concerned with movement. It *does* rather than *is.* It is method rather than matter. It is chiefly involved with bringing about a condition, rather than discovering or testing a condition. Even psychology, which is more nearly the special province of rhetoric than is any other study, is descriptive of conditions, but not of the uses of those conditions.

rhetoric: concerns relationship of ideas to human attitudes and/or behavior

So far as it is method, rhetoric is like the established procedures of experimental science and like logic. As the method for solving problems of human action in the areas of the contingent and the probable, however, it does not enjoy a privilege which is at the same time the great virtue and the great limitation of science and logic—it cannot choose its problems in accordance with the current capacities of its method, or defer them until method is equal to the task. Rhetoric will postpone decision as long as feasible; indeed one of its most valuable uses in the hands of good men, is to prevent hasty and premature formulation of lines of conduct and decision. In this it is one with science—and good sense. But in human affairs, where the whole is usually greater than the most complete collection of the parts, decisions—makings up of the mind—cannot always wait until all the contingencies have been removed and solutions to problems have been tested in advance. Rhetoric, therefore, must take undemonstrable problems and do its best with them when decision is required. We must decide when the blockade is imposed whether to withdraw from Berlin or to undertake the air lift, not some time later when perhaps some of the contingencies may have been removed. And the making of the choice forever precludes trying out and testing the other possibilities under the circumstances which would have prevailed had we chosen differently at first. Likewise we must make a choice on the first Tuesday in November, whether we are scientifically sure or not. In each case, rhetoric, good or bad, must be the strategy of enlightening opinion for that choice.

[15] "Of Studies."

To restate our central idea still another way: rhetoric, or the rhetorical, is the function in human affairs which governs and gives direction to that creative activity, that process of critical analysis, that branch of learning, which address themselves to the whole phenomenon of the designed use of language for the promulgation of information, ideas, and attitudes. Though it is instrumental in the discovery of ideas and information, its characteristic function is the publication, the publicizing, the humanizing, the animating of them for a realized and usually specific audience. At its best it seeks the "energizing of truth," in order to make "reason and the will of God prevail." But except in science, and no doubt theology, the promulgation of *truth,* sure or demonstrable, is out of the question. Normally the rhetorical function serves as high a degree of probability as the combination of subject, audience, speaker, and occasion admits. Rhetoric may or may not be involved (though the speaker-writer must be) in the determination of the validity of the ideas being promulgated. Such determination will be the province in any given situation of philosophy, ethics, physics, economics, politics, eugenics, medicine, hydraulics, or bucolics. To rhetoric, however, and to no other rationale, belongs the efficiency—the validity if you will—of the relations in the idea-audience-speaker situation.

FUNCTIONING OF RHETORIC

We are ready now, perhaps, if we have not been ready much sooner, to proceed to the question of how rhetoric works, what it accomplishes in an audience. Speaking generally, we may say that the rhetorical function is the *function of adjusting ideas to people and of people to ideas.* This process may be thought of as a continuum from the complete modification or accommodation of ideas to audiences (as is sometimes said, "telling people only what they want to hear") at the one extreme, to complete regeneration at the other (such perfect illumination that the "facts speak for themselves"). This continuum may, therefore, be said to have complete flattery (to use Plato's unflattering epithet) at one end and the Kingdom of Heaven at the other! Good rhetoric usually functions somewhere well in from the extremes. There, difficult and strange ideas have to be modified without being distorted or invalidated; and audiences have to be prepared through the mitigation of their prejudices, ignorance, and irrelevant sets of mind without being dispossessed of their judgments. The adjustment of ideas to people, for example, was being undertaken

rhetorical function: mutual accommodation of people and ideas by the Earl of Chatham in his speech for the repeal of the Stamp Act, when he agreed that Parliament had legislative supremacy over the Colonies but that legislative supremacy did not include the right to tax without representation. And when Booker T. Washington assured the Southern white folk that they and the Negroes could be as separate as the fingers in social affairs and as united as the hand in economics, he was adjusting people to the idea of real freedom for his race.

mutual accommodation not, in itself, an ethical problem

The moral disturbances which rhetoric and rhetorical activity seem to breed do not usually result from this process of mutual accommodation itself. Most of them arise when the speaker tries so to adjust ideas to people that the ideas are basically falsified, or when he attempts so to adjust people to ideas as to deform or anesthetize the people. Report has it that after Senator Hiram Johnson had campaigned through rural New England charging that England would have three votes to one for the United States in the League of Nations, he was taxed by a critic with misrepresenting the nature of the British Empire. One could not assume, so Johnson's critic declared, that Canada and South Africa would vote with England as a single bloc. "That may be," Johnson is said to have replied, "but New England farmers do not know the nature of the British Empire, and they do know common arithmetic." That is adjusting ideas to people so far as to falsify the basic idea. In the other direction, stimulating the "Red-menace-in-the-air-we-breathe" terror in order to adjust people to the idea of giving up their right of dissent is an effort to dispossess people of their judgments.

In terms of the old, but still convenient, faculty psychology, the terms in which rhetoric is most frequently attacked—reason, imagination, passions (emotions), judgment, will—rhetoric may still be described as the method of applying "reason to imagination for the better moving of the will." To complete our broad idea of the scope of rhetoric we should add "and the better clarification of the understanding." That is Francis Bacon's succinct statement of how rhetoric functions in the audience,[16] and it is still a good one. It establishes rhetoric squarely as an instrumental learning which manages the creative powers of the whole logical-psychological man toward a single dynamic end.

knowledge of psychology and logic essential for speaker

Rhetoric, therefore, has the greatest possible involvement with the logical and psychological studies. These learnings must be the core of the speaker's equipment. They are the

[16]From *The Advancement of Learning.* See Karl R. Wallace, *Francis Bacon on Communication and Rhetoric* (Chapel Hill, 1943), p. 27.

sine qua non in the knowledge through which rhetoric must function. In the good rhetoric which Plato described in the *Phaedrus,* after knowledge of the truth, he saw the equipment of the rhetorically skilled man to consist in knowledge of the various possible kinds of arguments, knowledge of the various kinds of souls, and knowledge of which kinds of souls will be affected by which kinds of arguments—that is, knowledge of the rational processes and knowledge of the mutual adaptation of these processes to audiences. Furthermore, in the great counter-Platonic *Rhetoric* of Aristotle, the first Book is devoted chiefly to the rational processes of rhetoric, and the next Book is the first extant comprehensive treatise on individual and group psychology. Likewise, in one of the best of the recent books on liberal education, which is, therefore, something like a basic statement on rhetoric, Hoyt Hudson sees the fundamental equipment of the liberally educated man to require three parts: the Arm of Information, the Arm of Operative Logic, and the Arm of Imagination.[17] Of these, in practical affairs, rhetoric is based on the second and third, and the first must be the starting place of the speaker in each particular situation.

Where in this pattern, then, does emotion come in, that famous roughneck who is said to spoil the rational life and vitiate the logic of behavior? As Hudson and many others have observed, and as Bacon knew well, emotion is a derivative of both reason and imagination. Love of truth and of the good life must be the results of any genuinely rational functioning, that is, of operative logic; and vivid realization of experience, which is imagination, can hardly occur without those strong emotional accompaniments which, in practice, have given rise to the identifying of emotion with imagination. This point seems hardly to need laboring over again. Hudson's book gives it adequate coverage, and I have summarized the traditional position of rhetoric and rhetoricians on it in the essay already mentioned.[18] The position is that a complete rhetoric, and that is the kind of rhetoric which we are discussing, knows the whole man and seeks to bring to bear the whole man in achieving its ends—what he is and what he thinks he is, what he believes and what he thinks he believes, what he wants and what he tells himself he wants. Towards its special ends, rhetoric recognizes the primacy of rational processes, their primacy in time as well as in importance, as Bacon's definition implies—applying reason to the imagination. Just so poetry

[17] *Educating Liberally* (Stanford University, 1945), pp. 10 ff.
[18] Above, note 14.

recognizes the primacy for its purposes of the imagination. But rhetoric has always been akin to poetry—for long periods of history it has in fact annexed poetry—in its recognition of the honest and highly important power of imagination and of that emotion which does not supplant but supports reason, and sometimes even transcends it. Thus Sir Philip Sidney and most literary theorists of the renaissance attributed to poetry the distinctly rhetorical function of using imagination to create what might be called historical fictions to give power and life to ideas. Rhetoric recognizes the strength of the fictions men live by, as well as those they live under;[19] and it aims to fortify the one and explode the other. Rhetoric aims at what is *worth* doing, what is *worth* trying. It is concerned with *values,* and values are established with the aid of imaginative realization, not through rational determination alone; and they gain their force through emotional animation.

We have observed that psychology, human nature, has been a staple of rhetorical learning through the ages. No doubt, therefore, scientific psychology will have more and more to contribute to modern rhetoric. The first notable attempt to ground rhetoric in a systematic modern psychology was made by George Campbell in his *Philosophy of Rhetoric* (1776), in which he stated as his purpose

> to exhibit . . . a tolerable sketch of the human mind; and, aided by the lights which the poet and the orator so amply furnish, to disclose its secret movements, tracing its principal channels of perception and action, as near as possible, to their source: and, on the other hand, from the science of human nature, to ascertain with greater precision, the radical principles of that art, whose object it is, by the use of language, to operate on the soul of the hearer, in the way of informing, convincing, pleasing, moving, or persuading.[20]

That same purpose governs our contemporary writers of treatises and textbooks on public speaking, argumentation, and persuasion, and most of them include as up-to-date a statement as possible of the psychological and the rational bases of rhetoric. It is a commonplace that of the studies recently come to new and promising maturity, psychology, especially social psychology, and cultural anthropology have much to teach modern rhetoric and to correct or reinterpret

[19] See the very relevant analysis of some of the fictions in the ideology of American business in C. Wright Mills, *White Collar* (New York, 1951), Ch. 3, "The Rhetoric of Competition."

[20] 7th edn. (London, 1823), pp. vii–viii.

in traditional rhetoric. The same may be said of the various new ventures into the study of meaning, under the general head of semantics. How language *means* is obviously important to the rationale of informative and suasory discourse. Nevertheless, in spite of I. A. Richards' book,[21] the theory of meaning is not *the* philosophy of rhetoric, any more than is the psychology of perception. Rhetoric is the organizer of all such for the wielding of public opinion.

ADVERTISING, SALESMANSHIP, AND PROPAGANDA

Now that we have sketched the rhetorical process functioning at its best for the exposition and dissemination of ideas in the wielding of public opinion, with the ethical and pathetic modes of proof in ancillary relation to the logical, with the imagination aiding and reenforcing the rational, let us turn to some of the partial incomplete, perhaps misused, rhetorics which I have already mentioned briefly.

It is axiomatic that men do not live by reason alone or even predominantly, though reason is such a highly prized commodity and stands in so high a repute even among the unreasoning and unreasonable, that men prefer to tell themselves and to be told that they make up their minds and determine their choices from reason and the facts. Intellectual activity, both learning and thinking, is so difficult that man tends to avoid it wherever possible. Hence education has almost always put its first efforts into cultivating the reasonable portion of the mind rather than the imaginative or emotional. Furthermore, the strength and accessibility of imaginative and emotional responses is so great in spite of education that though men seldom make effective reasonable decisions without the help of emotion, they often make, or appear to make, effective emotional decisions without the help of rational processes or the modification of reasonable consideration. Inevitably, therefore, the available reason in rhetorical situations will vary tremendously, and the assistance which imagination must provide towards the moving of the will must vary accordingly. Except in Swift's unexciting land of the Houyhnhnms, however, imagination will always be there.

Ever since men first began to weave the web of words to charm their fellows, they have known that some men can impose their wills on others through language in despite of

[21] *The Philosophy of Rhetoric* (New York, 1936).

reason. Almost as long, other men have deplored and feared this talent. If the talent were wholly a matter of divine gift and were wholly unexplainable, the only alternative to succumbing to the orator would be to kill him. In time it appeared, however, that this skill could be learned, in part at least, and could be analyzed. Thus if it were good, men could learn to develop it further; and if it were bad, they could be armed in some measure against it. Hence rhetoric, and hence the partial rhetoric of anti-reason and pseudo-reason. And hence the appeal of such rhetorical eruptions as Aldous Huxley's total condemnation of oratory in *The Devils of Loudon*.[22] His indictment of public speakers is indeed skillful, and ought to be taken seriously. If the talent of his golden-voiced Grandiers be indeed magic, then we will have to agree that the fate of man before such wizards is hopeless. Rhetoric teaches, however, that the method and the power of this kind of discourse can be analyzed, at least in large part, and if its subtleties cannot be wholly *learned* by every ambitious speaker, the characteristics of its operation can be understood, and if understood, then controlled, for better or for worse.[23]

mankind not necessarily at the mercy of unscrupulous oratory

The oratory which Huxley would extirpate presents a rewarding approach to the rhetoric of advertising and propaganda, of which it is the historic prototype. In them the techniques of suggestion, reiteration, imaginative substitution, verbal irrelevance and indirection, and emotional and pseudological bullying have been developed beyond, one might hazard a guess, the fondest dreams of the sophists and the historic demagogues. This development does not represent a change in intention from them to our contemporaries, but an advance in knowledge and opportunity and media.

advertisers and propagandists seek rhetorical solutions

If you have a soap or a cigarette or a social order for quick, profitable sale, you do not neglect any method within your ethical system of making that sale. That is the paramount problem of the advertiser and the propagandist, and their solutions are very much alike. They are rhetorical solutions, at their best very carefully gauged to the mass audience, adapted to special audiences, and varying basically only as the initial sale or the permanent customer is the principal object. What advertising is in commerce, propaganda is in politics, especially international politics. Neither scorns reason or the likeness of reason, the rhetoric of information and logi-

[22](New York, 1952), pp. 18–19.

[23]Observe the tradition of rhetoric as a systematic study, summarized in my "Aspects of Rhetorical Tradition," *QJS*, XXXVI (April 1950), 169–172.

cal argument, if the message and the audience seem to make that the best or only means to the sale. Neither, on the other hand, prefers that method to the shorter, quicker ways to unconsidered action. They concentrate—forcibly where possible, rhetorically where necessary—on the exclusion of competing ideas, on the short-circuiting or by-passing of informed judgment. By preference they do not seek to balance or over-balance alternative ideas or courses of action; they seek to obliterate them, to circumvent or subvert the rational processes which tend to make men weigh and consider. As Adlai Stevenson said, slogans, the common staple of advertising and propaganda, "are normally designed to get action without reflection."

That advertising should enjoy a happier reputation than propaganda in a competitive, commercial-industrial nation such as the United States, which is only just now learning the term *psychological warfare,* is not to be wondered at. We do not have a public service institution for the defensive analysis of advertising, like the Institute of Propaganda Analysis, which assumed that propaganda is something from which we must learn to protect ourselves. The ethical superiority of our advertising is no doubt a compliment to our dominant business code—and to our laws. Still, if one wishes to know what the ungoverned rhetoric of advertising can be, he may get a suggestion by listening to some of what is beamed to us from certain radio stations south of the border.

The kinship of advertising and salesmanship, and their somewhat denatured relatives "public relations" and "promotion," to conventional public address, the established vehicle of rhetoric, may be embarrassing at times, but it must be acknowledged. The family resemblance is too strong to be ignored and too important to be denied. The omnipresence of the rhetoric of advertising, as I have suggested, gives it a standing which must be reckoned with, no matter what opinion the student of public address may hold of it. The rhetoric of public address, in this country at least, must function, whether or no, in a public mind which is steeped in the rhetoric of advertising, a rhetoric whose dominating principles must be recognized as adaptations of a portion of the fundamentals of any rhetoric. One need only compare a textbook or handbook of advertising methods with standard, conventional rhetorics—textbooks in public speaking and persuasion—especially in the handling of such topics as interest, suggestion, and motivation, to be convinced of the coincidence of method if not of philosophic outlook. Many times in adult

undeniable kinship of advertising, public relations, propaganda to rhetoric

evening classes in public speaking, have I heard speeches on the secrets of successful salesmanship, and as often have I found myself being offered a more or a less competent parody of certain portions of our textbook, which for some reason the student had omitted to read. Not by mere chance, one must confess, does the non-academic public take great interest in the four "miracle" courses to be found among the offerings of many universities—advertising, salesmanship, psychology, and effective speaking. Nor is it remarkable, though one may think it deplorable, that appearances of the officers of our national government before the mass audience of the citizens are characteristic products of the country's leading advertising agencies.

techniques of unethical advertising, propaganda: long-known rhetorical techniques gone wrong

Likewise propaganda and its brother "information" borrow and refine upon certain portions of rhetoric. No doubt it serves a useful purpose to identify propaganda with the vicious forces in the modern world, with the German Government of World War I and with the Nazi and Soviet totalitarianisms of the present time. At the same time, however, it would be the better part of wisdom to recognize that most of the major techniques of this propaganda are long-known rhetorical techniques gone wrong, that propaganda is not a new invention which we have no ready equipment for combatting, let alone fumigating and using for our honorable ends. The understanding of propaganda will be founded in the understanding of rhetoric first of all, whatever else may be necessary.[24] Both Ross Scanlan and Kenneth Burke have demonstrated the enlightenment which can come from the application of rhetorical criticism to both the internal and external propaganda of the Nazis;[25] and two articles by Scanlan and Henry C. Youngerman in the first issue of *Today's Speech* (April, 1953) are grounded on the assumption of a close kinship between rhetoric (or its corollary, "public address") and propaganda.[26] In fact, one of Scanlan's concluding statements indirectly makes both the identification and the basic distinction: "Today it is to be hoped that America will find means to match enemy propaganda in effectiveness without sacrificing the standards of morality and intellect that distinguish democracy from the totalitarian order."

[24]See, for example, Everett L. Hunt, "Ancient Rhetoric and Modern Propaganda," *QJS*, XXXVII (April 1951), 157–160.

[25]Burke, *The Philosophy of Literary Form* (1941), pp. 191–220; Scanlan, "The Nazi Party Speaker System, I & II," *SM*, XVI (August 1949), 82–97, XVII (June 1950), 134–148; "The Nazi Rhetorician," *QJS*, XXVII (December 1951), 430–440.

[26]"Two Views of Propaganda," pp. 13–14; "Propaganda and Public Address," pp. 15–17.

RHETORIC AS A METHOD OF INQUIRY

More than once in the preceding pages I have in passing assigned to rhetoric a secondary function of the discovery of ideas, contributory to its prime function of the popularizing of ideas. That is the consequence of the division of *inventio,* the term applied in Roman rhetoric to the systematic investigative procedures by which rhetoric sought to turn up all the relevant arguments or considerations in any given situation. As part of *inventio,* for example, the elaborate doctrine of *status* was developed, through which by the application of analytical criteria it was possible to determine just what was the core, the central issue in any given case, just what had to be proved as a *sine qua non,* and where the lines of argument for proving it would lie if they were available. In general the division of *inventio* constituted a codification of the *topoi* or *places where arguments are to be found;* for instance, in *fact past, fact future, more and less, etc.* Rhetoric, thus, as we have said, provides scientific assistance to the speaker in discovering what questions to ask and how to go about answering them. It serves the speaker as laboratory procedures for analysis serve the chemist—by systematic inventory it enables him to determine with reasonable completeness what is present and what is absent in any given case.

We need not be surprised, therefore, that so useful a method tended to be incorporated into other arts and sciences where its original provenience was often forgotten. Historically, some of the studies to profit greatly from this borrowing from rhetoric have been the law, theology, logic, and poetic.[27] The Polandizing of rhetoric, one of the characteristic phenomena of its history, accounts in large part for the splinter meanings and the distortions which we have seen as typical of its current and historic significance. It has been the fate of rhetoric, the residual term, to be applied to the less intellectual segments of itself, while its central operating division, *inventio,* has been appropriated by the studies and sciences which rhetoric serves.

The functions of a complete rhetoric, however, have usually been operative under whatever temporary auspices as the whole art of discourse, even as they were in the renaissance tripartite grammar-logic-rhetoric. This splintering may go so far

inventio borrowed from rhetoric by many disciplines

[27] See Richard McKeon, "Rhetoric in the Middle Ages," *Critics and Criticism, Ancient and Modern,* ed. R. S. Crane (Chicago, 1952), pp. 260–296, reprinted from *Speculum,* January, 1942; and Marvin T. Herrick, "The Place of Rhetoric in Poetic Theory," *QJS,* XXXIV (February 1948), 1–22.

towards specialism, however, that the investigative function of rhetoric, the method of *inventio,* may be diverted from that to which it most properly applies. This diversion may very well be the tendency today, where a complete rhetoric hardly exists as a formal discipline except in those classically oriented courses in public speaking, debate, group discussion, argumentation, and persuasion whose central focus is on *inventio*—the investigation and discovery of lines of argument and basic issues. Mostly rhetoric today survives, as we have seen, under other names and special applications in those specialties which contribute to it or draw upon it or appropriate selectively from its store of method—psychology, advertising, salesmanship, propaganda analysis, public opinion and social control, semantics, and that which is loosely called "research" in common parlance.

May I attempt in summary of this matter to bring rhetoric back to its essential investigative function, its function of discovery, by quoting from Isocrates, the Athenian politico-rhetorical philosopher, and from Edmund Burke, the eighteenth-century British statesman-orator? Wrote Isocrates in the *Antidosis,* "With this faculty we both contend against others on matters that are open to dispute and seek light for ourselves on things which are unknown; for the same arguments which we use in persuading others when we speak in public, we employ when we deliberate in our thoughts."[28] Twenty-two centuries later, the young Burke included in his notebook digest of the topics of rhetoric, which he headed "How to Argue," the following succinct, Baconian statement about the functions of *inventio:*

> To invent Arguments without a thorough knowledge of the Subject is clearly impossible. But the Art of Invention does two things—
>
> 1. It suggests to us more readily those Parts of our actual knowledge which may help towards illustrating the matter before us, &
>
> 2. It suggests to us heads of Examination which may lead, if pursued with effect into a knowledge of the Subject.
>
> So that the Art of Invention may properly be considered as the method of calling up what we do know, & investigating that of which we are ignorant.[29]

[28] *Isocrates,* trans. George Norlin (Loeb Classical Library, New York, 1929), II, 327.

[29] From an original manuscript among the Wentworth-Fitzwilliam papers in the Sheffield City Library, used with the kind permission of Earl Fitzwilliam and the trustees of the Fitzwilliam settled estates.

RHETORIC IN EDUCATION

If the burden of the preceding pages is not misplaced, the importance of rhetoric in the equipment of the well-educated member of society can hardly be in doubt. I am not inclined, therefore, especially in this journal, to offer to demonstrate the desirability of speech as an academic study. Our conventions and our journals have been full of such demonstration for, lo, these thirty years.[30] If enlightened and responsible leaders with rhetorical knowledge and skill are not trained and nurtured, irresponsible demagogues will monopolize the power of rhetoric, will have things to themselves. If talk rather than take is to settle the course of our society, if ballots instead of bullets are to effect our choice of governors, if discourse rather than coercion is to prevail in the conduct of human affairs, it would seem like arrant folly to trust to chance that the right people shall be equipped offensively and defensively with a sound rationale of informative and suasory discourse.

study of rhetoric essential for preservation of our society

In general education, especially, rhetoric would appear to deserve a place of uncommon importance. That is the burden of a recent article by Dean Hunt of Swarthmore. Rhetoric is the organon of the liberal studies, the formulation of the principles through which the educated man, the possessor of many specialties, attains effectiveness in society.[31] A complete rhetoric is a structure for the wholeness of the effective man, the aim of general education. But, as Dean Hunt concludes, the rhetorician himself must not become a technical specialist:

rhetoric deserves special emphasis in education

> He will keep his wholeness if he comes back again and again to Aristotle, but he must supplement those conceptions with what modern scientists have added to the mirror for man; he must illuminate the classical rhetoric with psychology, cultural anthropology, linguistics and semantics, special disciplines, perhaps, but disciplines in which he can lean heavily on interpreters who speak to others than their professional colleagues. Departments of speech which have emphasized training in rhetoric have a new opportunity to establish their place in general education. Their very claim to wholeness has been a source of distrust in an atmosphere of specialism. If now they can relate themselves to newer conceptions in the sciences, social sciences, and humanities, they can show that the ideal of the good man skilled in speaking is like the sea, ever changing and ever the same.[32]

[30] See, for example, one of the latest, W. N. Brigance, "General Education in an Industrial Free Society," *QJS,* XXXVIII (April 1952), esp. p. 181.

[31] "Rhetoric and General Education," *QJS,* XXXV (October 1949), 275, 277.

[32] *Ibid.,* 279.

So much for rhetoric in education as a study directed at the creation and at the analysis and criticism of informative and suasory discourse—at the ability, on the one hand, "to summon thought quickly and use it forcibly,"[33] and on the other to listen or read critically with the maximum application of analytical judgment.

Rhetoric would appear thus to be in certain senses a literary study, or as Wichelns wrote, at least "its tools are those of literature." It is a literary study as it is involved in the creative arts of language, of informing ideas. It is a literary study also as it contributes substantially to literary scholarship. Not only have literature and literary theory been persistently rhetorical for long periods—during much of the renaissance, for example, the seventeenth and eighteenth centuries in England, and for most of the short history of American literature—but writers and readers until fairly recently had been so generally educated in rhetoric that it provided the vocabulary and many of the concepts in terms of which much literature was both written and read. Clark's *Milton at St. Paul's School* may be cited as one conclusive demonstration of the importance of rhetoric in renaissance education and its importance in renaissance literature. This importance is now being recognized by literary scholars, and rhetoric is taking on considerable proportions in their studies, especially among those who are studying the renaissance. Myrick's study of Sir Philip Sidney as a literary craftsman,[34] for example, demonstrates how thoroughly Sidney was schooled in rhetoric and how carefully he constructed his defense of poetry on familiar rhetorical principles. If Myrick has been in error in his construction of the specific genealogy of Sidney's rhetoric, the fact of Sidney's rhetorical system is nevertheless in no doubt.

The plain truth is that whatever the inadequacies in specific cases of the analytical method ingrained in our educated ancestors, they *had* method, the method of formal rhetoric; whereas a general characteristic of our contemporary education is that it inculcates *no* method beyond a rather uncertain grammar and a few rules of paragraphing and bibliography. Rigidity of method is doubtless a grievous obstacle to the greatest fulfillment of genius in either belles lettres or public address; but the widespread impotence and ineptitude even of our best-educated fellows when faced with the problem of

[33] Herbert A. Wichelns, "Public Speaking and Dramatic Arts," in *On Going to College: A Symposium* (New York, Oxford University Press, 1938), p. 240.

[34] Kenneth O. Myrick, *Sir Philip Sidney as a Literary Craftsman* (1935).

constructing or analyzing any but the most rudimentary expository or argumentative discourse, much less a complicated literary work, are surely worse. Rhetoric supplies the equipment for such practical endeavor in the promulgation of ideas, and twenty centuries have learned to use it to supplement and perfect chance and natural instinct.

That such method has at times become sterile or mechanical, that at other times it has been put to uses for which it was least adapted is amusing, perhaps lamentable, but not surprising. The remote uses to which rhetorical methods of analysis and description have been put, in the absence of a more appropriate method, are well illustrated by the following passage from Sir John Hawkins' *History of Music,* first published in the late eighteenth century:

> The art of invention is made one of the heads among the precepts of rhetoric, to which music in this and sundry instances bears a near resemblance; the end of persuasion, or affecting the passions being common to both. This faculty consists in the enumeration of common places, which are revolved over in the mind, and requires both an ample store of knowledge in the subject upon which it is exercised, and a power of applying that knowledge as occasion may require. It differs from memory in this respect, that whereas memory does but recall to the mind the images or remembrance of things as they were first perceived, the faculty of invention divides complex ideas into those whereof they are composed, and recommends them again after different fashions, thereby creating variety of new objects and conceptions. Now, the greater the fund of knowledge above spoken of is, the greater is the source from whence the invention of the artist or composer is supplied; and the benefits thereof are seen in new combinations and phrases, capable of variety and permutation without end.[35]

From its lapses and wanderings, however, rhetoric when needed has almost always recovered its vitality and comprehensive scope, by reference to its classic sources. But that it should be ignored seems, as Dean Hunt suggests, hardly a compliment to education.

Rhetoric as a serious scholarly study I have treated in my former essay, and I shall not go over the same ground again. That there is a body of philosophy and principle worth scholarly effort in discovery, enlargement, and reinterpretation is beyond question, and fortunately more competent scholars each year are working at it. Rhetorical criticism and the study

serious scholarly study of rhetoric must continue

[35](2 vols., London, 1875), I, xxv.

of rhetoric as a revealing social and cultural phenomenon are also gaining ground. New and interesting directions for research in these areas are being explored, or at least marked out; they are based on newly developed techniques and hitherto neglected kinds of data. One might mention, for example, those new approaches listed by Maloney:[36] the quantitative content analysis as developed by Lasswell; the qualitative content analysis as used by Lowenthal and Guterman; figurative analysis such as applied to Shakespeare by Caroline Spurgeon; and intonational analysis. Extensive and provocative suggestions are to be found in quantity in the text and bibliography of Brembeck and Howell's *Persuasion: A Means of Social Control,*[37] especially in Part VI. Lucrative also are the new attempts at the analysis of the rhetoric of historical movements, such as Griffin's study of the rhetoric of the anti-masonic movement and others under way within the Speech Association of America. Elsewhere in this issue Thonssen's review of recent rhetorical studies illustrates amply both the new and the traditional in rhetorical scholarship; and the section on rhetoric in the annual Haberman bibliography is convincing evidence of the vitality of current enterprise.[38]

Though new avenues, new techniques, new materials such as the foregoing are inviting to the increasing numbers of scholars whose interests and abilities—to say nothing of their necessities—lie in rhetorical research, especially those new directions which lead to rhetoric as a cultural, a sociological, a social-psychiatric phenomenon, the older literary-historical-political studies are still neither too complete nor too good. In any event, each new generation probably needs to interpret afresh much of the relevant history of thought, especially the thought of the people as distinguished from what is commonly considered the history of ideas. For this the scholarship of rhetoric seems particularly adapted. Towards this purpose, I find no need to relocate the field of rhetorical scholarship as envisioned by Hudson and Wichelns, nor to recant from the considerations which I outlined in the *QJS* in 1937.[39] One may find it reassuring to observe, however, that much which was asked for in those essays has since then

---

[36] "Some New Directions in Rhetorical Criticism," *Central States Speech Journal,* IV (February 1953), 1–5.

[37] (New York, 1952).

[38] "A Bibliography of Rhetoric and Public Address," ed. F. W. Haberman, formerly appearing annually in the *QJS,* latterly in *SM.*

[39] See above, note 1.

been undertaken and often accomplished with considerable success. Especially is this true of the study of public address in its bulk and day-to-day manifestations: in the movement studies, the "case" studies, the sectional and regional studies, the studies of "debates" and "campaigns" such as the debates on the League of Nations and the campaigns for conservation.

There remains much to do, nevertheless, and much to re-do in the more familiar and conventional areas of research and interpretation. The editing and translation of rhetorical texts is still far from complete or adequate. The canon of ancient rhetoric is, to be sure, in very good shape, and when Caplan's translation of the *Ad Herennium* is published in the Loeb Library there will hardly be a major deficiency. In post-classical, mediaeval, and renaissance rhetoric the situation is not so good, though it is improving. There are still too few works like Howell's *Rhetoric of Alcuin and Charlemagne* and Sister Therese Sullivan's commentary on and translation of the fourth book of St. Augustine's *De Doctrina.* Halm's *Rhetores Minores,* for example, is substantially unmolested so far.

English and continental rhetoric of the sixteenth, seventeenth, and eighteenth centuries is slowly appearing in modern editions by scholars who know rhetoric as the theory of public address. Our bibliographies show increasing numbers of these as doctoral dissertations, most of which, alas, seem to be abandoned almost as soon as finished. Only a few works of the sort, like Howell's *Fénelon,* represent mature, published work.

In the history and historical analysis of rhetoric, nothing of adequate range and scope yet exists. Thonssen and Baird's *Speech Criticism,* ambitious as it is, is only a beginning. The general history of rhetoric, and even most of the special histories, have yet to be written. Works now under way by Donald L. Clark and Wilbur S. Howell will make substantial contributions, but rhetoric from Corax to Whately needs far fuller and better treatment than it gets in the series of histories of criticism by the late J. W. H. Atkins.

Towards the study of the rhetorical principles and practice of individual speakers and writers the major part of our scholarly effort seems to have been directed. The convenience of this kind of study is beyond question and is hard to resist, either in public address or in literature. And this is as it should be. The tendency to write biographies of speakers, however, rather than rhetorico-critical studies of them, must be kept in check, or at least in proportion. Again for reasons of convenience, if not also of scholarly nationalism, the studies of American speakers are proportionately too numerous. British and foreign public address is still far too scantily noticed by competent rhetorical scholars.

RHETORIC AND POETIC

This would not be the place, I think, even if Professor Thonssen's review of rhetorical works were not appearing in this same issue of the *QJS,* for a survey of rhetorical scholarship. The preceding paragraphs are intended only as a token of decent respect to accomplishment and progress in a discrete and important branch of humane scholarship. A further area where rhetorical scholarship may be very profitably pursued, however, perhaps deserves some special consideration.

Even if it were not for the contributions of Kenneth Burke, the study of rhetoric in literature and of the relation of the theory of rhetoric to the theory of poetic would be taking on renewed importance at the present time. The lively revival of rhetorical study in renaissance scholarship which I have mentioned is only one phase of the problem. A renewed or increased interest in satire, deriving in part, perhaps, from the excellent work which of late has been done on Swift, leads directly to rhetoric. The rhetorical mode is obviously at the center of satire, and any fundamental analysis of satire must depend upon the equipment for rhetorical analysis. Likewise a complete dramatic criticism must draw upon rhetoric, both practically and philosophically. The internal rhetoric of the drama was specifically recognized by Aristotle when he referred readers of the *Poetics* to the *Rhetoric* for coverage of the element of *dianoia,* for the analysis of speeches in which agents try to convince or persuade each other. What, however, is the external rhetoric of the drama? What is the drama intended to do to an audience? Herein lies the question of the province of poetic as opposed to the province of rhetoric. When Antony addresses the Roman citizens in *Julius Caesar,* the existence of an internal rhetoric in the play is clear enough; the relation between Antony and his stage audience is unmistakably rhetorical. But what of the relation between Antony and the audience in the pit, or the Antony-stage-audience combination and the audience in the pit? The more we speculate about the effect of a play or any literary work on an audience, the more we become involved in metaphysical questions in which rhetoric must be involved.

Much contemporary poetry or pseudo-poetry in any generation is rhetorical in the most obvious sense—in the same sense as the epideictic oration. It "pleases" largely by rhetorical means or methods. It "reminds" us of experience instead of "organizing" or "creating" experience. It appeals to our satisfaction with what we are used to; it convinces us that what *was* still may be as it was, that old formulas are pleasantest if not best. It is not so much concerned with pointing up the old elements in the new, even, as establishing the identity of the old and the contemporary. "What oft was thought, but ne'er so well expressed" is a distinctly rhetorical attainment, and it would not have occurred to Pope to suppose that the poetic and the rhetorical were antithetical, if indeed they were separable. Though sporadically the effort of critics and theorists has been to keep *rhetoric* and *poetic* apart, the two rationales have had an irresistible tendency to come together, and their similarities may well be more important than their differences. When the forming of attitude is admitted into the province of rhetoric, then, to Kenneth Burke, rhetoric becomes a method for the analysis of even lyric poetry. Hence a frequent term in certain kinds of literary analysis now is *poetic-rhetoric,* as for example in the first two sentences in Ruth Wallerstein's analysis of two elegies: "I want this paper to consider two poems, John Donne's elegy on Prince Henry and Milton's *Lycidas,* in the light that is shed on them by seventeenth-century rhetoric-poetic as I understand it. Both the significance of that rhetoric and the test of my view of it will reside in its power to illuminate the poems."[40]

Undoubtedly there are basic differences between *poetic* and *rhetoric,* both practical and philosophical, and probably these differences lie both in the kind of method which is the proper concern of each and the kind of effect on audiences to the study of which each is devoted. The purely poetic seeks the creation or organization of imaginative experience, probably providing for reader or audience some kind of satisfying spiritual or emotional therapy. The rhetorical seeks a predetermined channeling of the audience's understanding or attitude. Poetry works by representation; rhetoric by instigation. The poetic is fulfilled in creation, the rhetorical in illumination. "An image," wrote Longinus, "has one purpose with the orators and another with the poets; . . . the design of the poetic image is enthralment, of the rhetorical, vivid description. Both, how-

---

[40]"Rhetoric in the English Renaissance: Two Elegies," *English Institute Essays, 1948,* p. 153.

ever, seek to stir the passions and the emotions. . . . In oratorical imagery its best feature is always its reality and truth."[41] Poetry, declared Sir Philip Sidney, cannot lie because it affirms nothing; it merely presents. Rhetoric not only presents but affirms. That is its characteristic. Both poetic and rhetoric attain their effects through language. If the poet's highest skill lies in his power to make language do what it has never done before, to force from words and the conjunction of words meanings which are new and unique, perhaps it is the highest skill of the speaker to use words in their accepted senses in such a way as to make them carry their traditional meanings with a vividness and effectiveness which they have never known before.

SUMMARY

In brief we may assign to rhetoric a four-fold status. So far as it is concerned with the management of discourse in specific situations for practical purposes, it is an instrumental discipline. It is a literary study, involving linguistics, critical theory, and semantics as it touches the art of informing ideas, and the functioning of language. It is a philosophical study so far as it is concerned with a method of investigation or inquiry. And finally, as it is akin to politics, drawing upon psychology and sociology, rhetoric is a social study, the study of a major force in the behavior of men in society.

[41] Trans. Rhys Roberts, sec. 15.

SUGGESTED FURTHER READING

Hostettler, Gordon F., "Trends in the History of Rhetoric," *The Communicative Arts and Sciences of Speech,* ed. Keith Brooks. Columbus, Ohio: Charles E. Merrill Books, Inc. (1967), 17–33.

Hudson, Hoyt H., "The Field of Rhetoric," *Quarterly Journal of Speech,* IX (April, 1923), 167–180. (See Footnote 1 above.)

Hunt, Everett Lee, "Rhetoric as a Humane Study," *Quarterly Journal of Speech,* XLI (April, 1955), 114–117. (See also footnote 24 above.)

Murphy, Richard, "Preface to an Ethic of Rhetoric," *The Rhetorical Idiom,* ed. Donald C. Bryant. Ithaca, New York: Cornell University Press (1958), 124–144.

Wallace, Karl R., "An Ethical Basis of Communication," *Speech Teacher,* IV (January, 1955), 1–9.

Wilson, John F. and Carroll C. Arnold, *Public Speaking as a Liberal Art.* Boston: Allyn and Bacon, Inc., 1968.

Wrage, Ernest J., "Public Address: A Study in Social and Intellectual History," *Quarterly Journal of Speech,* XXXIII (December, 1947), 451–457.

Toward a Meaning-Centered Philosophy of Communication

Dean C. Barnlund

A philosophy of training is essential in determining the aim, fixing the boundaries and evaluating the methods of any field. Yet formulating such a philosophy is an uncommon, formidable and sensitive venture. Uncommon, because in the daily round of classes, research projects, student conferences and faculty meetings, few teachers have the time or the perspective to canvass their purposes. Formidable, because to evolve such a philosophy is an immense undertaking requiring one to question the nature of our discipline, the legitimate boundaries of our scholarship and the character of our actions as teachers. Sensitive, because at every point one is forced to expose assumptions and motives that are only vaguely known or admitted even in the most mature human being. Each step in such an evaluation touches a raw nerve ending somewhere in that complex called the human ego. Yet this sort of periodic re-evaluation is absolutely essential. Loyalty to a discipline does not lie in an unquestioning acceptance of the status quo; it requires a continuous and vigorous testing of the postulates and practices of any field.

In attempting to phrase a more acceptable philosophy of communication training, I have been guided by a simple, but germinal, idea that can be succinctly stated. It is that a sound philosophy of training is implicit in a sound philosophy of communication. Whatever pedagogical decisions must be made—concerning the proper scope of the curriculum, the legitimacy of certain kinds of research, or the spirit and temper of student–teacher relations—they turn ultimately, if sometimes obscurely, on the nature and goals of successful communication. One cannot have a superficial, or narrow, or

Note: This paper was presented originally at the SAA Convention in New York in 1961 under the title "A Philosophy of Communication Training."

opportunistic concept of communication and be a thorough and responsible teacher of that same subject.

The question, therefore, of our role as scholar–teacher (and both the ordering and linking of those terms is deliberate) involves us in a circuitous, but essential, return to the communication process itself. Like the modern architect, one begins by discovering the "nature of his material." To be acceptable, a philosophy of communication should fulfill the following criteria: (1) It should provide a satisfactory explanation of the aim of communication. (2) It should provide a technically adequate description of the process of communication. (3) It should provide a moral standard that will protect and promote the healthiest communicative behavior. Once this process is defined and its nature exposed, the way should be clear for facing the practical decisions involved in giving effective instruction.

AIM OF COMMUNICATION

We begin by asking, why [do] men communicate? What human need does it, or shoud it, satisfy? While there is almost universal agreement that communication is tied to the manipulation of symbols, there is widespread disagreement as to what constitutes effectiveness in this endeavor. A brief review of some abortive explanations of communication is essential because, in spite of repeated criticism, these conceptions continue to influence current training in speech.

two restricted attempts to explain communication

One of these theories is that the aim of communication is to transmit information. Success hinges on mastery of the facts, effective arrangement of materials and strength of expression. It is a message-centered philosophy of communication. And it is largely amoral. Critical standards for determining the effectiveness of communication, as in the critical evaluation of literature, are internal; they are found within the message itself. When a writer or speaker or critic asks, "Was it well said?" he is usually viewing communication as a mode of expression. The training in communication that follows from this premise and perspective is destined to be truncated and unrealistic. Talk is not a guarantee of communication. Facts and ideas are not shared because they are articulated loudly or even well. Messages do not influence automatically because of being broadcast on the mass media. The inadequacy of this approach lies in its neglect of the listener as terminus of the communicative act, in its failure to provide an expla-

message-centered philosophy views communication as mode of expression

nation of how meaning arises through communication and in its disregard for all but public and continuous discourse.

speaker-centered philosophy:—lacks satisfactory theory of meaning

A second theory is that the aim of communication is to transfer ideas from one person to another. Here the listener is admitted as part of the communicative situation. The focus, however, in research and training, is upon the message formulator. Effectiveness in communication is thought to turn not only on the content and phrasing of the message, but on the intelligence and credibility of the source. Relatively little attention is paid to the listener other than to note that messages should be adapted to his interests. It ends by becoming a speaker-centered philosophy. Communicative events are explained largely in terms of the experiential milieu that shaped the mind of the speaker and find expression in his messages.

—tends to neglect the listener

As an an explanation of communication it, too, fails in several important respects. First, the listener tends to be regarded as a passive object, rather than an active force in communication. Unfortunately, it is not that simple to deposit ideas in another mind. Teachers of great intelligence and high purpose often find their lessons disregarded or misapplied. Messages flowing through an industrial complex are not received undistorted like images in a hall of mirrors. Second, this approach also fails to provide a satisfactory theory of meaning, and of how messages from highly credible sources can provoke so many and such contradictory meanings. Finally, it is too parochial. It neglects man's communication with himself—an area that is fast becoming one of the most vital in communication research—and it fails to account for the fact that communication is as often a matter of hiding or protecting what is in men's minds as it is a matter of revealing their thoughts and intentions.

—neglects man's communication with himself

Neither of these schools of thought, of course, omits the constituent elements in communication altogether. It is, rather, a question of emphasis. Questions of emphasis, however, are not irrelevant or inconsequential in establishing a productive orientation for a discipline. The pedagogical consequences of both of these approaches is to place a disproportionate emphasis (in research, courses and textbooks) on the source and message elements in communication. Both schools of thought tend, also, to minimize or overlook completely, the interactive and dynamic nature of the communicative process.

messages generated from external stimuli

Communication, as I conceive it, is a word that describes the process of creating a meaning. Two words in this sentence are critical. They are "create" and "meaning." Messages may be generated from the outside—by a speaker, a television screen, a scolding parent—but meanings are generated from within. This position parallels that of Berlo when he writes, "Communication does not consist of the transmission of meaning. Meanings are not transmitted, nor transferable. Only messages are transmittable, and meanings are not in the message, they are in the message-user."[1] Communication is man's attempt to cope with his experience, his current mood, his emerging needs. For every person it is a unique act of creation involving dissimilar materials. But it is, within broad limits, assumed to be predictable or there could be no theory of communication.

meanings not transferable: meanings are in people

The second, and more troublesome word, is "meaning." Meaning is not apparent in the ordinary flow of sensation. We are born into, and inhabit a world without "meaning." That life becomes intelligible to us—full of beauty or ugliness, hope or despair—is because it is assigned that significance by the experiencing being. As Karl Britton put it, "A world without minds is a world without structure, without relations, without facts."[2] Sensations do not come to us, sorted and labeled, as if we were visitors in a vast, but ordered, museum. Each of us, instead, is his own curator. We learn to look with a selective eye, to classify, to assign significance.

Communication arises out of the need to reduce uncertainty, to act effectively, to defend or strengthen the ego. On some occasions words are used to ward off anxiety. On other occasions they are means of evolving more deeply satisfying ways of expressing ourselves. *The aim of communication is to increase the number and consistency of our meanings within the limits set by patterns of evaluation that have proven successful in the past, our emerging needs and drives, and the demands of the physical and social setting of the moment.* Communication ceases when meanings are adequate; it is initiated as soon as new meanings are required. However, since man is a homeostatic, rather than static, organism, it is impossible for him to discover any permanently satisfying way of relating all his needs; each temporary adjustment is both relieving and disturbing, leading to successively novel ways of relating himself to his environment.

aim of communication: transform chaotic impressions into coherent, useful relationships

To say that communication occurs whenever meaning is assigned to internal or external stimuli is to enlarge greatly the span of our discipline. Communication, in this sense, may

[1] David Berlo, *The Process of Communication* (New York: Holt, Rinehart, Winston, 1960), p. 175.

[2] Karl Britton, *Communication: A Philosophical Study of Language* (New York: Harcourt, Brace, 1939), p. 206.

occur while a man waits alone outside a hospital operating room, or watches the New York skyline disappear at dusk. It can take place in the privacy of his study as he introspects about some internal doubt, or contemplates the fading images of a frightening dream. When man discovers meaning in nature, or in insight in his own reflections, he is a communication system unto himself. Festinger refers to this as "consummatory communication." The creation of meanings, however, also goes on in countless social situations where men talk with those who share or dispute their purposes. Messages are exchanged in the hope of altering the attitudes or actions of those around us. This can be characterized as "instrumental communication," as long as we remember that these two purposes are not mutually exclusive.

consummatory communication

What I am describing is a meaning-centered philosophy of communication. It admits that meaning in the sender, and the words of the messages are important, but regards as most critical the state of mind, the assumptive world and the needs of the listener or observer. The impact of any message from "See me after class" to "What's good for General Motors is good for the country" is determined by the physical, personal and social context, the most critical ingredient of which is the mind of the interpreter. Communication, so defined, does not require a speaker, a message, or a listener, in the restricted sense in which these terms are used in the field of speech. All may be combined in a single person, and often are.

meaning-centered philosophy of communication

A theory that leaves out man's communication with himself, his communication with the world about him and a large proportion of his interactions with his fellowman, is not a theory of communication at all, but a theory of speechmaking. Indeed, it seems applicable to speechmaking only in the most formal and restricted sense of that word. There is little in the traditional view of speech that is helpful in the analysis of conversation, interviewing, conflict negotiations, or in the diagnosis of the whole span of communicative disorders and breakdowns that are receiving so much attention currently. Upon so limited a view of communication it is unlikely that there can develop theories of sufficient scope and stature to command the respect of other disciplines or of the larger public that ultimately decides our role in the solution of man's problems. The field of speech seems to be fast approaching what the airlines call a "checkpoint" where one loses the freedom to choose between alternative flight plans, between a limited interest in speechmaking and a broad concern with

traditional view of speech: not helpful in analyzing much of our communication

the total communicative behavior of man. Be defining communication operationally, by examining a wider range of communicative acts, the way might be prepared for making the startling theoretical advances that have, so far, not characterized our field.

THE COMMUNICATION PROCESS

A satisfactory philosophy should also provide a starting point for the technical analysis of communication. One way of accomplishing this is to ask what characteristics would have to be built into a scientific model that would represent, at the same time and equally well, the entire spectrum from intrapersonal to mass communication. It should not be a model that is mechanically or structurally faithful, but one that is symbolically and functionally similar. Space is too limited here to more than suggest a few of the principles that would have to be reflected in such a model.

(1) Communication is not a thing, it is a process. Sender, message and receiver do not remain constant throughout an act of communication. To treat these as static entities, as they often are in our research, is questionable when applied to the most extreme form of continuous discourse, is misleading when used to analyze the episodic verbal exchanges that characterize face-to-face communication, and is totally useless in probing man's communication with himself. Changes in any of these forces, and few forces remain constant very long, reverberate throughout the entire system. Students of communication are not dissecting a cadaver, but are probing the pulsing evolution of meaning in a living organism.

communication: a process involving the total personality

(2) Communication is not linear, it is circular. There are many situations in life where a simple, linear, causal analysis is useful. One thing leads to another. A, then B, then C. I push over the first domino and the rest, in turn, topple over. But this sort of thinking is not very helpful, though quite appealing in its simplicity, in studying communication. There is not first a sender, then a message and finally an interpreter. There is, instead, what Henderson calls "mutual dependence" or what I have termed "interdependent functionalism." The words "sender" and "re-

communication process: circular, irreversible, unrepeatable, complex ceiver" no longer name the elements in a communicative act, but indicate the point of view of the critic at the moment.

(3) Communication is complex. Someone once said that whenever there is communication there are at least six "people" involved: The person you think yourself to be; the man your partner thinks you are; the person you believe your partner thinks you are; plus the three equivalent "persons" at the other end of the circuit. If, with as few as four constants, mathematicians must cope with approximately fifty possible relations, then we, in studying communication, where an even greater number of variables is concerned, ought to expound with considerable humility. In this age of Freudian and non-Freudian analysts, of information theory specialists, of structural linguists, and so on, we are just beginning to unravel the mysteries of this terribly involved, and therefore fascinating, puzzle.

(4) Communication is irreversible and unrepeatable. The distinction being suggested here is between systems that are deterministic and mechanical, and those that are spontaneous and evolutionary. One can start a motor, beat a rug, or return a book. But you cannot start a man thinking, beat your son, or return a compliment with the same consequences. The words of a teacher, even when faithfully repeated, do not produce the same effect, but may lead to new insight, increased tension, or complete boredom. A moment of indifference or interest, a disarming or tangential remark, leave indelible traces.

(5) Communication involves the total personality. Despite all efforts to divide body and mind, reason and emotion, thought and action, meanings continue to be generated by the whole organism. This is not to say that some messages do not produce greater or lesser dissonance, or shallower or deeper effects on the personality; it is only to hold that eventually every fact, conclusion, guilt, or enthusiasm must somehow be accommodated by the entire personality. The deeper the involvement produced by any communication, the sooner and more pervasive its effects upon behavior.

Research or instruction that disregards these characteristics of the communicative act would appear both unsound and of dubious value.

THE MORAL DIMENSION

The perennial and legitimate concern with ethics in the field of speech arises out of the inherent moral aspect of every interpersonal communication. As was noted earlier, the aim of communication is to transform chaotic sense impressions into some sort of coherent, intelligible and useful relationship. When men do this privately, either in confronting nature or in assessing their own impulses, they are free to invent whatever meaning they can. But when men encounter each other, a moral issue invades every exchange because the manipulation of symbols always involves a purpose that is external to, and in some degree manipulative of, the interpreter of the message. The complexity of communication makes it difficult to know in advance, and with certainty, the impact of any bundle of words upon the receiver of them. The irreversibility of communication means that whatever meaning is provoked by a message cannot be annulled. A teacher may erase a blackboard, a colleague apologize, or an employer change his mind, but there is no way of erasing the effect of a threatening ultimatum, a bitter remark, or a crushing personal evaluation.

interpersonal communication: a context for considering the element of ethics

Meaning, in my opinion, is a private preserve and trespassers always run a risk. To speak of personal integrity at all is to acknowledge this. Any exchange of words is an invasion of the privacy of the listener which is aimed at preventing, restricting, or stimulating the cultivation of meaning. Briefly, three types of interference may be distinguished. First, there are messages whose intent is to coerce. Meaning is controlled by choosing symbols that so threaten the interpreter that he becomes incapable of, and blind to, alternative meanings; second, there are messages of an exploitative sort in which words are arranged to filter the information, narrow the choices, obscure the consequences, so that only one meaning becomes attractive or appropriate; third, there is facilitative communication in which words are used to inform, to enlarge perspective, to deepen sensitivity, to remove external threat, to encourage independence of meaning. The values of the listener are, in the first case, ignored, in the second, subverted, in the third respected. While some qualification of this principle is needed, it appears that only facilitative communication is entirely consistent with the protection and improvement of man's symbolic experience. Unless a teacher is aware of these possibilities and appreciates the differences in these kinds of communication, it is unlikely that he will communicate responsibly in the classroom.

IMPLICATIONS FOR PREPARATION

communication: a study of meaning, and symbols and circumstances producing meaning

The outline of any philosophy must be expressed in abstract terminology. For that reason some will see little in this philosophy that is inconsistent with current practice in the field of speech. If so, my meaning has been less than clear. Once one accepts that communication is a study of meaning, and of all of the symbols and circumstances that give rise to meaning, he assumes new and formidable responsibilities as a scholar. Once he agrees that communication is a complicated, irreversible process, and accepts the moral obligation that inheres in such a conception, he embraces a new role as a teacher. Lest the practical consequences of endorsing such a philosophy go unexamined, let me attempt to translate the foregoing abstractions into more concrete form. What habits of preparation, what research interests, what sort of curriculum and what instructional methods follow from a commitment to a "meaning-centered philosophy of communication"?

All instruction begins with the discovery of knowledge, in this case with knowledge about communication. And the vast bulk of current information about communication is to be found not in the literature of our field but in the experimental investigations and theoretical systems of men in other disciplines. For this reason it would be difficult to imagine anyone committed to a meaning-centered philosophy of communication who was not already conversant with, or wanted to become conversant with, the men and works listed in the brief "Sampler in Communication" that follows. Each of these works is concerned at a sophisticated level with some aspect of meaning.[3]

meaning-centered philosophy: demands multi-disciplinary knowledge about communication

Sampler in Communication

Allport, F. *Theories of Perception and the Concept of Structure.* (New York: Wiley, 1955).

[3] This is not intended to be a definitive bibliography, only a suggestive sampling of sources. Substitutes could easily be made in every division of this bibliography. For example, in psychotherapy one could as easily recommend Ruesch's *Disturbed Communication* or Hoch and Zubin's *Psychopathology of Communication;* in cybernetics there is Walter's *The Living Brain* and Latil's *Machines That Think;* in literary criticism I. A. Richard's *Principles of Literary Criticism* or Burke's *Grammar of Motives;* in perception theory, Blake and Ramsey's *Perception: An Approach to Personality* and Beardslee and Wertheimer's *Readings in Perception;* in nonverbal communication one could recommend Hall's *The Silent Language* or Birdwhistell's *Introduction to Kinesics;* in semantics, Hayakawa's *Language in Thought and Action,* Korzybski's *Science and Sanity,* or Weinberg's *Levels of Knowing and Existence.* The purpose of the "Sampler" is only to indicate the broad scope of germinal studies of communicative behavior.

Anschen, R. *Language: An Enquiry into its Meaning and Function.* (New York: Harper, 1957).

Berlo, D. *The Process of Communication.* (New York: Holt, Rinehart, Winston, 1960).

Brown, R. *Words and Things.* (Glencoe, Ill.: The Free Press, 1958).

Burke, K. *A Philosophy of Literary Form.* (Baton Rouge: Louisiana State University Press, 1941).

Festinger, L. *A Theory of Cognitive Dissonance* (Evanston, Ill.: Row, Peterson, 1957).

Fromm, E. *The Forgotten Language.* (New York: Rinehart, 1952).

Hovland, C., Janis, I., and Kelly, H. *Communication and Persuasion.* (New Haven, Conn.: Yale University Press, 1953).

Langer, S. *Philosophy in a New Key.* (New York: Mentor Books, New American Library, 1948).

Osgood, C., Suci, G., and Tannenbaum, P. *The Measurement of Meaning.* (University of Illinois Press, 1957).

Rogers, C. *Client-Centered Therapy.* (New York: Houghton Mifflin, 1951).

Ruesch, J. *Communication: The Social Matrix of Psychiatry.* (New York: Norton, 1951).

Ruesch, J. and Kess, W. *Nonverbal Communication.* (Berkeley: University of California Press, 1956).

Wheelwright, P. *The Burning Fountain.* (Bloomington, Ind.: Indiana University Press, 1956).

Wiener, N. *The Human Use of Human Beings.* (New York: Anchor Books, Doubleday, 1950).

The breadth of this list, stretching from perception theory to symbolic processes, from cybernetics to psychotherapy, from literary criticism to cultural anthropology, matches the breadth of viewpoint intended in the phrase a "meaning-centered philosophy of communication." It is what George Miller seemed to have in mind when he wrote as preface to the first text in communication theory, "When one tries to assemble the facts about this important social event . . . the data come from all the fields of science."[4]

RESEARCH IMPLICATIONS

Preparation for offering training in communication, however, cannot depend upon sponging on the discoveries of others; it must, if our field is to survive, be advanced by empirical studies and theoretical constructs of our own. Tenure in the academic community is rightly contingent upon respect for the original contributions of a discipline. And, in this respect, it would be difficult to deny our theoretical sterility during the

[4] George A. Miller, *Language and Communication* (New York: McGraw-Hill, 1951), p. v.

past forty years. A large part of the fault seems to lie in the truncated view we hold of human communication. Medicine would scarcely have obtained recognition if it had limited itself to a study of the human arm. Sociology would be unknown today if it had never gone beyond the classification of criminals. Most of us would find unacceptable a psychology of man based on studies of hypnotism. Yet in our exclusive, or nearly exclusive, interest in formal public address we seem to be attempting the impossible—to build an overall theory of communication based upon a significant, but altogether too restricted, sample of human speech.[5]

need to broaden
research perspectives

What is needed is a broadening of perspective as to what constitutes legitimate research in communication, combined with an intensification of our efforts as research workers. There is no reason why the public platform should monopolize our attention. There is a whole universe of communication currently being neglected that could, and should be, studied. Whenever men work out new meanings, or defend old meanings, whether it involves parent and child, worker and boss, or client and therapist, the student of communication should be there. Sound training in communication is dependent upon the availability of respectable theories and objective data and these will be most valid when they are based on the whole span of human communication. The laboratory and library legitimize instruction.

CURRICULAR IMPLICATIONS

The lopsidedness of current work in speech is also evident in the hierarchy of courses offered to students. College catalogues show an almost exclusive concern with the formal aspects of communication. There are courses in public speaking, advanced public speaking, public debate, forms of public address, history of public address and so on. Here and there is a course in propaganda, in semantics, in business communication. But the curricular monolith we have designed adds to the impression that the rostrum is the only setting where communication among men matters.

[5] This is dramatically underscored whenever copies of *Speech Monographs* and the *Journal of Abnormal and Social Psychology* arrive in the same mail. Seldom does the former carry more than one title of empirical research in communication broadly conceived. Yet the last four issues of the *Journal of Abnormal and Social Psychology,* whose contributors are supposedly unqualified and uninterested in speech, carry between eight and ten titles on various aspects of communication in each issue.

The acceptance of a broader conception of our responsibilities should lead to a better balance in the curriculum in communication. Much of what exists would remain. But there would be a shift in emphasis in some offerings, and a compensating development of new work in areas currently neglected. There is no reason, if scholarship supports it, why there should not be courses in interpersonal communication, in conflict resolution, in decision-making, in organizational communication, in phycholinguistics, in societal communication, in network theory and so on. These can all be accommodated within a department of speech as long as the unifying focus of the curriculum is the problem of meaning and the control of it through symbols.

need to broaden communication curriculums

While the magnitude of a discipline of communication may seem frightening to envision, it does not seem any more so than the conception of psychology as the study of human behavior, or sociology as the study of social institutions, or anthropology as the study of cultures. Indeed, to build a significant discipline seems hopeless unless it encompasses a sufficiently broad cross-section of human activity to give it substance and scope.

If there is objection to this conception of communication because the lines separating our interests from those of psychology and sociology would be blurred and overlapping, they would appear to be no less blurred and overlapping than those already separating the behavioral sciences from each other. If students of communication will need to know their psychology, political science and history, it should also be true that a substantial discipline of communication will require students in other fields to be equally familiar with our contributions. If a distinguishing and unifying theme is required for the field of speech let it be our interest in language and how the manipulation of symbols alters human behavior, human institutions and cultural patterns.[6]

a unifying theme: language and symbol manipulation in human behavior, institutions, and culture

PEDAGOGICAL IMPLICATIONS

We come, finally, to the question of instruction. As in any problem of communication, meaning is a response to tensions in the nervous system of the communicant. This tension may be triggered externally for students through lectures, films,

[6]The broad conception of communication urged here is also the most promising basis for stopping, or even reversing, the continuing fractionalization of departments of speech.

demonstrations, or any other directive teaching technique. Or it may be generated from within by providing a facilitative setting which permits subconscious feelings of inadequacy, ineffectiveness, or inconsistency, to be admitted. As long as this tension is productive rather than reductive, that is, as long as it is disturbing without becoming unmanageable, it creates an opportunity for the evolution of new discriminations and meanings.

index of types of learning or communication

The resulting tension may be resolved, and learning accomplished, at a number of different psychological levels. Indexing of these types of learning, *or communication,* may clarify their differences. Learning$_1$ consists of acquiring new facts, new information, new terms. This is the simplest type of communication and probably involves the least disturbance to the receiver, for considerable information can be accommodated without altering the existing personality structure. When facts are discrepant with the student's world view, they are denied or distorted to protect past meanings. Learning$_2$ involves changes in outward behavior. The student acquires new skills which are largely the product of conforming to the directives of a coach or teacher. Recent studies suggest that this type of role-taking is likely to alter the personality in some ways, not all of which are desirable. Learning$_3$ occurs when the student discovers and adopts new attitudes toward communication. He begins to question his own assumptions and values, develops insight into his own motives and assumes

the student's total personality involved in learning

more responsibility for his own behavior. Learning$_4$ operates at all the preceding levels. The total personality of the student is involved—his knowledge, his attitudes, his actions. Teaching of this type aims at helping the student to become more conscious of his reasons for communicating and how these are linked to larger philosophical issues. It assists him in becoming increasingly aware of the complicated nature of communication, and its variety of uses and settings. It acquaints him with the multitude of technical means for accomplishing certain ends, and their immediate and long-term consequences. But while it sensitizes and informs him it should, in my opinion, leave the student free to evolve his own style and standards of communicating.

integrative instruction in communication needed

Alfred North Whitehead once said that any discipline deserving a place in the curriculum must have a philosophy, a method and a technique. The statement is undoubtedly true, but somewhat incomplete if philosophy, method and technique exist as isolated units of instruction. Too often what results is that the technical and moral aspects remain separate, lacking any vital connection in the classroom, and more importantly, in the personality of the student. The result is schizophrenic communication. Men learn to blot out all but technical considerations when communicating in a coercive or prejudicial way, but turn around and attack someone else's communication on moral grounds when it proves technically superior to their own. It is this sort of inconsistency that fosters pathological communication and pathological personalities.

Integrative instruction in communication encourages the student to work out better meanings concerning his own communication with himself and his fellowmen. By "better" I refer to meanings that permit more consistency in his personality between what he assumes, what he sees, and what he does. By "better" I refer to meanings that will increase his openness, curiosity and flexibility. By "better" I refer to meanings that will make him more independent, and more confident of his own judgment.

Lest the point of view presented here be interpreted as a paragon of philosophical virtue, the best possible theory in this best of all possible worlds, let me suggest some of the real obstacles and difficulties that stand in opposition to it. First there is the risk, in embracing the whole gamut of human communication, of tackling too much so that it cannot possibly be brought under control. There is a risk, too, of finding so much complexity that we shall have to return to the view that communication is an art that defies scientific analysis. The problems in making such an all-out attack on so broad a field are great; a conscientious teacher of speech already runs the risk of spending so much time in allied literature there is no time for original investigation of his own specialty. The view of training presented here is, also, an exceedingly moralistic one which, of itself, makes an academic discipline suspect these days. But science and morality must be conjoined when evidence indicates that the warping of communication is one of the most important factors in personality distortion.[7] These, and other objections, must be raised before taking this philosophy seriously.

Writing in the final pages of his last book, John Dewey made the remark that "As philosophers, our disagreements with one another as to conclusions are trivial in comparison

[7] Others in the behavioral sciences are belatedly reaching the same conclusion. The most penetrating and persuasive statement of the argument for linking psychological science with human values is to be found in Sigmund Koch's article, "Psychological Science versus the Science–Humanism Antinomy: Intimations of a Significant Science of Man," in the *American Psychologist,* October, 1961.

with our disagreements as to problems; to see the same problem another sees, in the same perspective and at the same angle—that amounts to something. Agreement as to conclusions is in comparison perfunctory."[8] The hope is not that all will share my conclusions—for few may—but that all will admit the problem facing our discipline, and see it from somewhat the same angle. That, indeed, would be something.

[8] John Dewey and Arthur Bentley, *Knowing and the Known* (Beacon Press, 1949), p. 314.

SUGGESTED FURTHER READING

Berlo, David K., *The Process of Communication.* New York: Holt, Rinehart, and Winston, Inc., 1960, Chapter 1. (See footnote 2, plus bibliography above.)

McCroskey, James C., *An Introduction to Rhetorical Communication.* Englewood Cliffs, N.J.: Prentice-Hall, Inc., 1968, Chapter 1.

Miller, Gerald R., "On Defining Communication: Another Stab," *Journal of Communication,* XVI (June, 1966), 88–89.

Nilsen, Thomas R., "On Defining Communication," *Speech Teacher,* VI (1957), 10–17.

Shannon, C. E. and W. Weaver, *The Mathematical Theory of Communication.* Urbana: University of Illinois Press, 1949.

Stevens, S. S., "Introduction: A Definition of Communication," *Journal of the Acoustical Society of America,* XXII (1950), 689.

The Process of Human Communication

Jimmie D. Trent and Judith S. Trent

All social groups, whether they be schools, businesses, states, marriages, or friendships, involve interaction between human beings. The success of those relationships is dependent upon the ability of the individuals to communicate their ideas, emotions, and goals. Among the many problems symbolized by the social unrest in our society, one problem, the inability to communicate, operates as cause, catalyst, and result of many of the others. It is the first symptom of many problems and the first step to correction of many others.

It is no longer sufficient to think of communication as simply public speaking or discussion and a series of accepted techniques for conducting these activities. It is no longer sufficient to think of audiences as monolithic. We must begin to think of speech-communication as a process of interaction between complex organisms called human beings. Only as we understand people and the complex process through which they derive meaning can we hope to become more effective communicators.

This essay discusses the process of human communication. Part I presents a verbal-pictorial model of the process. Part II contains some comments on differences and similarities between public speaking and interpersonal communication.

I

to understand communication, study what factors affect meaning in people

Speech communication is the process through which a speaker induces meaning in a listener. If you are to understand this process, you must study speakers and listeners and the factors which affect the meanings that they infer.

The process of communication can be described most readily by constructing a verbal-pictorial *model.*

The advantage of using a model to describe a process comes from the model's ability to visually portray relationships between the various elements at a glance. You may find it easier to remember the process if you can carry a mental picture of the model.

The limitations of using a model to portray the communication process are similar to those of using a picture to represent a stream. You can take a picture of a stream and its surroundings. When the picture is developed it may represent the stream well enough to allow you to recognize the exact place where the exposure was made. But when you find the exact place you will not be able to observe the stream as it was when the picture was taken; the water was in the process of going downstream while the exposure was being made. Your picture is a static representation of a dynamic process. In the same way, a communication model is a static representation of a dynamic process. We stop the action of a model in order to examine the components, but the process occurs in a fraction of a second and continues to flow after our model ends.

models: helpful but limited; static pictures can't show interaction

A model of communication resembles a picture of a stream in yet another way. A picture represents reflected light; in this case, the light which is reflected from the top of the stream exposes the film from which the picture is printed. If water consisted of peelable layers like mica, we could peel off the top layer and take another picture a fraction of an inch deeper in the stream. And we could keep peeling layers and taking pictures until we reached the bottom. The picture you took of the top of the stream would be representative of the total but it would distort reality to believe that variations not shown in the picture were not occurring concurrently.

In much the same way, a communication model distorts reality. What is shown as a single message or signal is actually a cluster of messages or signals interacting and affecting meaning. For example, the assigned meanings of words interact with the way they are said but a communication model does not portray that interaction.

With these limitations in mind, we can examine the process of communication. Communication requires idea formulation by both the speaker and the listener. Meanings occur only within people; communication is the process through which one person formulates a meaning and induces a second person to formulate approximately the same meaning. Thus, explanation of the communication process must examine the individuals involved and the factors which connect those individuals in the mutual acquisition and comprehension of ideas.

meanings occur only within people

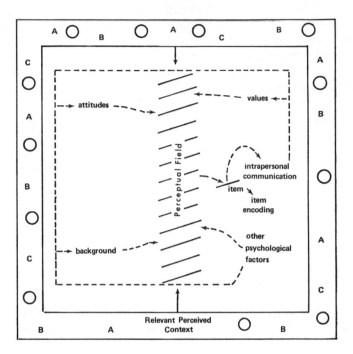

Figure 1.   THE PROCESS OF COMMUNICATION

Begin with the speaker or, as he is usually referred to in communication literature, the *source.* Examine the elements which determine the meanings which the source will formulate. Then examine the methods available to the source for affecting the meaning formulation of the listener or receiver.

THE SOURCE

meanings formulated in people's mental pictures of reality

The communication source formulates meanings in his *perceptual field,* which is affected by several factors. When the meaning is formulated, it is *encoded* for transmission and, at the same time, becomes an additional factor which affects the source's perceptual field in making judgments in the future. The source is portrayed in the model as shown in Figure 1.

Perceptual Field

people build realities based on experiences in their environments

The message originates in the source's mental picture of reality, that is, in his perceptual field. Meaning does not exist distinct from people; people create meanings according to the way they perceive reality. Meanings are inferences which people make from signs that they have received. Each individual builds his own picture of reality based upon his perceptions of experiences in his environment.

Meanings are formulated in ways which will be consistent with perceptual conclusions which already exist. For example, if while walking on campus on a sunny day, someone behind you calls for you to wait, you will derive a friendly meaning from the call. But when someone calls for you to wait when you are walking alone in a high crime district on a moonless night, you will formulate a threatening meaning.

Factors Affecting the Perceptual Field

The perceptual field is affected by several factors. The factors are represented in the model as though they are separate from the perceptual field, but they are actually a part of the source's mental picture of reality. This separation was made deliberately in order to illustrate through the use of arrows that the factors exert pressures which determine the nature of the field.

source's mental picture: internal factors plus perceived relevant context

Some of the factors are relatively long-lasting and operate to varying degrees in all decisions the source makes. Such factors, shown in the model as *attitudes, values, background,* and other psychological factors are internal in the sense that the source carries them with him regardless of changes of his immediate environment.

A less permanent factor affecting the psychological field is the *relevant perceived context* of the source. The communication event occurs in a context of physical objects, people, time, related and unrelated events, and the source's conception of the receiver in relation to himself. The context affects the source only to the extent that he perceives it as being relevant to the particular situation. Although there are many possible elements in the relevant perceived context (indicated by A, B, and C in the model), one of the most important when a deliberate attempt is being made to communicate, is the intended *receiver* (indicated by a circle in the model).

The internal factors and the relevant perceived context interact to create certain "determining tendencies" which influence the formation of the source's conception of reality and his perceptual conclusions about any specific item.

internal factors and perceived relevant context interact to form source attributes

The factors and context also determine what the source will attempt to communicate. For example, whites who have limited backgrounds in dealing with blacks will frequently mention their admiration of prominent black athletes or entertainers in social conversations with blacks. What does this tell us about the source? Situations can also affect item selection; immediately after the assassination of Martin Luther King, white people felt compelled to speak to blacks on the street.

Selection and Encoding

information items
encoded into signals

From the source's perceptual field, an information item (perceptual conclusion) is selected to be communicated. It cannot be communicated directly because thoughts are non-transferable. The information item must be encoded into *signals* which can be transmitted between people. Words are one form of *code.*

many speech
techniques important
as means of encoding
a message

It is at this point that the source makes decisions (at some level) regarding certain speech techniques which are commonly stressed in textbooks for basic courses in public speaking. Such variables as organization, style, evidence, and delivery are all means of encoding the message. Each of these variables operates as a complex signal; thus, communication is most effective when they are consistent.

The elements in the relevant perceived context are important in determining how information items will be, or should be, *encoded.* Changes in situations can change the agreed upon meaning of signals (words said between friends could start a war if said between diplomats). Again, in terms of item

receiver: an important
element in selecting
signals for encoding

encoding, the receiver is an important part of the relevant perceived context. The source will, or should, adapt his selection of signals to his perception of the receiver and the effect that he wishes to have upon the receiver. If he wants to have his message considered favorably, he will attempt to identify himself and his message with what he perceives to be the goals and self-identity of the receiver.

complete agreement on
the meaning of signals
is impossible

Another important consideration in the process of encoding is the selection of signals according to the meaning which the receiver is likely to assign. Words, like other signals, have no meaning *per se;* meanings are assigned to signals by people and communication depends upon the source and receiver approaching agreement on the meaning.

Of course, even if there is near agreement on the meaning of signals, the encoded item can never be the same as the information item which was formed in the source's perceptual field. The original information item or perceptual conclusion was formulated in the context of the source's perceptual field. No source is capable of encoding the experiences which affected his original inference.

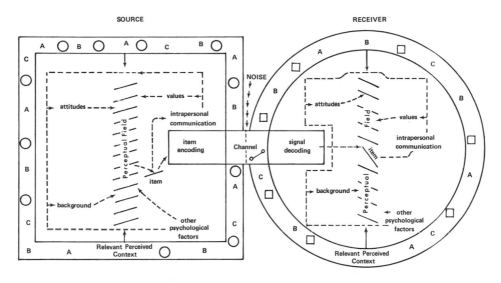

Figure 2.   THE PROCESS OF COMMUNICATION

Intrapersonal Communication

In addition to communicating to the receiver the source also communicates to himself and in this circular process changes himself at least to the extent that he makes salient certain of his attitudes and values. The process, depicted on the model by dotted lines and arrows, proceeds in this way: by selecting one item from his perceptual field the source calls attention to the item and gives it salience for himself (perhaps reducing in importance another cluster of attitudes) and then when he transmits this encoded message he commits himself both rhetorically and ideologically to the receiver. Thus *intra-personal* communication can ultimately have a significant effect on the source in the future commitments it may make for him, the choices it may close to him, and the image it portrays to which he must adjust.

With our discussion of the source completed, we are now ready to complete our model, as shown in Figure 2.

source communicates simultaneously to receiver and to himself

CHANNEL

After the item is encoded into a signal, it is transmitted through a *channel* which most commonly consists of light waves or air. The image of writing, for example, is carried as reflected

channel commonly consists of air and light waves

light waves. Vibrations in the air form what the receiver conceives as sounds. Variations in the gases which compose the air form different sense reactions in the receiver (i.e., different smells) and can signal that dinner will soon be ready or that the kitchen is on fire.

Note again that signals, not information items or perceptual conclusions, are transmitted through the channel. This is indicated in the model by changing the shape of the item while it is in the channel.

signals transmitted in channel often interrupted or distorted by noise

The signal may be interrupted or distorted while it is in the channel. Such interruptions are called *noise.* While noise may refer to sound, its meaning is interpreted more broadly by writers in communication theory. Anything which interrupts the channel sufficiently to prevent the listener from receiving an undistorted signal is called *noise.* For example, a bright light shining on the listener might so dominate his attention that he will not perceive an oral or written signal; in that case, the light would be noise. The possibility of noise is indicated in the model by a broken line through the channel.

noise: interruption of air or light waves in the channel

sources often unaware of noise in the channel

Noise is a receiver variable. It has occurred when the receiver's channel is interrupted. The source completes his portion of the communication act when the signal enters the channel. Noise occurs in the channel as perceived by the receiver. The source may not be aware that noise interrupted the channel. The receiver may not be aware that a signal was sent.

RECEIVER

When the signal reaches the receiver, the process described as happening in the source is reversed. The process will be discussed in terms of *decoding,* interpreting, intrapersonal communication, and response.

Decoding

receiver decodes signals into recognizable symbols

When the signal is received, it is composed of light variations or air vibrations; it must be changed to a recognizable symbol as the first step in the receiver's process of formulating meaning. If the symbol is to approximate the meaning intended by the source, it must have a similar denotation for the receiver. Even common symbols have different meanings for people with different backgrounds; for example, the word ''tough'' means rough for some people and neat or attractive for many college students.

Interpreting

The decoded item will be interpreted according to the perceptual field of the receiver. (The model indicates this by changing the slant of item when it reaches the receiver's perceptual field.) The item must be perceived by the receiver as being consistent with his concept of reality if it is to be believed and assimilated. In order to make an inconsistent item consistent, the individual may interpret it only partially or he may alter it to make it fit (the second possibility is illustrated in the model).

receiver interprets decoded items according to his perceptual field

consistency important to believing, assimilating decoded items

Even if the item is generally consistent with the receiver's perceptual field, it will still be interpreted according to the field and the pressures exerted upon it. As with the source, factors such as attitudes, values, background experiences, and the relevant perceived context have an effect on the way the receiver interprets the item. Connotations will be added to the denotative meanings which were assigned to the symbol in decoding. Since each person's total perceptual field is unique, each will interpret messages slightly differently.

messages interpreted slightly differently by each unique person

The elements in the relative perceived context of the receiver will always be different from those in the source's context. As indicated by the squares in the model, one of the more dominant contextual elements for the receiver is his perception of the source. The receiver may perceive the source with respect, trust, and goodwill; he may also perceive the source with disrespect, distrust, and hostility. The receiver's perception of the source can alter the interpretation of the symbols. For example, Joe's boss says, "Joe, you have been working too hard lately. Bill has just finished another job and I don't have anything for him to do, so I am going to have him do part of your work. And Joe, while you're at it, why don't you teach him to do the rest of your job, just in case you want to take a day off some time?" How will Joe interpret this message? While the denotations seem rather clear, the connotations may be far more important. Note how the connotations differ when the boss is viewed with hostility and when he is viewed with goodwill.

receiver's perception of source affects interpretation of symbols

Intrapersonal Communication

After the item is interpreted, it becomes a part of the perceptual field and a factor which affects the field. The receiver is changed; his mental picture of reality is altered; future items relative to the interpreted item will be interpreted in terms of their consistency with his altered world. This change

receiver slightly changed after the message has been transmitted can be expected to be less effective than the comparable change in the source was. The source reinforced his changed perception through public commitment; unless the receiver chooses to assume the role of source in another sequence of communication, he will not have made a public commitment and will thus avoid the restrictions on future conclusions and behavior.

RESPONSE

feedback: receiver's reaction to source and message

The receiver will react in some way to the item. If the reaction is received by the source (or what was the source of the original item), *feedback* will have occurred. Feedback involves the same process as the original communication act. It is important because it provides data from which the original source can make inferences regarding the success of his attempt at communication. Communication of complex or unusual ideas may require several interchanges before the receiver's formulation of meaning will approximate the source's perceptual conclusion. The source cannot hope that the receiver's perceptual conclusion will be exactly the same as his; what the source can hope for is similarity sufficient for operational understanding.

II

As you can see, even in its simplest form the process of human communication is complex. When two people attempt to communicate, the complexities of each must in some way interrelate if both are to formulate approximately the same meaning.

When we think of public speaking, the speaker's problems are compounded still further by the rules, both formal and informal, and expectations, both actual and imagined, of the group. Fortunately, most members of a group will belong because they have some major characteristics in common. Without this commonality, it would probably by impossible to communicate more than the simplest noncontroversial ideas to any group.

But the common bond which holds audiences together depends upon many variables. Why are they together? Were they a group before they came to hear you speak? Or are they strangers to each other who happen to find you or your subject interesting? Is this their primary group or do most of the members have stronger loyalties to other groups? What situations are influencing their beliefs and thus influencing their reformulation of your messages? These questions are only suggestive of the myriad of variables which can affect your attempt at communication.

If you are to be a successful communicator, you must be prepared to deal with the variables which are present. In order to adjust, you must learn what it is that forces your adjustment and you must develop a variety of skills from which you can select behavior appropriate for the situation you will face.

SUGGESTED FURTHER READING

Barker, Larry and Gordon Wiseman, "A Model of Intrapersonal Communication," *The Journal of Communication,* XVI, No. 3 (September, 1966), 172–179.

Berlo, David K., "Model," *The Process of Communication.* New York: Holt, Rinehart and Winston, Inc., 1960, 72.

Cherry, Colin, *On Human Communication.* Cambridge, Massachusetts: Technology Press of MIT, 1957.

Deutsch, Karl W., "On Communication Models in the Social Sciences," *The Public Opinion Quarterly,* XVI (Fall, 1952), 356–380.

Keltner, John W., *Interpersonal Speech Communication: Elements and Structure.* Belmont, California: Wadsworth Publishing Company, 1970.

Martin, Howard H. and C. William Colburn, *Communication and Consensus: An Introduction to Rhetorical Discourse.* New York: Harcourt Brace Jovanovich, Inc., 1972.

McCroskey, James C. and Carl E. Larson and Mark L. Knapp, *An Introduction to Interpersonal Communication.* Englewood Cliffs, N.J.: Prentice-Hall Publishing Co., 1971, Chapter 1.

Ross, Raymond, *Speech Communication: Fundamentals and Practice.* Englewood Cliffs, N.J.: Prentice-Hall Publishing Co., 1970.

Schramm, Wilbur, *The Process and Effects of Mass Communication.* Urbana: University of Illinois Press, 1955, 3–26.

ACTIVITIES

1. How did Bryant define rhetoric? Write a paragraph in which you explain the key differences between Bryant's concept of rhetoric and Barnlund's concept of communication.

2. Based upon your experiences and observations, list what you consider to be the qualities or characteristics of an effective communicator. Examine your list and, considering the definitions of communication and rhetoric presented in Part I, draft your own definition of speech communication.

3. Informally discuss with the members of your class the proposition, suggested in the Trent and Trent essay and the Barnlund essay, that "meanings are not transferable, meanings are in people."

4. Begin a communication journal in which five of your attempts at communication are recorded each day. Determine for each whether the attempt was successful. What could you have done to make the attempt more successful?

5. Consider the model presented in the Trent and Trent essay. Diagram your own model of communication. Include elements you think are essential to the communication process.

Part 2.

Concepts of Source and Message

2.

Introduction (by Jimmie D. Trent). Whether we are thinking about interpersonal communication or public speaking, the most important element is the meaning formulated by the listener. If we could alter listeners to make their perceptual fields identical with our own, we would not have to worry about the conclusions they derive from our attempts to communicate. Listeners' meanings would duplicate our own. Obviously, this is not possible. We must approach listeners as they are.

What we can do is learn about listeners and adapt our messages. We can be conscious of the meaning our verbal and nonverbal behavior will have for a listener. Whether in conversations, negotiations, or large audience situations, we will have to take responsibility for the meanings derived from our messages. Thus, while the listener is important, much of our emphasis in improving communication must be directed to concepts of sources and messages.

The source and the message can be studied separately or together. While thinking of the source and the message as separate entities is not an uncommon practice, a more accurate view of the speech-communication process must consider them interdependent. Every message has a source and, in one way or another, the source is represented in the message. In addition, as you learned in Part One, the source is potentially part of the message and the message also affects the source or speaker. Thus, consideration of source and message as separate entities must be presented in a context which acknowledges their interrelationships.

It is, of course, obvious that every message has a source. On an elementary level, it is obvious that the source or speaker is represented in the message; the subject choice, beliefs expressed, and the purpose obviously originate with the source.

In order to test this concept, we might try to deny it by speculating about totally ghost written speeches. Such speeches are sometimes prepared for delivery by governmental officials. The official merely reads what someone else has written. We might argue that the subject choice, beliefs, and purpose did not originate with the speaker. But such an argument would involve mere semantic game-playing; the true source would then be the person who wrote the speech rather than the person who delivered it. The person who delivered the speech would be part of the channel that the message went through in arriving at its destination.

We might also argue that a source can consciously prepare a deceptive message; one designed to distort his feelings, beliefs, or goals.

Would such a messge not represent the source? Probably it would, but the deception would be part of the message. If the deception were discovered, it would become the dominant element. What was said or what will be said in the future will probably not be as important to the receiver as the knowledge that the source or speaker tried to mislead him. The deceptive message would represent the source, both in the present and in future contexts.

Source and message are also interrelated because the source is part of the message. As was discussed in Part One, the listener will reconstruct the message from the signals he receives. The source or speaker's delivery and appearance are signals which affect the meaning which the listener will assign to words.

The listener's attitudes toward the source will also affect the meaning assigned to signals. For example, if the listener trusts the source and believes that they have common goals, the interpretation which will be placed on signals may differ significantly from what it would have been in a context of distrust.

In addition to the listener and message being affected by the source, the source is himself affected by the message he constructs and presents. As a source or speaker decides which ideas he will present and how he will phrase and develop ideas, his own thinking is crystalized and structured. Depending upon the importance of the message, varying amounts of the source's future thinking will be affected.

The source or speaker will also be affected by the degree of public commitment that he makes when he presents the message. When he goes on record with a particular point of view, he will be forced to rationalize a change in view before he can present opinion.

Thus the source and his message are interrelated because the message represents the source, the source is part of the message, and the message affects the source.

Does this mean that the source and message can never be considered separately for pedagogical purposes? Obviously not. Before the individual decides to speak, he exists and has characteristic attitudes and behavior.

And the potential source or speaker can learn many skills which are not message-specific. For example, a wide range of delivery skills can be developed which will have potential application regardless of the message.

The message can also have characteristics which do not relate to the source per se. For example, a speech might be said to follow a problem-solution pattern of organization without revealing anything about its content or source. The speaker or the message can be studied, discussed, theorized, or learned about in isolation; but, as we turn to a consideration of articles, we should keep in mind the total communication process and the interaction between the variables.

The first article, "A Fresh Attitude toward Rationalism" by Robert L. Scott, is primarily about the message but is based upon the limitations of man, whether he be speaker or listener. Scott examines the basic tenet of twentieth-century speech education that man is a rational animal capable of operating solely on the basis of logic if he is given a chance. In a paradox which Scott points out himself, a rational case is built advocating that rationality is not possible. Scott's proposal for a fresh attitude represents an attempt to approach rationality pragmatically in order to preserve the advantages accrued from attempting to be logical.

Without committing ourselves to his position, we can look at Scott's approach as a framework for consideration of the articles within this section. Each article attempts to talk about communication attempts or effects in relation to the way man is, rather than to the way we wish he were.

The second article, "The Substance of Rhetoric: Good Reasons," by Karl R. Wallace, encourages scholars to study the themes and content of speeches as well as the structure and style. Wallace argues that the basic materials of discourse are ethics and values and that these are applied in the stating of good reasons for belief. Scholars are asked to study speeches to determine what successful speakers have considered to be "good" in the past, in the hope that it will provide a list of value applications which might be used in future messages. You should gain understanding of the way values determine what you and others say.

"Finding Good Reasons" by Jimmie D. Trent is the second essay written especially for this volume, and it builds on Wallace's article. Accepting the premise that speeches are built around good reasons, the Trent essay explores in greater depth the nature of values and decisions based upon values. The article stresses that while it is useful to learn the values used by speakers in the past, it is essential in speech planning to discover the values of the specific audience which will judge the reasons we present. A method is presented for learning the values of a specific audience.

Professor Ronald H. Carpenter's original essay, "The Problem of Style in Presidential Discourse," explains, and applies to speech criticism, a concept which many students and scholars have found troublesome. After defining style operationally, Carpenter discusses it as a variable which has an effect on audiences. By utilizing familiar presidential discourse, Carpenter both enriches our understanding of those historical events and makes concrete the application of stylistic devices for effect. As you read this scholarly but frequently amusing article, you might think of ways that stylistic devices can help you communicate more effectively.

Another original essay, "A Summary of Research on Order Effects in Communication" by Professor Loren J. Anderson, discusses the decisions a speaker must make about the organization of his message. Anderson summarizes the findings of experimental research and explains what they mean in answering three questions which a speaker might ask: (1) Should I place my strongest argument first, or last? (2) Should I outline the solution before discussing the problem, or vice versa? (3) Should I discuss one or both sides of the issue? Anderson's answers, like the research, accept the achievement of the desired effect as criterion for judgment. Organizational patterns are considered to be only one variable which affects audience reaction to both the message and the speaker.

Since Aristotle's time, the audience's opinion of the speaker has been called *ethos* and considered to be one of the three factors affecting persuasion, the other two being logic and emotion. Professor Paul I. Rosenthal questions both the tripartite division and the classical definition of *ethos* in his article "The Concept of Ethos and the Structure of Persuasion." After defining logic and emotion in terms of the physiological reactions they represent in the listener, Rosenthal argues that ethos is a distinct level of persuasion which contains elements of both logic and emotion. He further specifies conditions which will make ethos the controlling factor in influencing opinions. Ethos is present as a complex variable which can become the dominant factor or which can be relatively insignificant.

The last two articles in this section each take cognizance of the experimental findings which deny the long-accepted belief that evidence is necessary for effective speaking. While the authors accept that evidence is not required in every speaking situation where belief is sought, they argue that evidence is a variable which interacts with other variables and, which depending on the nature of the other variables, may be either essential or of no effect. Professor William R. Dresser, in "The Impact of Evidence on Decision Making," formulates hypotheses about situations which require evidence from the writings of experimentalists, semanticists, and case studies of famous speakers. The last study, Professor James C. McCroskey's "A Summary of Experimental Research on the Effects of Evidence in Persuasive Communication," reports not only the findings of other experimenters but also the results of a series of studies which he and his students conducted with the specific purpose of isolating variables which determine the effectiveness of evidence.

The eight articles in Section Two present some of the best thinking available in the field today on the variables which affect the communication process. While there are variables omitted, those discussed here should provide an adequate background for you to begin to make your own judgments about what communication behavior is most important in a particular speaking situation. The emphasis is on the speaker and his message but only in so far as variations in those factors affect the response which can be expected from the audience.

As you read this section, think about the principles you have learned. To what extent are they applicable in a particular situation? When will you have to make exceptions in your speech communication behavior in order to accomplish your purpose? The articles which follow should help you to make such judgments.

A Fresh Attitude
toward Rationalism

Robert L. Scott

What impressed Prince Andrey as the leading characteristic of Speransky's mind was his unhesitating, unmovable faith in the power and authority of the reason. It was plain that Speransky's brain could never admit the idea—so common with Prince Andrey—that one can never after all express all one thinks. It had never occurred to him to doubt whether all he thought and all he believed might not be meaningless nonsense. And that peculiarity of Speransky's mind was what attracted Prince Andrey most.[1]

If one were to take from Tolstoy's *War and Peace* the character of Speransky to typify the consistent bias of twentieth century speech education, he would overdraw the portrait. The picture would be caricature. Yet in caricature some value might be discovered.

Since the definition of man as a rational animal has dominated the thinking of Western man, one should not be surprised to find that speech texts, curricula, and declarations of good intentions on behalf of the field have featured descriptions of rational behavior. These descriptions become formulae for the student to follow—means of patterning assertions and data to create public speeches which will manifest the rational process, or, turning to discussion, steps to follow in cooperative problem solving, or some variation on stock issue analysis in school debates.

The complex meaning which ordinarily surrounds the utterance, "Man is a rational animal," tends to exhibit two distinct characteristics. First, it calls attention to the process

Note: Robert L. Scott (Ph.D., University of Illinois, 1955), is Professor of Speech, Communication, and Theatre Arts, University of Minnesota.

[1]Leo Tolstoy, *War and Peace,* Part Six, Chapter 6 (Constance Garnett trans., Modern Library Giant, p. 398).

of reasoning, that is, to man's capacity to draw conclusions from evidence. Secondly, it assumes the efficacy of reasoning; put another way, it suggests that man can act harmoniously with his reason and that in doing so he can create good. The act of invoking *rationality* ordinarily suggests that man *has* an ability that distinguishes him from other animals and that he *should* depend upon it.

A *partitio* at this point may be appropriate. After inquiring briefly into the origins of the notion of rationality in the discipline of speech, this essay will argue that the notion has been and must be severely questioned. A proposal will then be set forth. Although modest, it will claim several advantages.

rational bias probably
derived from Aristotle

Is it not inevitable that any speech teacher who goes back to the beginning of things cite Aristotle? As departments of speech became established in this century, scholars drew heavily on classical tradition and particularly on Aristotle. Although his work has been subjected to numerous interpretations, these interpretations exhibit a strong tendency to present him as making reason primary. Edwin Black has argued tellingly that for Aristotle rhetoric was fundamentally a matter of making rational judgments, that the other modes of argument are subordinated to the logical.[2] One can discard Black's case and make distinctly different interpretations, but eventually these interpretations will lead back to the same conclusion. Perhaps Black was right to label as "neo-Aristotelianism" the critical adaptations often made; at any rate, interpretations of Aristotle probably account for much of the rational bias in speech texts and courses.

enlightenment thinkers
encouraged growth of
the rational bias

One must be struck, moreover, with the climate of thought in which this Aristotelianism flourished. Apparently nothing could have been much more conducive to its hardy growth than the buoyant American belief in progress as the fruit of the free, informed mind. The great break with the past, first intellectual and then political, came in the seventeenth century (now referred to as the Age of Reason) and flowered in the eighteenth. The Enlightenment thinkers bequeathed the optimism that still permeates most utterances of man-is-a-rational-animal. Carl L. Becker's summation of the Enlightenment is justly famous. He makes it in four propositions:

(1) man is not natively depraved; (2) the end of life is life itself, the good life on earth instead of the beatific life after death; (3) man is capable, guided solely by the light of reason and

[2] Edwin Black, *Rhetorical Criticism* (New York: The Macmillan Co., 1965), see esp. pp. 125–128.

experience, of perfecting the good life on earth; and (4) the first and essential condition of the good life on earth is the freeing of men's minds from the bonds of ignorance and superstition, and of their bodies from the arbitrary oppression of the constituted social authorities.[3]

The third proposition is of most concern here, but note how neatly it interlocks with the others.

Becker's typification of the Enlightenment helps locate an aspect of the sense of rationality—of what it is and what it does. This is not to say that from the eighteenth century to the present every utterance has been in praise of the efficacy of reason—strong criticisms have been entered from several points of view—but rationality is still the strongest tenet of twentieth century speech education. So strong is the belief in *being rational* that an attempt to call the premise into question may seem difficult to understand, if not silly, perverse, or downright diabolic.

The argument which will follow concludes not simply that the ordinary sense of rationality ought to be called into question but that it ought to be discarded as unsupportable. This argument will draw from three points of view.

the ordinary sense of rationality is unsupportable

It is a familiar fact that for centuries the word "philosophy" was the term which applied to human inquiry and learning generally. The use of the term "natural philosophy" pointed to a series of forks in the road. Science became a clearly marked and separate path, and soon other disciplinary divisions became apparent until today we live in a thoroughly departmentalized intellectual world.

Psychology became a distinct discipline in the late nineteenth century. Perhaps the most apparent example of a specialist in this realm to cite as challenging the picture of man as a rational animal would be Sigmund Freud for "consciousness is the *surface* [emphasis Freud's] of the mental apparatus. . . ."[4] Under his lead "rationalization" became the term for the use of reason to deceive the self; an overwhelmingly common phenomenon. To Freud, and to psychoanalysts generally, the conscious is but a function of the outermost portion of the *ego* which in turn is a function of the *id* generally, the *id,* of course, being a name for the reservoir of instinctual impulses. Reason has a role in depth psychology, but the role

psychology rejects rationality

[3] *The Heavenly City of the Eighteenth-Century Philosophers* (New Haven: Yale University Press, 1959), pp. 102–103.

[4] *Ego and Id,* Trans. James Strachey, *Standard Edition of the Complete Works of Sigmund Freud,* XIX (London: Hogarth, 1961), p. 19.

seems fundamentally a subordinate one; it operates not only in rationalization but in such mechanisms as repression and transference. It belongs to our surface experiences.

But one need not depend on Freud to reject the ordinary notion of rationality. The dominant American school of psychology is behaviorism. As complex as the work of the behaviorists has become, an examination of their general tendencies from nearly any angle reveals the unsupportability of a primary position for rationality. For example, if there is a key word for behaviorism generally, it probably is *conditioning.* The simple model of stimulus-response bonds may need numerous modifications to explain complex human behavior, but if it is accepted as the fundamental operation in determining behavior, rationality must be a subsidiary function.

This conclusion does not deny the reality of cognitive experience. Cognition, in fact, may be looked on as a part at least of the important function of mediation, which is to admit that for the most part human behavior is not simple reflex, nor just the product of a number of simple reflexes. But giving a mediating role to cognition is not to grant it the sort of domination that rationality assumes in speech texts and classes.

sociology rejects rational control of environment

The fundamental assumptions of sociology may also be invoked to call into question the primacy of rationality. Sociology has been built on the proposition that society is organismic. From this proposition, one must argue that the human, or any animal, may be studied as a distinct organism, but that such a study must fall short of explaining the nature of the object of interest. The individual organism is not only formed by but is a continuing part of the dynamic social unit. Whereas this view does not reject reason, it cannot grant to individual, rational man sovereignty over his physical and social environment, nor over himself.

A philosophic position may also be entered as a vantage point from which to argue that man-is-a-rational-animal is not a supportable definition. Any definition will be in some way a reduction of reality. If one attends to all aspects of any set of phenomena, he will not be able to define at all. He must select some features to settle on as essential to his purposes. Most persons will probably agree that the process of definition is in an important way arbitrary. An objection to a definition is apt to be an objection to omitting certain features.

In part the objection developed in this essay to the rationalist bias in speech education is such an objection. The rationalist bias tends to omit the contradictoriness that gives richness to human experience. But, since this objection may seem to be purely a matter of taste, and since it has been argued at length recently,[5] a different line of argument must be developed.

Most agree that in a rational process there must be a starting place, some proposition or propositions that are root. No one is surprised to find that a disagreement, when examined, reveals that the parties began at different starting points. Sometimes those who disagree are able to resolve their differences by reinterpreting their assumptions. At other times they are able to reduce the importance of disagreement by agreeing arbitrarily, recognizing and allowing to stand, differences either apparent or suspected.

rationality depends on obtaining a complete set of axioms

The dream that has haunted rationalists since Plato is to reduce everything to an axiomatic system. That is to say, to discover a finite set of propositions that can be accepted without proof and on the basis of which theorems can be derived with no other means than logic. Thus the axioms will be the foundation of the system and the theorems its superstructure. The model, and most successful approximation of the ideal to date, is Euclidean geometry.

Some twentieth century scientists are coming to the conclusion that an axiomatic ideal is unattainable. In his book, *Computers and Commonsense,* Mortimer Taube poses a key question: can mathematics be reduced to a complete and consistent system?[6] Until 1931, Taube says, mathematicians would have answered this question "yes"; today, few will. In that year, Kurt Gödel published a revolutionary paper. A long quotation from Newman and Nagel's recent book, *Gödel's Proof,* indicates the revolution in thinking Gödel's work necessitates:

> Within the past two centuries the axiomatic method has come to be exploited with increasing power and vigor. New as well as old branches of mathematics, including the familiar arithmetic of cardinal (or "whole") numbers, were supplied with what appeared to be adequate sets of axioms. A climate of opinion was thus generated in which it was tacitly assumed that each sector of mathematical thought can be supplied with a set of axioms sufficient for developing systematically the endless totality of true proportions about the given area of inquiry.

[5] See Robert L. Scott, "Some Implications of Existentialism for Rhetoric," *Central States Speech Journal,* XV (November 1964), 267–278; and "Rhetoric Is Epistemic," *Central States Speech Journal,* XVIII (February 1967), 9–17.

[6] Mortimer Taube, *Computers and Commonsense* (New York: Columbia University Press, 1963), p. 9.

Gödel's paper showed that this assumption is untenable. He presented mathematicians with the astounding and melancholy conclusion that the axiomatic method has certain inherent limitations, which rule out the possibility that even the ordinary arithmetic of the integers can ever be fully axiomatized. What is more, he proved that it is impossible to establish the internal logical consistency of a very large class of deductive systems—elementary arithmetic, for example—unless one adopts principles of reasoning so complex that their internal consistency is as open to doubt as that of the systems themselves. In the light of these conclusions, no final systematization of many import areas of mathematics is attainable, and no absolutely impeccable guarantee can be given that many significant branches of mathematical thought are entirely free from internal contradiction.[7]

Gödel's proof shows the ideal to be unattainable

Gödel's proof should be a death blow to the notion that, even if there are clear truths apparent to the mind, a complete and consistent system can be built from them. The tendency to teach students that their thought can be somehow purified by a cleansing with logical forms, by de-personalizing it in effect, is a pernicious one, and one which must be rejected on the grounds of consistency since it draws its strength from an appeal to an ideal which turns out to be unattainable.

Although the case against what has been referred to in this paper as the rationalist bias is complete, there are some paradoxes arising from the arguments which must be considered. If one finds himself tending to agree that the bias is not supportable, his agreement probably rests on his predispositions. Agreement has been sought consistently in this essay as a basis for further agreement. If one agrees that the case against the rationalist bias is important, the sense of importance probably springs from ambivalence, that is, one is attracted to the rationalist bias at the same time he is repelled from it.

man encounters paradox when his reason tell him to reject reason

From the outset the argument of this paper has had an aura of absurdity about it. The degree to which an attempt to build a rational case against rationalism is successful, to that degree the case refutes itself. In short, a man encounters paradox when his reason tells him to mistrust reason. Recognizing the paradox does not relieve the tension caused by the contrary forces. How may the dissonance be reduced? Must the maxim man-is-a-rational-animal be discarded as a foundation for texts and courses in speech?

A courageous answer to this question is, "Yes and no."

[7]Ernest Nagel and James R. Newman, *Gödel's Proof* (New York: New York University Press, 1965), pp. 5–6.

Yes, the ordinary conception of rational man must be discarded as a dead weight. It is a dead weight in two ways.

First, the old rationalist modes are suspect. Speech teachers must be much less confident of their ability to describe the way that human beings think and on the basis of those descriptions to recommend the shape that speeches ought to take. Any attempt to reduce theory to an axiomatic scheme is especially dubious.

Secondly, the attitude that accompanies the old bias is especially detrimental. Speech teachers must relinquish the old faith in the efficacy of reason. The old optimism is dangerous because in the face of its shoddiness men are losing faith not only in reason but in man. The present is marked by cynicism and self-centeredness. Men suspect that salvation will not follow quickly from the free exercise of their reason. This suspicion has become an invitation to exploit one another by the instruments of social science and mass communication. The exploitation has greatly worried some of the leaders in speech education. The remedy, however, is not to insist shrilly on the efficacy of reason.

Man's faith in rationality must be built on a fresh foundation. This recommendation may seem quite inconsistent with the case just constructed. But rationality must be given new meaning, and the first step toward the necessary change will be a different attitude toward the familiar maxim, one more consistent with what the analysis just completed shows the strength of rationality to be. To affirm one's faith in the rationality of man, in the face of what the last few centuries has taught us about man, is to affirm one's faith in man at his weakest.

affirming faith in rationality affirms faith in man at his weakest

To affirm one's faith in this manner is not to claim that through the exercise of his reason man will or that any one man can triumph—in terms of success, happiness, or whatever. It is to say that there is something in one's experience that makes him want to be as rational as he is able, recognizing that his ability is weak and hoping that he may strengthen it, but with no expectation of consistent success.

an affirmation: man wants to be as rational as he is able

The attitude suggested is one which has been expressed many times. One of the most famous and most beautiful expressions is Pascal's:

> Man is only a reed, the weakest to be found in nature; but he is a thinking reed. It is not necessary for the whole of nature to take up arms to crush him: a puff of smoke, a drop of water, is enough to kill him. But, even if the universe should crush

him, man would still be more noble than that which destroys him. The universe knows nothing of this.

All our dignity, then, consists in thought. It is upon this that we must depend, not on space and time, which we would not in any case be able to fill. Let us labour, then, to think well: this is the foundation of morality.[8]

Clearly enough Pascal does not say that it is man's reason which is weak, but man himself. It is not untrue to the spirit of Pascal, however, to designate man's unconscious, or the force of history, or of society as that capable of crushing man but not capable of knowing. If man can be identified with all of nature, as atoms, themselves formed of energy, which is conserved even though the specific manifestations change constantly, then man as nature knows not. Rational man is the reed.

acting with faith in rational man brings benefits

Accepting faith in rational man and acting consistently with this faith may bring about several benefits. Our activity and attitudes will give us an alternative to the two concerns that fill so much of our time as speech teachers and researchers: the cold-blooded search for effective means of persuasion and the frantic, frustrated demand for involvement and commitment as somehow antidotes to the consequences that apparently many suspect are inherent in service to the criterion of effect.

Teaching students to be consistent with an attitude of belief in the rational in spite of its weakness ought to teach them to be tolerant of the efforts of others to express persuasively their beliefs. Differences will be more readily recognized as the result of uniqueness and limits of individuality rather than attributed to pernicious self-interest which subverts truth rationally observable from the proper point of view, the latter, of course, being one's own. Tolerance should spring not only from a recognition of man's weakness but from a sense of the necessity of the participation of the other in the communication process in order to make maximum the feeble power that each possesses.

The mutual dependence of speaker and audience, fellow participants in conferences, or opponents in debates, should be highlighted rather than consistency with some standards which may be known objectively and manipulated with the sort of certainty the rationalist bias suggests.

Clearly, then, saying that one ought to declare a faith in rationality in full recognition of its weakness is not to be

[8]*Pensees.* Chapter XIII.

pessimistic. Once freed of the false notion that man can make what he thinks fully rational, that he can if he simply presents his thought in proper form win the assent of all worthy listeners, perhaps speech teachers can find ways to enable man to take more nearly complete advantage of those powers of reason that he does possess.

SUGGESTED FURTHER READING

Blan, Joseph L., "Public Address as Intellectual Revelation," *Western Speech,* XXI (Spring, 1957), 77–83.

Bryant, Donald C., "Aspects of the Rhetorical Tradition: The Intellectual Foundation," *Quarterly Journal of Speech,* XXXVI (April, 1950), 169–176.

Oliver, Robert R., "Human Motivation: Intellectually, Emotionally and Rationalization," *Quarterly Journal of Speech,* XXII (February, 1931), 67–77.

Rank, Vermont, "Rationalization as a Factor in Communication," *Speech Teacher,* IX (April, 1956), 10–21.

Scott, Robert L., "Some Implications of Existentialism for Rhetoric," *Central States Speech Journal,* XVIII (February, 1967), 9–17. (See footnote 5 above.)

————, "Rhetoric is Epistemic," *Central States Speech Journal,* XVIII (February, 1967), 9–17. (See footnote 5 above.)

The Substance of Rhetoric:

Good Reasons

Karl R. Wallace

Rhetorical theorists have always recognized that speeches have content and substance, and that the content of a particular speech is derived from the setting and occasion. Yet unlike classical rhetoricians who presented systems of invention, modern writers who offer theories of rhetoric are unclear and uncertain what to say about the materials of discourse. They will include in their theories statements about methods, principles, techniques, and styles of discourse; that is, they talk of the forms and the handling of ideas and are mostly silent about the substance of utterance. Perhaps they are silent for three main reasons. Under the influence of structural linguistics, rhetoricians may uncritically believe that language is like the symbols of music and mathematics—empty and devoid of substantial meanings. Or they may overlook the full implication of Donald Bryant's reference to rhetoric as an art of adjusting ideas to people and people to ideas.[1] The notion of adjustment—and for that matter, adaptation—directs attention chiefly to acts of manipulation and treatment. It is easy to forget that one cannot engage in manipulation without manipulating something, and that speakers and audiences stand on common ground only through commonalities of meaning and partial identities of experience. If this simple fact is acknowledged, there always bobs up that old, bothersome question: With what ideas, with what materials do speakers adjust and adapt to their hearers? Finally, for the last century or so students of rhetoric seem to have been trapped into accepting a sort

Note: [when this article first appeared in October, 1963,] Karl R. Wallace [was] Head of the Department of Speech and Theatre at the University of Illinois and author (with Donald C. Bryant) of Fundamentals of Public Speaking.

[1] The point of view is fully expressed in Donald C. Bryant, "Rhetoric: Its Functions and Its Scope," QJS, XXXIX (December 1953), 401–424.

of scientific realism, or perhaps I might better say, a naive realism. The argument runs something like this: Since man derives his substantial information and knowledge through his sensory apparatus and since the natural sciences have successfully claimed for themselves both the acquisition and interpretation of sensory materials, discourse is left with nothing to say about the real world that does not properly belong to the sciences. Furthermore, since the behavioral sciences and the disciplines of philosophy and ethics have asserted property rights over the study of human experience and conduct, rhetoric has nothing to say about the behavior of speakers and listeners that these sciences cannot say with greater reliability and authority. Ergo, the substance of discourse comes from finding the right scientific and historical facts and of consulting the right authority. To me this is very much like saying that rhetoric is nothing more than the art of framing information and of translating it into intelligible terms for the popular audience.

1.

basic materials: ethical and moral values

My position is this. First, rhetorical theory must deal with the substance of discourse as well as with structure and style. Second, the basic materials of discourse are (1) ethical and moral values and (2) information relevant to these. Third, ethics deals with the theory of goods and values, and from ethics rhetoric can make adaptations that will result in a modern system of topics.

In developing these ideas we must try at the outset to indicate what we mean by *substance*. The concept has carried many meanings, but the ones that are relevant here may be suggested by calling attention to certain words as correlatives. On one side are *substance, matter, material, content,* and *subject matter*. On the other are *form, structure, order, arrangement, organization, shape,* and *figure*. The words on each side reveal overlapping meanings. This fact must be recognized, of course. But what is important is that the terms on one side are not fully intelligible in the absence of the terms on the other. The notion of form is useless without the notions of matter and material; the notions of order and arrangement are senseless without the notions of matter and substance—of something to be ordered and arranged. In every case we recognize the relationship of figure and shape to that which is figured and shaped, the relationship of form to that which is formed—to that which is material and substantial. In the same sets of words there is also lurking the idea of substratum—of that which stands under, of support. In this sense, form is inconceivable without something as its basis. One does not arrange and order bricks, or think of arranging or ordering them, without having bricks or the idea thereof. One does not build a house without a foundation, nor an oration without spoken or written words and the meanings they carry.

In what sense, then, do we understand substance? An attempt to meet this question requires us to regard an utterance, a linguistic event, a speech, as an object. There are natural objects. These exist, or come into being, without the agency of man. They are the things of land and sea, vegetable and mineral. We say, depending upon our point of view, that natural objects are made by God, by Nature, or by some mysterious force. There are artificial objects, and these are said, in our language, to be man-made. Among these are language itself and whatever one makes with language—novels, poems, commands, instructions, laws, speeches, et cetera. If speeches are objects, rhetoric is related to speeches as theory is related to behavior. Since a theorist tries to explain the particular group of objects, events, and behaviors in which he is interested, a rhetorician endeavors to explain what speeches are, and this task involves his setting forth what speeches are about and how they come about. If speeches exhibit substance and materials—and it is nonsense to say that they do not—the rhetorician must, among other things, characterize the substance of speeches, the materials of which they are made. Theories of rhetoric in the classical tradition, as we know, almost always said a good deal about the substance and materials of speeches. Under the heads Invention and Topics, they described the general materials of speeches and their chief kinds, together with lines of argument that often recurred. Except for Kenneth Burke, the principal writers on modern rhetorical theory—e.g., I. A. Richards—neglect substance and concentrate on processes, methods, techniques, and effects. Most of our textbooks pay little attention to what speeches are about; rather, their point of view is pedagogical. They concentrate on how to make a speech and deliver it. I do not think this condition of affairs could long endure if rhetoric were to rediscover and reassert its concern with subject matter.

Rhetoric, then, ought to deal with the substance, the substratum or foundations of speeches. What is this stuff? In answer to this question, I shall offer three propositions. First,

rhetoric is related to speeches as theory is to behavior

rhetoricians must characterize the substance of speeches

the underlying materials of speeches, and indeed of most human talk and discussion, are assertions and statements that concern human behavior and conduct. They are prompted by situations and contexts that present us with choices and that require us to respond with appropriate decisions and actions. Second, such statements are usually called judgments and appraisals. They reflect human interests and values, and the nature of value-judgments and the ways of justifying them are the special, technical, and expert concern of ethics. Third, the appearance and use of value-judgments in practical discourse are the proper, although not the sole, concern of the theory and practice of rhetoric.

appearance and use of value judgments: proper concerns of rhetoric

Probably most thoughtful persons will at once agree that the foundation materials of speeches are statements that are evoked by the need to make choices in order that we may act or get ready to act or to appraise our acts after their doing. Furthermore, choosing itself is a substantive act and the statement of a choice is a substantive statement. Rhetoricians will recall that the time-honored classifications of speeches are based upon the typical choice-situations that audiences confront. The deliberative or political kind of speech helps an audience decide what it *ought* to do, and the materials most often appearing are those that bear on the particular audience's ends and purposes and the means to those ends. More specifically, so Aristotle thought, these things give rise to considerations of what is good and evil and what is useful, and these again with respect to the problems of war and peace, of national defense, of taxation (or support of the state in relation to the citizen's purse), of the standard of living (or the welfare of the citizen), and of the making of laws and the good that laws can do. The forensic or legal speech helps a jury to decide upon the manner of treating a person who is accused of breaking the moral codes enshrined in law. What is justice in the case at hand? Is the man guilty or innocent? And if guilty, how should he be treated? The epideictic speech helps an audience to assess the ethics and morality of a person's actions. Whether the decision is to praise or blame him will depend upon whether his acts are judged virtuous, noble, right, and good. Evidently, then, large numbers of speeches employ statements whose content is ethical or moral, or they use language in a setting and in ways that logically imply ethical and moral ideas.

Still it may be asked whether there are not speeches in situations that have nothing to do with ethics and morality? What about discourse that is called informative, expository, or scientific?

We consider this question by pointing out that we often label a speech informative when in its proper context it is persuasive. Thomas Huxley's famous lecture, "On a Piece of Chalk," consists predominantly of factual sentences, yet to its English audiences in the 1870's it functioned as a plea for evolution. Much discourse and discussion that is thought of as didactic is probably persuasive in effect if not in intent. The character and bias of the state and nation function to select what is taught in the public schools. The teacher-learner relationship is accordingly less neutral and colorless than we think. Moreover, many teachers employ a method of learning that encourages students to think for themselves, to weigh and consider, to be intelligently appreciative and critical, to select and reject ideas and information that function indirectly, if not directly, to build attitudes and determine preferences. Furthermore, much newspaper discourse is in response to the widespread belief that knowledge is a good thing, and that certain kinds of materials and events are interesting, useful, and satisfying to readers, and other kinds are not. In brief, it would appear that expository speaking and writing recognizes choices and values that differ from those of persuasive discourse principally in that they are more remote and less apparent. So in saying that the materials and the substrata of speeches come about in response to contexts that present alternative possibilities, I want to include what is ordinarily thought of as informative utterance. First, much exposition is functionally persuasive, whether in intent or effect. This fact we have just remarked upon. Second, scientific discourse in itself cannot be utterly devoid of value. It owes its being to two assumptions: (1) knowledge in itself is a good thing, and (2) the information transmitted is accurate, reliable, valid, and true. Furthermore, scientific reporting of observations and experiments—and the criticism thereof—involves *what* a scientist did and did not do, *how* he did it and did not do it, and *why* he did it in one way rather than another. The scientist cannot escape choices, whether he is addressing other scientists or a popular audience. His decisions are anchored in contexts governed by rules, conventions, and practices, whether they be those of the scientist or those of the nonscientist public.

values are only less apparent in expository speeches

scientists cannot avoid choice

2.

Although the basic substance of speeches comprises statements that are made when human beings must make choices, the consideration of such statements in their special and technical character is the proper concern of ethics. To support this assertion I must indicate what students of ethics today seem to be focusing on.[2] Despite differences in their special points of view and in the treatment of their material, they see the human being as he uses his reason in practical situations that involve choice and decision. Practical reason is revealed in judgments that guide man's conduct, i.e., judgments are statements having to do with action, motives, feelings, emotions, attitudes, and values. They are responses to one of two fundamental kinds of questions: What shall I do or believe? What ought I to do?[3] Both Toulmin and Baier talk in terms that are familiar to every historian and theorist of rhetoric.[4] Practical reason, for example, appears in three types of behavior: deliberation, justification, and explanation. Deliberation uses reason prior to the act. Justification and explanation use reason after the act. When we justify, we praise or blame; we use terms like right and wrong, good and bad; in general we *appraise.* When we explain, we show what moved the agent and use terms untinctured by praise or censure. Because these three types of rational behavior are carried on almost exclusively in symbolic and linguistic terms, some writers tend to treat ethics as consisting of statements, of kinds of statements, and of the content of statements. Of proper concern are statements in whose predicates are the words, *is a desirable thing, is morally obligatory, is morally admirable or reprehensible, is a good thing, is praiseworthy,* and the like.[5] Included, furthermore, are all statements that imply, though they do not specify, such evaluative words. Edwards achieves considerable simplicity when, following Broad and Findlay, as he says, he presents his theory in terms of two classes of judgments.[6] The first is the value-judgment or moral judgment in which key predicate words are *good, desirable, worthwhile,* and their equivalents. The second is the *judgment of obliga-*

[2] My chief informants have been Richard B. Brandt, *Ethical Theory: The Problems of Normative and Critical Ethics* (Englewood Cliffs, N.J., 1959); Kurt Baier, *The Moral Point of View: A Rational Basis of Ethics* (Ithaca, N.Y., 1958); Paul Edwards, *The Logic of Moral Discourse* (Glencoe, Ill., 1955); P. H. Nowell-Smith, *Ethics* (Baltimore, Md., 1954 [Penquin Books]); Philip Blair Rice, *On the Knowledge of Good and Evil* (New York, 1955); Charles L. Stevenson, *Ethics and Language* (New Haven, 1944); and Stephen Edelston Toulmin, *An Examination of the Place of Reason in Ethics* (Cambridge, Eng., 1961).

[3] Baier, p. 46.

[4] For example, see Baier, pp. 148–156.

[5] See Brandt, pp. 2–4.

[6] Edwards, p. 141.

tion, as signalled by words like *ought, oblige,* and *duty.* We may say, then, that students of ethics are concerned with choice situations that are always signalled by the question, "What ought I to do?" They are concerned, also, with the rational and reasonable responses that human beings make to the question, i.e., with the judgments that we use in making choices and in justifying them.

Since judgments either state values directly or imply them indirectly, ethics as a study examines all values that influence action and are imbedded in judgments. It attempts to explain value-terms and how they are used, to classify them, and to find values that apply widely to our actions. Those of greatest generality are called standards or criteria of conduct. Some of them are compressed in concepts with which all of us are familiar: good and evil, pleasant-unpleasant, duty, obligation, self-interest, altruism, truth-telling, promise-keeping, honesty, fairness, courage, law-observance, utility, right and wrong, and the like. They appear typically in general statements called rules of conduct, regulations, laws, codes, principles, and moral maxims. With such values in mind, ethics also asks and tries to answer questions like these: Why these values rather than some other ones? And are the methods employed to identify them valid and trustworthy? In a word, modern ethics undertakes to present a theory of values which includes an account of how value-judgments are justified.

It would seem apparent, accordingly, that ethics as a study derives its materials in large measure from men's linguistic behavior when they must choose among alternatives. Their behavior constitutes judgments, and these appear in their reasonings when they deliberate, explain, and justify their choices. It is possible to observe such behavior systematically, to analyze it and theorize about it, and this ethics does. It is also possible to observe such behavior, to note what judgments all men, or most men, or wise men, or the wisest of men in practice accept or reject, and to perceive which of these recur in the materials and premises of men's reasonings. This is what classical rhetorical theory did, and this is what modern rhetorical theory should do. If the modern rhetorical theorist feels that he cannot in his textbook present a workable account of the material basis of speeches, perhaps much as Aristotle did in his *Rhetoric,* at least he can assert that rhetoric is related to ethics as theory is to practice. He can point out that the science of ethics deals with moral principles and standards of conduct as they are abstracted from practice, and that the art of rhetoric encounters moral principles in

ethics: observing, analyzing, theorizing about judgment behavior

rhetorical theory should record values which recur in practice

particular situations, in specific cases in which man in his social and political roles must make up his mind and act in concert, or be ready to act in concert.

If the materials of rhetorical discourse are fundamentally the same as the materials of ethics, it should be possible to derive a scheme of rhetorical topics from the study of ethics. Indeed, this can be done. I shall present now a brief outline of *topoi*. In doing so I am not suggesting that it is a perfect product and ready for incorporation into a textbook on public speaking. I aim only to point the way to a practical instrument.

an ethical scheme for *rhetorical topics*

First I shall sketch the general categories of values that help us to decide whether our decisions and actions are good or bad, right or wrong. There appear to be three, all-embracing classes—the desirable, the obligatory, and the admirable or praiseworthy, and their opposites.[7]

desirability depends on goals

Whether or not something is desirable depends upon one's motives, goals, or ends—upon that for the sake of which we act. We act to reduce certain painful or unpleasant tensions. We rid ourselves of disease and illness to restore health; we banish hunger by seeking and eating food. On the other hand, some tensions produce pleasure, the chief among these being activity associated with sexual behavior, competitive activity in both work and play, and aesthetic excitement. Pleasurable tensions are involved, too, in activity that is venturesome and that involves learning and knowing. We desire things, also, that are in our own interests. Among interests, some are primarily self-centered, such as property and security (although both of these directly depend on social institutions and practices). Some interests are directly social—those for the sake of the general welfare. Other interests are professional, vocational, and recreational in nature. Desirable, furthermore, is personal and group achievement and its attendant pleasure and exhilaration. We derive satisfaction in making and creating something. We take pleasure and pride in achieving the "right" self-image. With this image is associated status—the respect and deference of others to us, and the power and ability to do what we wish. Desirable, moreover, is freedom of choice and action; undesirable are arbitrary restraints. A much-prized good is being loved and liked by others. Finally, there is an overriding, hedonistic desire, that of seeking anything that gives us pleasure and of avoiding acts and states of being that are painful or unpleasant. These, then, are things generally regarded as desirable and good. They are

---

[7] In developing general categories of values, I have been most helped by Brandt.

reflected directly or indirectly in the statements through which we make choices and explain or defend them.

Things that are morally obligatory and acts that are praise-worthy seem to acquire their meaning and force in the sort of regard that others have for us. The self-image is built up through the approvals and disapprovals of others, and thus we learn what is "right" and "wrong." Our integrity, our re-spect for ourselves, is a function of social rewards and sanc-tions. On the other hand, acts that are desirable and conduct that is goal-directed and that is said to be motivated, all seem to be built around, and come to focus on, the individual orga-nism. The distinction between the desirable and the obligatory appears to be imbedded in our language. It is acceptable to say that playing golf is a good thing to do, but it is odd to say that playing golf is a right thing to do, or that golf playing is a matter of duty.

moral obligations acquire force from regard that others have for us

Within the class of things obligatory are duties. These are acts specified by one's position or role in a group or in a social institution. With respect to the family, a father has duties. With respect to his profession, a physician, a lawyer, a teacher has duties. With respect to the state, a governor has duties, and so does the citizen. There are obligatory actions so deeply woven into the social fabric that, once learned, they are rarely examined. They are truth-telling, promise-keeping, the paying of debts, and obeying of law. Finally, there are the *mores* of the group, as revealed in codes, customs, commandments, and moral maxims, and enforced by unwritten, social sanc-tions.

The last class of goods and values is that of the praise-worthy-blameworthy, the admirable-reprehensible. These value-terms are meant to refer to character traits, to behavior classes that have become stable, to what in the older literature of ethics were usually called *virtues.* Among these is consci-entiousness, a term that refers not to some mystical, innate sense of the good, but to a concern for living up to one's own self-image and for fulfilling one's obligations. There are, too, the familiar virtue names—kindliness, fairness, courage, verac-ity, honesty, prudence, persistence, tolerance, reliability, and good will (i.e., concern for the welfare of others). Although space does not permit the elaboration of these behavior traits, two or three observations should be made. Some writers call these traits *extrinsic* goods, or instrumental goods, because possession of them leads to the acquisition of other goods and ends. Honesty, for example, leads more often to desirable ends and less often to punishments than stealing and cheat-

praiseworthy values become stable through extended acceptance

ing. Although these terms may enter into all kinds of value-judgments, their long usage and genetic development suggest that they typically apply to behavior that is completed and past. Hence, to some writers they are technical terms of appraisal, and we use them most appropriately when we size up conduct that has become history. Yet terms of appraisal often appear in deliberative or policy contexts with persuasive intent. As Aristotle once observed, to praise a man is to hold him up for the imitation of others.

3.

rhetorical value scheme can be derived from ethics

This sketch of value categories has been presented entirely from the point of view of ethics. The categories represent a sort of *topoi* of values. Doubtless it is evident that rhetorical topics can be derived from them. One has only to recall the ordinary ways of analyzing a problem—the Dewey steps in problem-solving, for example, and the surveys for a proposition of fact and a proposition of policy—to perceive that they refer to situations in the present and the past and point to the possible future in terms that are ethical and moral. Such schemata of analytical thought originally had their basis in the logic of choice, decision, and conduct. Their long use and ready application have turned them into formulae whose derivation has been forgotten.

In presenting *topoi* of ethical values, I am not forgetting that the system must also include political values. Although this is not the place to spell out the significant differences between politics and ethics, we do well to remember that politics can be properly included within the scope of ethics, for the art of government is the art of adjusting the desires and values of the individual to the desires and values of others. Accordingly, rhetorical topics derived from ethics will point to political topics in the ways that genus relates to species, in those ways that the general idea suggests the specific idea. So some ethical premises will in use be indistinguishable from political premises. Take, for example, Kant's famous categorical imperative: Do only that thing which you would will all others to do. It appears to apply to political conduct as well as to individual conduct.

politics can be included in study of ethics

Nevertheless, some rhetorical topics will be characteristically political. We all know where to look for them. Government may be viewed as the formal instrument whereby individuals accept a system of law for the benefit of themselves and of each other. Hence from the point of view of politics there is always a triadic relationship of parties: the individual, the political group in which the individual plays the role and goes under the name of *citizen,* and the governor or ruler. With this relationship in mind, one can at once locate the foci of political explanations and arguments. These will center on such concepts as the powers, obligations, and duties of both the ruler and the citizen. These in turn derive much of their meaning from the concepts of liberty, freedom, and justice, and from our ideas about rights, both individual rights and civil rights. From these spring the standards, rules, and maxims of political conduct. Some political theorists, for example, believe that Roman law settled our custom of defining "private affairs in terms of rights, and public affairs in terms of power and responsibilities."[8] Political rules become the substantial bases and premises of appraisals and judgments. They also dictate the method and tone of rational criticism. These, perhaps, are our special heritage from the Greeks.[9] Possibly the deep-rooted, long-unquestioned habit of waiving aside the "constitutionality" of debate propositions has led debaters to ignore the real sources of arguments that are simultaneously material, moving, and interesting.

political rules become premises of appraisals and judgments

To see that a *topoi* of values would indeed be possible we need only to glance swiftly at the debater's issues and sources of argument. The debater refers to "evils" and "difficulties" that give rise to "problems." These terms, I suggest, can refer only to situations, persons, groups, or institutions that have experienced unpleasant tensions of one kind or another. They are frustrated because they haven't secured their desires, their goals, their pleasures, and their interests. Somebody is threatening their freedoms, their status, or their power. Somebody is accused of breaking the law, and his character and that of witnesses and of the trial system itself are put to the test. Self-interest, vested interest, or the entrenched power of some group or institution is interfering with the general welfare.

debaters' arguments illustrate use of value judgments

Once the debater has located the evils of the situation, he defines the problem. His explanation of it cannot avoid value-judgments and even his facts that support explanation function in a context of values. If the question be medical care for the aged, the description of the present state of medical

[8] D. G. Hitchner and W. H. Harbold, *Modern Government: A Survey of Political Science* (New York, 1962), p. 175.

[9] *Ibid.,* p. 174.

care may well support different interpretations of the problem and point to different decisions.

Such, then, are the kinds of materials which, assembled and analyzed, provide the basis of decision. The decision itself—the solution of the problem—emerges either as a proposition in which the words *should* or *ought* appear, or as a proposition in which value-terms are expressed or clearly implied—e.g., the party is innocent (or guilty), the state has an obligation to provide employment opportunities for everyone, this person or this institution is responsible for doing so-and-so. It is well to remark that the *ought* in a proposition of policy means more than a vague pointing to the future. It is a decision in response to the question, What ought we to believe or do? And this question is always, so Baier asserts, an ethical or moral one.[10] Moreover, an *ought* proposition carries a meaning of obligation about it, such that if one accepts the proposition one feels bound to do what is specified or implied.[11] With either individuals or institutions in mind, one can ask sensible questions: Are obligations to be found in the context of the problem? Who is obligated to whom? What is the nature of the obligation? Furthermore, an *ought* seems always to imply that the decision is the best thing to do; it suggests that the speaker has compared all relevant alternatives.[12]

Perhaps enough has been said to show that many rhetorical *topoi* may be readily derived from ethical and moral materials. Indeed, I believe that topics and lines of argument *inevitably,* in the nature of things, lead the investigator to ethical and moral considerations, guide him to decisions and propositions that are ethical and moral, and furnish him with most of the explanations and arguments that support his decision and in whose terms he will recommend it to the consideration of an audience. If modern rhetoricians will face the fact that language symbols are not empty symbols, like those of symbolic logic and mathematics, that the language of practical discourse bears meanings that testify to man's attempt to identify and solve problems of action and conduct, modern rhetoric will formulate a theory of invention and will present a plan of *topoi* in the language of ethics and morals.

language of practical discourse: man's attempt to identify, and solve problems of conduct

[10] Baier, p. 86.

[11] Brandt, esp. pp. 353–354.

[12] *Ibid.*

4.

If rhetoricians would see the materials of speeches in this light, they would do well, I believe, to take a special term from the field of ethics and employ it, perhaps with minor adjustments. The term is *good reason,* or in the plural form, *good reasons.* What are these? A good reason is a statement offered in support of an *ought* proposition or of a value-judgment. Good reasons are a number of statements, consistent with each other, in support of an *ought* proposition or of a value-judgment. Some examples may prove illuminating.

a *good reason:* statement in support of an *ought* proposition

The Federal government ought to provide for the medical care of the aged. (Or, more technically: It is desirable that the Federal government. . . .)
  It will contribute to the security of the aged.
  It will be in the welfare of everybody.
  It is in the interest of equity.
    The aged spend a disproportionate amount of their income on medical care.
      Their bill for drugs is twice that of persons in age brackets below 60.
  The government has an obligation to finance medical care for the aged.
X should not have copied from Y's paper.
  It was an act of cheating.
  Cheating is wrong.
Jones made a good speech.
  It conformed to most of the principles and rules of speechmaking.
  Its consequences will be good.
This man ought not be elected sheriff.
  He is not qualified to hold the office.
  He cannot be depended on.

These illustrations serve to point out what good reasons are and what they support. If the rhetorician were to adopt the term, good reasons, he would have a technical label that refers to all the materials of argument and explanation.

There are advantages to the use of the term, good reasons. Both rhetorician and teacher would be ever reminding the speaker, as well as themselves, that the substance of rhetorical proof has to do with values and value-judgments, i.e., with what is held to be good. One can scarcely declare that something is desirable without showing its relevance to values. It may be desirable, for example, to adjust the balance of power between management and labor, on the ground that justice has become too partisan, that basic rights are not being respected, and the like. Moreover, the word *reason* indicates that the process of proof is a rational one and can be used to cover such traditional forms of reasoning as deduction and induction, the syllogism, generalization, analogy, causation, and correlation. Furthermore, the term *good reason* implies the indissoluble relationship between content and form, and keeps attention on what form is saying. If we could become accustomed to the concept, good reasons, we might cease worrying over our failure to find perfect syllogisms in the arguments of everyday life; rather, we would recognize, as the examination of practical reason seems to indicate, that reasons which govern practice are quite different from the syllogism as usually presented. I think that most ethicists would agree that the measurement of validity in practical discourse quite commonly resides in the general principle and its applicability. Brandt has this to say on the point: "Any particular ethical statement that is valid *can be supported by a valid general principle. . . .*"[13] X should not have copied from Y's paper, for in doing so he cheated, and cheating is wrong. In this case, clearly there are facts that could or could not be established. Clearly, the general principle, "cheating is wrong," is relevant and functions as a warrant. The principle is applicable, or is applicable as qualified, if particular circumstances call for qualification. The principle itself is valid to the extent that it corresponds with the beliefs and conduct of the group which gives it sanction. Such statements, Edwards observes, are objective in the sense that they are independent of the speaker's subjective attitudes. It is true, of course, that the speaker's attitude may prompt his giving a general principle as a reason; nevertheless, the general principle can be tested for its truth-value quite apart from his attitude.[14] What a good reason is is to some extent fixed by human nature and to a very large extent by generally accepted principles and practices which make social life, as we understand it, possible. In a word, the concept of good reasons embraces both the substance and the processes of practical reason. One could do worse than characterize rhetoric as the art of finding and effectively presenting good reasons.

rhetoric: the art of finding and presenting good reasons

[13] *Ibid.,* p. 20.

[14] Edwards, pp. 148, 157.

If rhetoricians could accept good reasons as the substance of discourse, we would immediately secure additional advantages. Any distinctions that modern rhetoric may be trying to maintain between logical, ethical, and emotional modes of proof would immediately become unreal and useless, except for purposes of historical criticism. For the practitioner, both communicator and respondent, the correct questions would always be: What is my choice? What are the supporting and explanatory statements? What information is trustworthy? It would be absurd to ask: Is my choice a logical one? Shall I support my position by logical, ethical, or emotional means? For the theorist, analyst, and critic of discourse, the disappearance of those weasel concepts, logical proof and emotional proof, would permit a description of the materials of practical discourse in terms of two broad categories: materials deriving from the specific occasion, and materials consisting of general value-judgments. Furthermore, perhaps practitioners would get into the habit of applying first and foremost to any instance of communication, the searching queries: Who or what is the responsible agent? What person or agent is taking the responsibility, or should take it? If the proposition be supported by reasons that immediately or ultimately relate to value-statements whose content reflects the desirable, the obligatory, and the admirable, then for whom is the message desirable and admirable? Upon whom do the obligations and duties rest? Discourse to which such questions are habitually applied cannot long remain abstract, distant, colorless, and unreal. Rather, it could well become personal and direct. The speechmaking of the Greeks, who understood ethos, was eminently personal.

this definition directs practioners to the correct questions

5.

It seems probable that if students of rhetoric looked to the substance as well as to the forms of practical discourse they would discover a set of statements or value-axioms that would constitute a modern system of invention. The axioms would consist of those political and ethical values that apply to public discussion. Derived in theory from politics and ethics and in practice from the rules and conventions that speakers appeal to explicitly and implicitly when they explain, advocate, deliberate upon, and justify their choices, the axioms would serve as a base for finding good reasons and thus for providing

studying substance of discourse is key to finding good reasons fundamental materials in any given case of rhetorical discourse. Eubanks and Baker have recently reminded rhetoricians of Aristotle's position that "If rhetoric has any sort of *special* subject matter province, that substance is constituted in the popular and probable value axioms related to the civil decision making of a free society."[15] The hypothesis should be put to the test.

---

[15] Ralph T. Eubanks and Virgil L. Baker, "Toward an Axiology of Rhetoric," *QJS,* XLVII (April 1962), 162.

SUGGESTED FURTHER READING

Brandt, Richard B., *Ethical Theory: The Problems of Normative and Critical Ethics.* Englewood Cliffs, N.J.: Prentice-Hall, Inc., 1959. (See notes 2, 5, 7, 11–13 above.)

Eubanks, Ralph T. and Virgil L. Baker, "Toward an Axiology of Rhetoric," *Quarterly Journal of Speech,* XLVIII (April, 1962), 162. (See note 15 above.)

Ray, Jack L., letter to the editor on "The Substance of Rhetoric: Good Reasons," *Quarterly Journal of Speech,* L (February, 1964), 71–73.

Rothman, Richard M., letter to the editor on "The Substance of Rhetoric: Good Reasons: Further Comment," *Quarterly Journal of Speech,* L (February, 1964), 74–75.

Wallace, Karl R., letter to the editor on "The Substance of Rhetoric: Good Reasons: Author's Rejoinder," *Quarterly Journal of Speech,* L (February, 1964), 73.

Finding Good Reasons

Jimmie D. Trent

Professor Karl Wallace defines the substance of rhetoric as consisting of "good reasons."[1] In doing so, he emphasizes the importance of values and value-judgments for speakers:

values and value judgments: the substance of rhetorical proof

> There are advantages to the use of the term, good reasons. Both rhetorician and teacher would be ever reminding the speaker, as well as themselves, that the substance of rhetorical proof has to do with values and value-judgments, i.e., what is held to be good.[2]

While Professor Wallace is aware of the importance of audiences, his essay on good reasons is directed primarily at the speaker's derivation and construction of the message. I agree that it is important to understand the values of speakers and that it is equally important for a speaker to understand his own values. But since the message which counts in the communication act is the message constructed by the listener, a speaker who wants understanding or acceptance of his ideas must learn to construct messages in terms of his audience's value system. And in order to adapt messages to the values of an audience, whether that be one or many people,

messages must be constructed in terms of audience values

the speaker must first be able to determine what listeners consider to be good or desirable.

For a speaker to develop his rhetoric according to his own concept of good may actually be counterproductive. For example, a father might try to convince his son to enter the family business by telling him that it would mean a nice home, expensive cars, a country club social life and the chance to have power, and then not understand when the son prefers to join the Peace Corps. The reasons which were good for the father were low on the son's priority list, at least, and might even

[1] Karl R. Wallace, "The Substance of Rhetoric: Good Reasons," *Quarterly Journal of Speech,* XLIX (October, 1963), 247. [See the preceding essay in this collection.]

[2] Wallace, *Ibid,* p. 248.

have been considered undesirable. If the father had prepared his message in terms of reasons that his son accepted as good, he might have told him that the family business was a way to maximize his effectiveness in helping others. Either set of good reasons could be expected as a possibility for the son if he had the flexibility and influence which comes with wealth, but only one has desirable connotations for the listener. Such is always the case; it is the listener who judges what is good and it is the listener to whom the effective speaker adapts.

the listener judges what is good

Adaptation to an audience is not a new concept. Every speech text since Aristotle has advocated it. But traditional public speaking textbooks have presented only general guidelines about examining the characteristics of audiences. They seldom mention the audience's values.

And while Professor Wallace takes us several steps further when he talks about values being the substance of rhetoric, his system is still message oriented. Wallace proposes this:

> It seems probable that if students of rhetoric looked to the substance as well as to the forms of practical discourse they would discover a set of statements or value-axioms that would constitute a modern system of invention. The axioms would consist of those political and ethical values that apply to public discussion. Derived in theory from politics and ethics and in practice from the rules and conventions that speakers appeal to explicitly and implicitly when they explain, advocate, deliberate upon, and justify their choices, the axioms would serve as a base for finding good reasons and thus for providing fundamental materials in any given case of rhetorical discourse.[3]

Wallace would have us prepare a list of axioms from which we would choose according to our audience. But the axioms would originate from studies of speakers and would therefore be limited to the value axioms which have proven useful for public discussion in the past. Would the same axioms be useful for private discussions? Have the speakers of the past utilized all of the value-judgments which listeners might potentially make? Perhaps, but if they have not, our list would merely bind us to the limitations of the past. And if the list did include all the value-judgments used by listeners, it would necessarily include every value known to mankind. Such a comprehensive list would not discriminate between values which are appropriate or inappropriate for a particular audience.

[3] Wallace, *Ibid,* p. 249.

study audience
values directly

 I believe that it is better to begin with the audience. If we can determine what our specific audience considers to be good or desirable, it will be totally unimportant whether some speaker in the past has thought it was the right axiom for his audience. If I am correct, the question we should be asking is "How do we study audience values directly?"

Rokeach's definition
of values

 In order to answer that question, we must first determine the nature of values and the manner in which they operate. There are many definitions of values but Milton Rokeach's is particularly useful for our purpose:

> I consider a value to be a type of belief, centrally located within one's total belief system, about how one ought or ought not to behave, or about some end-state of existence worth or not worth attaining. Values are thus abstract ideals, positive or negative, not tied to any specific attitude object or situation, representing a person's beliefs about ideal modes of conduct and ideal terminal goals. . . . Some examples of ideal modes of conduct are to seek truth and beauty, to be clean and orderly, to behave with sincerity, justice, reason, compassion, humility, respect, honor, and loyalty. Some examples of ideal goals or end-states are security, happiness, freedom, equality, ecstasy, fame, power, and states of grace and salvation.[4]

values determine choices
an individual makes

 Thus values are the factor which will determine the choice an individual will make when he must choose between courses of action. His selection of a course of action will reflect his judgment of the situation and an application of his values. If he perceives a situation as a problem, it will mean that it violates his "ideal mode of conduct" or because he perceives a blockage preventing his achieval of "terminal goals." If he adopts a course of action, it will be because such action represents his ideal mode of conduct or because he believes it will help him reach his terminal goals.

only salient values
affect decisions

 Of course, not all values will affect any particular decision; only those values which are perceived as salient to the situation will be involved. Those values which are not perceived as relevant will not be a factor in making the decision.

 In some situations, even some of the relevant values will not be reflected in decisions. This will occur when two or more values are relevant and they lead to contradictory decisions. For example, a jury member may value both justice and compassion but in a trial his decision may not be able to reflect both values. In such a situation, the juror would have to

---

[4]Milton Rokeach, *Beliefs, Attitudes, and Values* (San Francisco: Jossey-Bass, Inc., 1968), p. 124.

choose between the two values. If he values justice more highly than compassion, his decision may not reveal the existence of compassion but that will not mean that it does not exist. In another situation, where justice was not involved, compassion might be the controlling value.

values are arranged in a hierarchy

Such variations in the application of values occur because we arrange our values in a hierarchy. Some values are consistently more important to us than other values and, when two values seem to have equal relevance in a situation, the value higher in the hierarchy will always dominate the decision.

With this elementary understanding of the nature of values we can return to the problem of determining an audience's values.

The values of listeners, whether as individuals or as individuals in a group, are revealed in their acts. In order to determine an audience's values, it is necessary to study their acts. Every act has been committed because the person or group found the act or its goals consistent with his value system. And every refusal to act can be attributed to a fear of violating values. If we study acts, which in this context includes refusal to act and statements, we can determine the operational value system which controls behavior for the person or group we are studying.

values revealed in behavior

we determine values by studying behavior

Dr. Harold Spaeth studied the attitudes controlling the Supreme Court.[5] Spaeth collected and computerized 3000 post-1958 decisions in seventy-three categories. By feeding the computer data on particular controversial cases, the issues and the judges involved, Spaeth has successfully predicted the Court's decisions in ninety-one percent of the most controversial cases.

Note that Spaeth was studying attitudes rather than values. Attitudes are similar to values but are more specific. Like values, attitudes create a predisposition to action. But unlike values, attitudes represent beliefs toward a specific object or situation.[6] Attitudes are based upon the more generalized predispositions we refer to as values. For example, an individual who places high value on truth will hold this value as it applies to all objects and situations. When the value is applied to a specific situation or object, it is classified as an attitude.

attitudes represent beliefs toward a specific object or situation

If it were possible for a speaker to analyze his audience's

---

[5]George Bullard, "Michigan State University Professor Predicts High Court Rulings," Detroit News, July 25, 1971, p. 5-B.

[6]Rokeach, *Beliefs, Attitudes, and Values,* p. 127.

attitudes, it would present a more specific basis for judgments he might make about particular audiences or situations. Unfortunately, it is frequently not possible to determine what an audience's attitude is toward the object or situation with which the speaker is concerned simply because no analogous act is known to have been committed. What a speaker can learn is an audience's more general value system on which attitudes are based. The values can then be applied to situations or objects in order to obtain "good reasons."

learn the general value system on which attitudes are based

I said earlier that we must study an audience's acts if we wish to learn its values. There are several steps to this process. First we must make a list of all the past actions which we can determine that the audience had the power to determine. Restrictions on the audience's power to decide may force it to act against its values; thus only those acts which are freely determined can be regarded as value revealing.

list all freely determined past actions

The second step is the making of educated gueses (forming of hypotheses) about the motivation for the act. Several factors are involved here. First, examine the situation which existed before the action was taken and the apparent goals of the action. What existed before was apparently considered less desirable than the goals of the action. The next step is to break the action into constituent parts. Two basic parts are the method of procedure and the result; these parts parallel the value categories that Rokeach characterized as modes of conduct and terminal values.[7] Each part can then be reduced to its constituents. After the various elements of the action and its expected effects are determined, you will have to make judgments about which elements were the controlling factors.

form hypotheses about motivation for actions

Let us look at an example. A manufacturer made a large loan to the leader of the union which represented the workers in his plant. A jury refused to convict the manufacturer in spite of the fact that his action represented a clear violation of the Taft-Hartley Act. Was bribery the motivation for the loan was the question. That it was classified as such by law was beyond question. The defense attorney argued that neither the method by which the loan was made nor the motivation for the loan indicated that the manufacturer was attempting to influence the union official's behavior in negotiations. No attempt had been made to conceal the loan. (The mode of conduct was honest.) And many years earlier, the attorney argued, the union official had saved the manufacturer's business by arranging a large loan for him. Repayment of a debt, not bribery, was argued to be the motivation.

[7] Rokeach, *Beliefs, Attitudes, and Values,* p. 124.

Before the jury found the accused not guilty, he was threatened with a large fine and/or imprisonment. The jury's action removed that threat. The method of procedure was determined for the jury; its only function was to determine guilt or innocence. Therefore the values which came into play, the controlling factors, were terminal values, the values represented in the situation which would exist after their decision was implemented.

At this point we may guess that the jury's act was motivated by a belief that the manufacturer had met a personal obligation. If the jury had returned a finding of guilty, we would have to assume that they had considered his violation of the law to be the most important factor in their decision.

If we were to state the jury's motivation in terms of values, we would say that under the conditions which existed in this case, meeting a personal obligation is considered more important than obeying the letter of the law. We can not say that obeying the letter of the law is considered undesirable because another value dominated the decision. What we can say is that "personal obligation (self respect) is higher in the audience's hierarchy of values than is respect for law."

Thus with the analysis of one act, we begin to formulate the audience's hierarchy of values. But it is only a beginning. We do not know at this point whether respect for law is considered undesirable or simply less desirable than another value. In order to determine this, we would have to examine a series of actions relating to that value. If it is consistently rejected in favor of other values or preferably when no other values are involved, we may conclude that respect for law is considered to be undesirable. But if we find that some people are found guilty, we will have to conclude that respect for law is held as a value even though it is not the controlling value in all situations. *with analysis of one act, begin formulating a hierarchy of values*

If we wish to compile a fairly complete hierarchy of values, it will be necessary to examine a great many acts. Less satisfactory, but more efficient, than compiling a complete hierarchy is conducting a specialized examination to determine the beliefs relating to the value to which we want to appeal in forming good reasons. A specialized examination would involve analysis of only those acts which obviously involve the value in question. For example, if power is the value in which we are interested, we would have to look for and examine all opportunities which the listener had to obtain additional power. In those instances where the individual acted to increase his power, we would find values which are lower in his hierarchy. In instances where the opportunity to gain *examine many acts to compile a complete hierarchy of values*

specialized examination analyzes only acts relevant to values in question

power was not taken, we would find values which are higher in the hierarchy. Using this information, we can plan whether the obtaining of power is a "good" relative to other values operable in the situation of immediate concern.

values are the key
to human behavior

Values are the key to human behavior. We decide what actions we will take on the basis of what we believe will create good results. As we examine alternatives, we attempt to determine results of each. Then, according to our individual value systems, we decide whether those results are good or bad. If our value systems say the results are good, we try to obtain them. If our value system labels the results as bad, we try to avoid them.

to influence others,
present potential
results they value
as good

Audiences operate in the same fashion. If we wish to influence the actions of others, we have to present potential results that their value systems will label as good. It is not enough that we think they are good; the audience must agree. When we speak of good reasons, we are talking about the results of an action which an audience will accept as being good. If we wish to influence beliefs, we must study the acts of our audience to determine what they consider good. Only after we understand our audience's values, can we proceed with confidence in preparing good reasons.

SUGGESTED FURTHER READING

Gronbeck, Bruce E., "From 'Is' to 'Ought': Alternative Strategies," *Central States Speech Journal,* XIX (1968), 31–39.

Leys, Wayne, A. R., *Ethics For Policy Decisions.* Englewood Cliffs, New Jersey: Prentice-Hall Inc., 1952.

Miller, Gerald R., "Questions of Fact and Value: Another Look," *Southern Speech Journal,* XXVIII (1962), 116–123.

Rokeach, Milton, *Beliefs, Attitudes, And Values.* San Francisco: Jossey-Bass Inc., Publishers, 1968. (See notes 4, 6, 7 above.)

Stevenson, Charles L., *Facts And Values.* New Haven: Yale University Press, 1963.

Toulmin, Stephen E., *An Examination of the Place of Reason in Ethics.* Cambridge England: Cambridge University Press, 1961.

The Problem of Style in Presidential Discourse

Ronald H. Carpenter

Style in discourse is a troublesome topic. In the context of the presidency, style in discourse is a particularly troublesome topic, often evoking thoughts of bombast, excess and ornamentation, ostentation for the sake of ostentation. And permeating those thoughts may be apprehensions of obfuscation, that somehow this thing called style in discourse is the means of language maneuvering by which meaning is hidden or distorted. Such a nonfunctional and negative outlook toward style has no relevance here. For there is an inescapable fact: in moments of greatest functional urgency, the most direct of statements in presidential discourse also have been characterized to large extent by what rhetoricians know as style. As overture to developing further understanding of style and its function in presidential discourse, or *any* rhetorical endeavor for that matter, an operational definition is in order.

an operational definition of style is needed

Style in discourse evolves from selection of words and their arrangement in sentences. Whether or not a specific selection of word or syntax *is* stylistic, however, depends upon whether or not that choice favors an option which, while grammatical, nevertheless departs from what would be the customary and familiar idiom for the speaker's language. For example, for the conception that Americans should not ask what their country can do for them, the common idiom suggests "Don't ask what your country can do for you." This is customary and familiar language usage. Phrased as an imperative which conforms to norms for more formal address, perhaps, the statement more likely might be "Do not ask what your country can do for you." But this, too, really is customary and familiar usage. Phrased with an inversion which departs from normative syntax, however, the utterance becomes "Ask not what your country can do for you." This is style. As a principle of language behavior, style is evinced when a grammatical state-

style: a lexical and/or syntactic departure from generally perceived norms ment departs from the lexical or syntactical norms for the conception being phrased.[1]

In discourse, several factors may inhibit evincing style. At the syntactical level, flexibility in arranging words is limited by constraints in favor of using the syntax with which the language user is most familiar, usually the customary word orders which characterize the common idiom. Deviation from these syntactical norms requires both effort as well as, perhaps, some awareness of other available options and their possible functions in discourse. Whether on the level of a highly sophisticated knowledge of the effects of language variation, or merely on the level of intuitive, imitative appreciation of some particular stylistic model, that awareness leads to the relative syntactical flexibility prerequisite to evincing style.

factors limiting syntactic flexibility

At the lexical level, evincing style is inhibited in large measure not only by the limitations of one's vocabulary but also by semantic constraints. Obviously, subject matter imposes severe limitations on the words used by a speaker. For instance, discourse on foreign policy requires terminology which simply is not applicable in speaking on organized crime. Another constraint upon a speaker's flexibility in lexical choice evolves from individualistic mannerisms of word and phrase that tend to be habitual for a person regardless of his topic. As a hypothetical illustration, consider Lincoln's "Gettysburg Address" as it might have been written by Dwight Eisenhower, probably beginning something like "Eighty-seven years ago, I think it was." It does not possess the style of the original text, but this version is not unusual in its reliance on what some people have come to think of as Eisenhower's highly individualistic tendency in discourse toward idiomatic language behavior.

factors limiting lexical flexibility

And remember that in large measure, style is personal and reflective of a man's singular condition. It is often, as stated in Buffon's celebrated epigram, "the man himself."[2] This does not mean, however, that one cannot change his personal style in discourse. Consider how a man of Richard M. Nixon's background and temperament could assume the very personal and different style of a man of John F. Kennedy's significantly divergent background and temperament. In *The Making of the President 1968,* Theodore White reported that phenomenon, hearing in Richard M. Nixon's speaking "the echo of the phrases of John F. Kennedy in 1960."[3] A stylistic analysis of Kennedy's Inaugural Address and Nixon's crucial Acceptance Address at the 1968 Republican National Convention illustrated that "echo" with several comparisons such as that

style is personal

it is possible to change customary stylistic tendencies

between Nixon's "We shall always negotiate from strength and never from weakness" and Kennedy's "Let us never negotiate out of fear—but let us never fear to negotiate."[4] To the stylist, it is evident that for his 1968 Acceptance Address, a New Nixon was Old Kennedy! Moreover, for Richard Nixon to change from the highly stereotyped idiomatic phrases of his 1960 campaign to the sylistic polish of his so personally prepared 1968 discourse required an effort that may have been motivated by a desire to imitate.[5] Richard Nixon admits to doing this before when the 1952 "Fund Speech" referred to his dog Checkers in conscious imitation of Franklin D. Roosevelt's reference to his dog Fala in the 1944 campaign.[6] Whether Nixon's 1968 effort really was an instance of deliberate stylistic imitation, though, is beyond the scope of this commentary. The noteworthy point here is a man's personal attempt to change his customary stylistic tendencies to evince for an occasion a different style intimately associated with another man. And what could be more noteworthy than a Richard M. Nixon with a John F. Kennedy style?

So although style is personal, it certainly can be changed—if not created entirely anew. For a president or his speech writers, however, any decision to overcome lexical or syntactical constraints and stereotypes must be predicated upon this assumption: attempts to evince style should not alter the essential conception to be phrased. The notion of style presumes a relative independence of matter from manner. That is, any manipulation which changes the meaning intended by the utterance is an alteration of content rather than form and is not in the realm of style.[7]

stylistic alterations that change meaning not in realm of style

uncommon syntax most likely source of distinct presidential style

Bearing this distinction in mind, what are the stylistic determinants which most often characterize presidential discourse? They are likely those of syntax more so than of lexicon. Assuming he is aware of the choices available to him, a president or his writers can alter the syntax of virtually any utterance to achieve a grammatical statement which also is stylistic. Attempts to select from among several lexical choices, however, may have results which are neither stylistic nor appropriate. If a lexical choice introduces a significant change in the meaning of an utterance, it has not achieved style so much as it has phrased a different conception; if a departure from lexical norms for the situation allows variant, unwanted interpretations of the statement, it has not fulfilled a crucial condition prerequisite to language usage in presidential discourse—the capability to evoke only intended, favorable meanings in respondents. During political maneuverings to secure the Republican presidential nomination in 1968, for example, George Romney said he was "brainwashed," to describe how he felt that officials had misled him about Viet Nam during his visit there. For many people, the unintended meanings evoked by the term (influenced no doubt by reporters and commentators,) led to unfavorable impressions about Romney and what should be a presidential candidate's important ability to perceive situations accurately. Therefore, because of the semantic problems that may arise from inappropriate word choices, the more prudent source of a president's style in discourse will be his uncommon syntax.

Within this framework, then, consider the following syntactical determinants of style prominent in the speaking of presidents such as Abraham Lincoln, Franklin Roosevelt, John Kennedy, Richard Nixon, and, by recent contrasting omission, perhaps Lyndon Johnson.

A major source of presidential style in discourse is an uncommon proximity or parallelism in which words are repeated. Because of vocabularly limitations or constraints of subject matter, people use an average of 10 to 15 words before repeating one of them. In terms of different words (types) appearing in a total number of words (tokens), a type-token ratio of .90 to .93 may describe a familiar proximity of repetition in segments of the common idiom that are 10 to 15 words or less in length. When arrangement is manipulated so that repeated words appear in still closer proximity, a construction's type-token ratio (TTR) tends to depart from idiomatic norms.[8] For instance, in Lincoln's "government of *the people,* by *the people,* for *the people,*" the 10 tokens and 6 types have a TTR of .60. In this context, consider the style, then, in a statement such as Franklin Roosevelt's "We have nothing to *fear* but *fear* itself." More recent examples can be drawn from the thirty parallel repetitions used in Nixon's 1968 Acceptance Address, such as when the future President spoke of those failures "*when the* strongest nation in the world can be tied down for four years in a war in Viet Nam with no end in sight, *when the* richest nation in the world can't manage its own economy, *when the* nation with the richest tradition of the rule of law is plagued by unprecedented lawlessness. . . ." The same phrase, "I see a day," began seven successive brief paragraphs. This usage was inspired by a memorandum from speech writer William Safire who recommended the device as typical of other famous speakers, including Franklin D. Roosevelt, Adlai E. Stevenson, Martin Luther King and—John F. Kennedy.[9]

parallelism: major source of presidential style

suspension: another
source of presidential
style

    While the common idiom is characterized by sentence conformations that are relatively easy to construct, it is possible to achieve constructions that postpone utterance elements for a later than customary appearance (because they impose a strain on memory, speakers or writers are apt to avoid such suspensions).[10] For instance, a salient suspension is the climax achieved by withholding the element of greatest semantic signification until the conclusion of a series, as in Kennedy's "All this will not be finished *in the first one hundred days,* nor will it be finished *in the first one thousand days,* nor *in the life of this administration,* nor even perhaps *in our lifetime on this planet.*" (And notice the parallel repetition here, too!)

syntactic inversion of
positional norms as
source of style

    Languages have customary ways of positioning functional elements within clauses and sentences. In English syntax, for instance, a positional norm for functional elements is illustrated by the familiar actor-action construction whereby the subject (actor) commonly precedes the predicate (action) in an utterance. These positional norms for a language may be inverted syntactically, however, to achieve sentences that are uncommon but nevertheless meaningful and grammatical, as is the case of course in Kennedy's "*Ask not* what your country can do for you."[11]

antithesis: a major
determinant of style

    When the next sentence is added, "Ask what you can do for your country," there is another major determinant of style: antithesis. Most instances of arranging words in sentences admit the possibility of adding the utterance elements that have contrasting semantic signification. When those semantically opposing elements are stated and arranged to be contiguous or in close proximity, antithesis is present.

    Antitheses are uncommon because of two constraints that seem to influence language behavior. First, a preference for affirmative rather than negative information may cause people to omit the obverse portions of such statements as "to be not a curse but a blessing." Second, idiomatic arrangement may favor the contiguous placement of words associated by similarity of meaning. For instance, if presented with "devil," "fearful," and "sinister," there is an automatic and unconscious tendency to respond with an associative word such as "dark" rather than antithetical terms such as "light" or "blessed." When arranging words in sentences, a person responds partly to the contexts afforded by preceding words, and he therefore may avoid antonymical juxtapositions such as those in Kennedy's "*support* any *friend* or *oppose* any *foe,*" or the antithesis between "the *many* who are *poor,*" and "the *few* who are *rich.*"[12] Or, consider these examples of antitheses combined by Kennedy with stylistic repetition: *"Let both sides* explore what problems *unite* us instead of belaboring those problems which *divide* us. . . . *Let both sides* seek to invoke the *wonders* of science instead of its *terrors."* As further illustration of Nixon's "Kennedy" style, recall from among the 40 antitheses characterizing the 1968 Acceptance Address: "After an *era of confrontation* the time has come for an *era of negotiation,"* or the more recent antitheses from Nixon's 1970 and 1971 "State of the Union" addresses: (A) *"Millions of Americans* are forced to go into debt *today* because the *federal government* decided to go into debt *yesterday,"* or (B) "It is time for those who make *massive* demands on *society* to make some *minimal* demands on *themselves,"* or a hauntingly Kennedyesque (C) ". . . *asking not what will government do for me, but what can I do, how can I contribute. . . ."*

Despite the caveats governing word choice in presidential discourse, there is a prominent lexical source of style to which presidents and their writers resort: metaphor. Essentially, metaphor may be defined as a stimulus-response event of language behavior in which a word or phrase is used contextually in a new, nonliteral way, thereby evoking an added affective dimension of meaning somewhat discrepant with that of the word's more normative usage.[13] Thus, John F. Kennedy's "New Frontier" as a linguistic stimulus to refer to programs in space and science and social reform may have been somewhat discrepant with a more conditioned literal usage of "frontier" in America in reference to events of westward expansion. In the context of technological progress, however, the resultant *psycho*linguistic response may have enhanced Americans' general positive attitude toward advancement with added affective overtones of the adventureous opportunity and fulfillment of our earlier frontier life. The metaphorical phrase caught on with the eighty-thousand people who listened in the Los Angeles Coliseum to Kennedy's acceptance of the Democractic nomination, and the phrase perservered through the campaign to become the name for his presidential administration.

metaphors: a prominent lexical source of style

Of course language need not always be metaphorical to be a source of style. Earlier reference was made to the first four words of Lincoln's Gettysburg Address. "Four score and seven" is literal but quite stylistic. A score is twenty, and four of these plus seven equal eighty-seven, and Lincoln would have been far more idiomatic if he had said instead "eighty-seven years ago." After all, this is what people know now as the customary way of phrasing a reference to that particular

non-idiomatic words as determinants of style

span of time. But think of what would have happened had Lincoln started the speech idiomatically. Nothing compared to the result of his stylistic beginning. "Four score and seven" is a phrase which virtually any literate American remembers despite the *very strong probability that it is undoubtedly many years since that person last read (or heard) the phrase.* In the jargon of advertising or public relations, the style of "four score and seven" makes it a "grabber." And to consider further this or any other functional aspect of uncommon language behavior is to shift the focus of this commentary from the determinants of style to the effects of style.

effects and objectives
of presidential style

Emphasis may be the most obvious functional effect of style. Characteristically, presidential speakers, or any speakers for that matter, are concerned with emphasis. In discourse, not all statements are of equal significance for the presentation of a point of view or for the development of an argument. Some statements are more important than others and are worthy of being *noticed* and *remembered.* [14] And the notice and memorability concomitant to emphasis is to be derived not only from audiences in general but in the case of televised speeches from the reporters and commentators who then repeat for mass audiences the statements that impress them. Typically, utterances in the common idiom are emphasized effectively by repeating them word for word, or by an increase in vocal force, a gesture, a pause, or some combination of these elements. For presidential discourse, style in language also may be a mode of emphasis capable of causing listeners to notice and remember a statement.

emphasis is a
functional effect

As a basis for any further consideration of this facet of stylistic functionalism, remember that emphasis is an attentional phenomenon. A statement's being noticed and remembered is a function of perceptual selectivity on the part of a listener. Facilitating adjustments, both psychological and physiological, enable the listener to focus on that statement rather than some other stimulus in his potential perceptual field. This act of perceptual selection has the important behavioral effects of an increase in the efficiency with which a stimulus can be noticed and, what is more important for political discourse, an increase in the capability to remember that "selected" stimulus.

novelty helps
statements be noticed
and remembered

One of the basic behavioral vehicles which influence perceptual selectivity and memorability is novelty. Human beings characteristically develop expectations about what would be customary and familiar in a given situation; and when a stimulus is discrepant with those expectations, it is novel and tends to be noticed and remembered. [15]

The same factor of novelty may influence the perceptual reaction to statements which are phrased grammatically but uncommonly. As a result of years and years of listening to language conformations which becomes customary and familiar, people develop expectations about the syntax they will hear; and a grammatical but uncommon statement departs from those expectations, it may be emphatically salient.

saliency: another effect of style

The history of discourse is replete with examples of such stylistic and salient statements. Consider further John Kennedy's "Ask not what your country can do for you—ask what you can do for your country." There is nothing particularly noteworthy or memorable about the meaning of the conception. There is certainly nothing particularly noteworthy or memorable about the words "country," "you," "what," "do," "can," "your," "ask," "for," or "not." The statement probably achieves much of its effect from its style, which endows the utterance with a saliency making it noteworthy and memorable for as long as there is an English language. It is likely that the epigram will be engraved on a monument to John F. Kennedy. You might speculate on whether or not Kennedy's Inaugural statement of principle would be preserved for posterity had it been phrased instead, as in an earlier version in Cadillac Square, Detroit, on September 5, 1960: "The new frontier is not what I promise I am going to do for you. The new frontier is what I ask you to do for your country."

Not only must a presidential style conduce to noteworthiness and memorability, but it also must lend itself to achieving ease and efficiency of comprehension on the part of recipients. For television in particular, with its severe limitations on time, it is imperative to achieve maximum efficiency of psychological response in a minimum amount of discourse. For this purpose, the language variable for *stylistic* manipulation is the attribute of redundancy.

Here, redundancy designates the decreased information and predictability of a symbol. For instance, from the words "The door was hermetically _____," a reader or listener (who understands these words) could predict that "sealed" would be the next word. Because "sealed" is the only word which could occur next in this sequence, it is completely predictable and adds no information to the statement. Conversely, the words "The ball was _____" do not allow a reader or listener to predict with certainty the next word. "Red," "purple," "over," "round," "bounced," "put in play," or a host of alternatives might appear next and add some amount of information to the statement. In this context, information is not an indication of semantic meaning but rather of the number of

stylistic redundancy increases efficient message assimilation

alternatives from which a symbol is chosen. The greater the freedom of choice exercised in the appearance of a symbol in a sequence, the more information it contains; the greater the constraints determining the appearance of a symbol in a sequence, the less information it contains. Decreased information, then, is a concomitant of predictability, and a predictable symbol is a relatively redundant symbol.

There seems to be a basic relationship between redundancy and psychological response: the more redundant or predictable a stimulus is, the potentially greater the efficiency with which it can be handled psychologically. Essentially, highly probable events are likely to place less demand on a nervous system than improbable ones and thereby receive relatively rapid response; and this manifestation of redundancy is a fairly consistent facet of human behavior.

Relate this concept of redundancy to the problem of style. Certainly customary and familiar usage tends to be redundant, with idiomatic lexical and syntactical sequences contributing to some degree of predictability and a relative efficiency of psychological response. When discourse manipulates syntax and lexicon to develop uncommon conformations with even greater than usual predictability of successive words or word types, it attains a *stylistic* redundancy which potentially could be a source of yet increased efficiency.[16] Burke offers an excellent illustration of how a formal climax, for instance, is particularly conducive to facilitating predictability: "He who controls Berlin controls Germany; he who controls Germany controls Europe; and he who controls Europe controls the _____."[17] By the time you react to the final portion of this utterance, the formality of the sequence enables you to predict with a relatively high degree of certainty that it will conclude with "World." This factor of predictability or redundancy should increase the efficiency with which the statement's conclusion can be handled psychologically. Phrased as a more idiomatic anticlimax construction, the utterance likely would decrease the efficiency with which the statement's conclusion can be handled psychologically. While one can grasp the trend of the climax from "Berlin" to "Germany" to "Europe" to "World," a sequence proceeding from "World" to "Europe" and thence anticlimatically would increase the alternatives from which the next items might be chosen. The statement could end just as well with "France" and "Paris," or "Yugoslavia" and "Belgrade," and less predictability is possible.

If used in sequence, antitheses may achieve a similar predictive effect: "*we* do *this,* but *they* on the other hand do *that; we* stay *here,* but *they* go *there; we* look *up,* but *they* look _____." [18] Compare this sequential regularity of opposites with Kennedy's host of antitheses preceding his peroration "Ask not what your country can do for you—ask what you can do for your country." By the time the first half of this statement occurred in the "Inaugural Address," some respondents could have been expecting its obverse resolution. If so, the conclusion of the antithesis was redundant. There is no doubt, however, that continued repetition of a specific antithesis is probably a more reliable means of conditioning to achieve redundancy. For instance, because of extensive exposure to a former cigarette commercial on television, it finally became necessary for the ad to say only "You can take Salem out of the country, but _____ _____ _____ _____ _____ _____ _____ _____."

Of all the possible stylistic determinants, parallel repetitions are among the most widely used in presidential discourse. These conformations also might achieve redundancy by creating expectancies that allow a respondent to predict accurately the appearance of successive items. Just as the formal regularity of *a a b a a b a a* _ facilitates completion of the sequence with *b,* the stylistic regularity in the formal "*of the people,* by *the people,* for the _____" provides readers or listeners with reasonably reliable predictions that it will conclude with *people.* Redundancy and efficiency of response may result whenever a speaker or writer begins successive phrases or short sentences with the same word or words, as in the several previously cited examples from both Kennedy and Nixon, or when he concludes those elements with the same word or phrase, as illustrated in the familiar repeated refrain in Hubert Humphrey's Vice-Presidential Acceptance Address to the 1964 Democratic Convention, ". . . but not Senator Goldwater" (a refrain that his immediate audience joined in vociferously after only the first few repetitions).

Certainly any attempt to achieve redundancy must be tempered, however, by a judicious concern for change, perhaps the most crucial of all attentional attributes. Because excessively repeated words and unchanging patterns might create an undesired monotony and cause listeners to "tune out," employment of a slight alteration at an appropriate place in an extended redundant pattern might enhance its effect all the more, as in Franklin Roosevelt's successive references in parallel to freedom of speech "everywhere in the world," freedom of worship "everywhere in the world," freedom from want "everywhere in the world," and freedom from fear "*anywhere* in the world." Here, capitalizing on the accumulated effects of novelty and repetition for emphasis as well as parallelism for redundancy, the final segment introduces a slight change which may make the last phrase even more emphatic.

The previous explication of emphasis and efficiency of comprehension deals with what are probably the more obvious facets of stylistic functionalism, ones which some people have grasped already, however intuitively. Now, some speculation may be in order about another facet of style in presidential discourse, one which has not been investigated systematically as yet but is deserving nevertheless of some initial inquiry.

In the context of presidential discourse, it may be time to add another dimension to the thinking about functional objectives. Traditionally, discourse is regarded as rhetorical if it seeks as objective some kind of alteration or adjustment in affect, attitude, or action. True, the overall objective of obtaining change does characterize much of presidential discourse. But another possible rhetorical objective that often seems to be particularly appropriate now may be devoid of basic intent to change, adjust, or modify, per se. Perhaps Richard Nixon provides a helpful focal point for further discussion of such "non-change" discourse and the basic functionalism of its style.

style to achieve
identification with
"silent majority"

Consider this interpretation of the success of his appeal to the "silent majority" of 1968. In America not too many decades ago, solitude was the order of the day at work in the fields or forest, in the small shop or business run by one person. The "crowd" such as it was, could be found in the Grange Hall or in the town meeting. There, one could speak his mind on his politics with full realization that he indeed could be heard and that he could be heard by a viable constituency whose voting behavior he might influence.

This is no longer the case. We are more and more urbanized. Now, upon completing his day's toil in crowded factories or offices, and combating rush hour traffic, the urban American will occasionally find relaxation with crowds at sports events or theaters, but he more often will seek the relative solitude offered by the closed door of his apartment or the fence of his yard. Home is not only one's castle but the "Keep" which places him in "solitary" away from the crowds. There, any partisan political interests are evinced in *listening* rather than speaking. For average Americans know full well that to influence any viable constituency of voters, one must have access to the mass media, particularly television, at an incredibly prohibitive cost. Moreover, the average American now probably feels that even if he did have access to television, how could he hope to compare favorable in ability to articulate a viewpoint with a mellifluous Walter Cronkhite, an urbane David Brinkley, and the host of oleaginous political commentators and candidates. The majority, or more accurately, *majorities,* are indeed silent.

That silence is no indication of political indifference, however, but rather more the end product of a complex, urban mass society. Resigned more and more by circumstance to political reticence, Americans will seek surrogate spokesmen. That is, political allegiance (and votes) will be rendered not so much to those speakers who attempt to change attitudes so much as to those who articulate well the prevailing predispositions which Americans have less and less opportunity to express for themselves in political arenas. To secure such allegiance via discourse and actually become surrogate spokesmen in this sense, presidents or presidential candidates will in many instances not be concerned with an objective of *modi*fication so much as one of *identi*fication.

In developing the concept of identification as the basis for rhetorical activity, Kenneth Burke has provided several insightful examples of stylistic language behaviors as they may help achieve a rapport and empathy whereby "the audience feels as though it were not merely receiving, but were itself participating in the poet's or speaker's assertion."[19] Some examples of those usages were cited earlier in this essay. And it is not too difficult a matter to think of contemporary political figures who seem to use language stylistically to achieve not only the "collaborative expectancies" described by Kenneth Burke, but also what may be a potentially persuasive reaction to style observed by the great critic Longinus: "a generous exultation to be filled with joy and pride," as though the respondents themselves originated the ideas they are hearing articulated so well.[20] At one level, conjure up an image of the way some people may have reacted positively at the beginning to Vice-President Spiro Agnew's colorful but stylistic language behaviors. Viewing the televised film clips, they probably nodded their heads in agreement as Agnew uttered what they only wished they could say, and perhaps they even then vocalized their approval with a middle American counterpart of "Right on, Spiro!" Or, for an example that may come closer to illustrating the Longinian concept of eloquence, remember that moment in the Kennedy Inaugural when all that had been articulated so stylistically before was climaxed with the rhetorical question: "Will you join in that historic effort?" What might have been just another unanswered rhetorical question was in that instance responded to with vocal affirmations in the immediate audience on January 20, 1961. Here certainly was the surrogate spokesman, albeit of a different mold, for another segment of politically reticent Americans.

style: only one element in effectiveness, but may be "main difference" today

Of course this is not to say that style alone can be a determinant of identification or any or all aspects of rhetorical effectiveness. The most important conclusion to this consideration of language behavior is that style is only the *manner* in which one most effectively phrases the crucial *matter* of presidential discourse—the arguments and the appeals to emotions and the efforts to create an image that in combination are the bases of rhetorical effectiveness. But in a day when more and more candidates may be offering nearly the same content and perhaps even the same image, it just might be that the "main difference" between the comparative effectiveness of speakers will be, due to what another great critic discussed at length as their individual style in discourse.[21] So if style *is* the man, the better men, stylistically, will continue to put their talents to work advantageously in discourse to complement all the other factors that conduce to political success.

REFERENCES AND FOOTNOTES

Note: Ronald H. Carpenter (Ph.D., University of Wisconsin, 1966) is Associate Professor of Speech, University of Florida. This essay was presented initially as guest lectures in the Spring of 1971 at American University and the University of Maryland.

1. This concept of style is developed in greater detail in Ronald H. Carpenter, "Style and Emphasis in Debate," *Journal of the American Forensic Association,* VI (Winter 1969), 27–31.

2. Buffon, "Address on Style," in *The Art of the Writer,* ed. Lane Cooper (Ithaca: Cornell University Press, 1952), p. 153.

   For an indication of how style may have some situational origins in addition to the dictates of individuality, see Ronald H. Carpenter and Robert V. Seltzer, "Situational Style and the Rotunda Eulogies," *Central States Speech Journal,* XXII (Spring 1971), 11–15.

3. Theodore H. White, *The Making of the President 1968* (New York: Atheneum Press, 1969), p. 131.

4. Ronald H. Carpenter and Robert V. Seltzer, "On Nixon's Kennedy Style," *Speaker and Gavel,* VII (January 1970), 41–43.

5. A brief account of Nixon's preparation of this particular speech appears in William H. Honan, "The Men Behind Nixon's Speeches," *New York Times Magazine* (January 19, 1969), 65.

6. Richard M. Nixon, *Six Crises* (New York: Doubleday and Company, 1962), p. 103.

7. For further discussion of this point, see Rulon Wells, "Nominal and Verbal Style," and Charles E. Osgood, "Some Effects of Motivation on Style of Encoding," both in *Style in Language,* ed. Thomas A. Sebeok (New York: John Wiley and Sons, 1960), pp. 215, 293–296.

8. Analyses supporting this conclusion about the TTR of smaller segments of the common idiom are cited in Ronald H. Carpenter, "The Essential Schemes of Syntax," *Quarterly Journal of Speech,* LV (April 1969), 162.

9. Honan, *loc. cit.*

10. See the discussion in Carpenter, "The Essential Schemes of Syntax," *op. cit.,* 163–164.

11. The syntactical inversion, or *anastrophe,* of functional elements is one of the basic recommendations for stylistic effectiveness, most notably perhaps in Herbert Spencer's "Philosophy of Style," in *The Art of the Writer,* op. cit., pp. 245–246.

12. Along with the various types of syntactical parallel repetitions, the specific varieties of antithesis comprise one of the largest categories of stylistic usage recommended in traditional rhetorical theory over the centuries. For further discussion of why antitheses are uncommon, as well as a compilation of all of rhetoricians' recommendations for uncommon word orders, see Carpenter, "The Essential Schemes of Syntax," *op. cit.,* 165–168.

13. This definition is derived from William J. Jordan's most interesting analysis of metaphor as a psycholinguistic phenomenon. See his "Psychological Explication of Aristotle's Concept of Metaphor," unpubl. Ph.D. diss. (Wayne State University, 1969).

14. Jon Eisenson, J. Jeffery Auer, and John V. Irwin, *The Psychology of Communication* (New York: Appleton-Century-Crofts, 1963), p. 250.

15. One of the better treatments of novelty and its influence on perceptual selectivity appears in William Dember, *The Psychology of Perception* (New York: Holt, Rinehart, and Winston, 1964), pp. 347–350.

16. For bibliographies of empirical studies relating to the effects of redundancy in this context, see Ronald H. Carpenter, "Stylistic Redundancy and Function in Discourse," *Language and Style,* III (Winter 1970), 62–68; or "Language, Redundancy, and Communication Efficiency," *Journal of Communication Pathology,* III (1970), 13–16.

17. Kenneth Burke, *A Rhetoric of Motives* (New York: George Braziller, Inc., 1955), pp. 58–59.

18. *Ibid.*

19. *Ibid.*

20. Longinus *On the Sublime* 7, trans. H. L. Havell (London: MacMillan and Company, 1890).

21. Dionysius of Halicarnassus *On Literary Composition* 3, trans. W. Rhys Roberts (London: MacMillan and Company, 1910).

SUGGESTED FURTHER READING

Blankenship, Jane, *A Sense of Style.* Belmont, California: Dickenson Publishing Company, Inc., 1968.

Cunningham, J. V., *The Problem of Style.* New York: Fawcett Publications, Inc., 1966.

Enkvist, Nils Erok and John Spencer and Michael J. Gregory, *Linguistics and Style.* London: Oxford University Press, 1964.

Lucas, F. L., *Style.* New York: Collier Books, 1962.

Ullman, Stephen, *Language and Style.* Oxford: Basil Blackwell, 1964.

A Summary of Research on Order Effects in Communication

Loren J. Anderson

Communication may be viewed as a goal-oriented process, a process in which the source develops and presents a message in hopes of securing the audience's understanding and/or acceptance of his proposal. In constructing a message, the source is faced with a myriad of choices. He must, for example, isolate his goal and the arguments he will use to support his position. He must choose the language to express his arguments. He must decide what, if any, evidence he will use to develop these arguments. Each of these choices may, in some circumstances, dramatically affect his chances of success.

clear organizational patterns benefit communicators

In preparing a message, the communicator also faces organizational decisions. There can be little doubt that a clear organizational pattern will benefit the communicator. Research has shown that a disorganized message, as might be expected, is more difficult to comprehend.[1] Disorganization may also have a negative effect on the source's image, reducing his credibility.[2]

But beyond developing a clear organizational pattern, the source faces decisions about the placement or order of his ideas. A source might ask: (1) Should I place my strongest argument first, or last? (2) Should I outline the solution before discussing the problem, or vice versa? (3) Should I discuss one or both sides of the issue? Like his other decisions, the choices that a source makes in answering these questions may influence his effectiveness.

This essay discusses the experimental research relevant to these organizational choices. Basically, this research is concerned with the effect a particular order of presentation has on receivers. Section I summarizes research on the placement of materials in a message. Section II discusses the "primacy-recency" controversy. Section III offers a perspective for viewing the results of this research.

I

Communication sources frequently deal with controversial issues. On such issues, there are arguments which support, and
others which contradict, the speaker's position. Thus, the
speaker must decide if he will include only those arguments
which support his position (a one-sided message) or if he will
consider opposing arguments as well (a two-sided message).
Studies comparing one and two-sided messages provide some
guidelines for answering this question.

The first research on this question was conducted by
Hovland, Lumsdaine, and Sheffield.[3] They found that a two-
sided message, which mentioned opposing arguments, was
more effective when the listeners were (1) initially opposed to
the speaker's position, or (2) were well-educated. Listeners
who initially agreed with the speaker or listeners with less
education were more influenced by the one-sided message.

An indirect explanation for these findings is suggested by
Chu.[4] He reasoned that listeners who were "familiar" with a
message topic would detect arguments which were omitted
in a one-sided presentation. The detection of these omissions
would make the speaker appear biased and, hence, less effective. Chu's findings support this rationale. Like the listeners
who are familiar with the message topic, well-educated receivers are likely to be better informed on the topic, and better
able to detect omitted arguments. Likewise those who oppose
the speaker's position are apt to be aware of issues not mentioned in a one-sided communication. In either case, Chu's
results indicate that the speaker may be seen as less objective
and his effectiveness may suffer.

In many situations, receivers are exposed to competing
persuasive appeals. In a political campaign, for example, the
voter listens to both Republican and Democratic speakers. In
such circumstances, Lumsdaine and Janis[5] and Insko[6] have
found that a two-sided message may be preferable. Listeners
who are exposed to a two-sided message are more resistant
to counter-persuasion (by a second speaker) than those who
hear a one-sided message. The two-sided message functions
to inform the receiver of the arguments he is likely to hear
from a subsequent, opposing source. This appears to make
the listener more resistant to the persuasive appeals of the
second communicator.

As a unit, these studies indicate that a two-sided message
is preferable when the audience is well-educated, hostile,
or likely to be exposed to counter-persuasion. Other experi-

"two-sided" message
for intelligent, hostile
audiences, subject to
counter-persuasion

ments offer additional suggestions for the use of two-sided messages.

A two-sided message presents arguments that favor the speaker's position (pro-arguments) and arguments that oppose the speaker's position (con-arguments). Should the pro-arguments be presented before the con-arguments? Janis and Fierbend[7] have investigated this question. They hypothesized that when the message topic was nonsalient and the message source highly credible, a pro-first order would be more effective. Pro-arguments discussed by the highly credible source should provide maximum motivation for acceptance. The con-arguments should have little effect because they contradict the highly credible source and the pro-arguments. The findings support the superiority of a pro-first organization.

Similar findings have been reported by McGuire[8] and Cohen.[9] McGuire found that a message was more effective if information highly desirable to the listeners was presented before the less desirable material. Cohen reported that a message was more effective if need arousal preceded, rather than followed, need satisfaction. This finding suggests the superiority of a problem-solution over a solution-problem organization.

Thistlethwaite, Kamenetsky, and Schmidt[10] have studied the type of refutation used in a two-sided message. They found no significant differences between a message which simply mentioned opposing arguments and a message which mentioned *and* refuted the contradictory issues.

Finally, studies by Holz and Rosnow,[11] Rosnow,[12] and Schultz[13] have isolated an interaction between "awareness" and sidedness. Awareness refers to the listener's knowledge of the source's intent to persuade. When aware of the source's intent, subjects responded more favorably to a one-sided message. The two-sided message, however, was more effective when no forewarning preceded the communication.

A one-sided message contains a series of arguments supporting the speaker's position. In such a message the most important or strongest argument may be presented first (anti-climax order) or last (climax order). Several studies have compared the effectiveness of these two approaches. Sponberg[14] found that anti-climax organization resulted in better comprehension of the message, but the two orders did not differ in persuasiveness. Cromwell[15] found that the climax order was more effective. Three additional studies found no difference between climax and anti-climax orders.[16]

Gulley and Berlo[17] compared the effectiveness of three

orders; anti-climax, climax, and pyramidal. In the pyramidal arrangement the most important material is placed in the middle of the message. Both the climax and anti-climax speeches were more effective than the pyramidal order. This study suggests that the most important material should be placed either first or last in the message.

One variable which may influence the choice of a climax or anti-climax organization is subject interest. Anti-climax order may be useful in arousing the attention of a disinterested audience while a climax order may be preferable if the audience is already interested in the source's topic. While such an approach seems reasonable, its effect has not been experimentally verified.

most important material
placed first or last

II

The general question of order effects is known as the "primacy-recency" controversy. Does material presented first (primacy) have a greater impact than that placed last (recency)? While this seems like a simple question, the research on this issue provides no clear answer.

The primacy-recency debate began in 1925 when Lund[18] proposed the "Law of Primacy." This principle suggested that the impact of the first communication is greater than the effect of a subsequent message. Later studies by Jersild,[19] Knower,[20] and Doob[21] supported Lund's theory. However, research reported by Cromwell,[22] Ehrensberger,[23] and Tannenbaum[24] produced findings inconsistent with a universal law of primacy. Hovland and Mandell's[25] systematic study of primacy-recency effects also sheds doubt on Lund's principle. In the Hovland and Mandell studies no clear primacy *or* recency effects were isolated. In total, there is little evidence to support the existence of a law of primacy or recency. Rather primacy and/or recency effects appear to depend on other variables in the communication setting. Subsequent studies have attempted to isolate some of these variables.

no *general* law of
recency or primacy;
dependent on other
variables

Familiarity

When two opposing persuasive communications are presented, several studies have identified a primacy effect if the receivers are familiar with the message topic.[26] Receivers who were unfamiliar with the topic reacted more favorably to the second message (recency). However, this finding may be lim-

familiarity in persuasive
communication has a
primacy effect

ited to persuasive messages. Research using descriptive communications have found that an *unfamiliar* topic resulted in primacy effects.[27]

Controversiality of topic

controversiality
and primacy effects

Some messages are more controversial than others. Lana[28] has identified a primacy effect if the topic is highly controversial for the listener. This primacy effect is absent when a less controversial subject is discussed.

Interest

interest and
primacy-recency effects

Like controversiality, a highly interesting message appears to produce primacy effects.[29] When the message is perceived as uninteresting, recency effects result.

Commitment

public commitment
and primacy effects

Hovland, Campbell and Brock[30] have found that public commitment can produce primacy effects. In this research, listeners were presented two communications. After the first message, they were asked to publicly express their position. As a result of publicly expressing their opinions, receivers were less influenced by the second message. The commitment must, however, be expressed publicly, rather than anonymously, if the primacy effect is to result.[31]

Reinforcement

Reinforcement theory suggests the possibility that a reinforcing event may produce either primacy or recency results. A "reinforcing event" refers to any occurrence in the communication setting that the listener perceives as satisfying or need-fulfilling. By contrast, any occurrence which is perceived as unsatisfying may be described as a "punishing event."

placement of reinforcing
or punishing events
affects primacy-recency

Reinforcement theory predicts that a message presented nearest the reinforcing event, or furthest from a punishing event, will be more effective. Accordingly, if a rewarding incident occurs before both messages, primacy effects are predicted. If the reinforcing incident follows both messages, the second communication should have more impact (recency). Conversely, a punishing event before both messages should produce recency while punishment following the communication should produce a primacy effect. Several studies which are basically supportive of this theory have been reported.[32]

The major impact of all primacy-recency studies has been to deny the existence of any universal order effect. Rather the superiority of either the first or second communication in a series is almost certainly tied to other variables. As Rosnow and Robinson conclude:

> Nonsalient, controversial topics, interesting subject matter and highly familiar issues tend toward primacy. Salient topics, un-interesting subject matter, and moderately unfamiliar issues tend to yield recency.[33]

Public commitment may result in primacy effects, while reinforcing or punishing events, depending upon their placement, may produce either primacy or recency results.

III

Research on order effects—one-sided versus two-sided messages, climax versus anti-climax, and primacy-recency—allows no absolute generalizations. It provides no formulas for "effective organization." Rather, the research indicates that the most effective order of material is affected by other variables in the communication process. The impact of a one or two-sided message appears to be influenced by the audience's prior attitude, education, familiarity with the topic, awareness of the persuader's intent, and the likelihood that they will be exposed to competing persuasive appeals. Climax and anti-climax order do not seem to differ in persuasiveness, but this may depend upon the interest level of the audience. Research has linked the occurrence of primacy or recency effects to the variables of familiarity, controversiality, interest, commitment, and reinforcement.

many variables in process of communication affect the most effective order

The lack of simple generalizations about order effects should not, however, be taken as a sign that the research is unproductive. Rather, it is a reminder that communication is an extremely complex process and that every message must be developed in terms of a unique audience and situation. The most effective placement of arguments depends upon these other variables. The question of order effects cannot be treated in isolation.

Nor should the absence of generalization lead to the conclusion that order effects are unimportant. In any communication setting, there are a multitude of factors which can influence the outcome. The speaker's delivery, his use of (or failure to use) evidence, or his use of fear appeals could, either singly or collectively, be crucial variables. The order of material is only one among many forces that may explain a speaker's success or failure. It is conceivable that a speaker may choose the most effective order of argument and still, perhaps because of his delivery, fail to achieve his objective. On the other hand, a speaker may use a less effective order and still be successful. In short, order effects are only one of the important variables which the communicator must consider in the construction of messages. This consideration is aided by a thorough understanding of order effects research.

REFERENCES AND FOOTNOTES

1. For summaries of research on this question see, K. C. Beighley, "A Summary of Experimental Studies Dealing with the Effect of Organization and of Skill of Speakers on Comprehension," *Journal of Communication,* II (1952), 58–65; C. Petrie, "Informative Speaking: A Summary and Bibliography of Related Research," *Speech Monographs,* XXX (1963), 79–91; and E. Thompson, "An Experimental Investigation of the Relative Effectiveness of Organizational Structure in Oral Communication," *Southern Speech Journal,* XXVI (1960), 59–69.

2. H. Sharp, Jr., and T. McClung, "Effects of Organization on the Speaker's Ethos," *Speech Monographs,* XXXIII (1966), 182–183; and J. C. McCroskey and R. S. Mehrley, "The Effect of Disorganization and Nonfluency on Attitude Change and Source Credibility," *Speech Monographs,* XXXVI (1969), 13–21.

3. C. I. Hovland, A. A. Lumsdaine, and F. D. Sheffield, "The Effects of Presenting 'One Side' versus 'Both Sides' in Changing Opinions on a Controversial Subject," in *Experiments in Persuasion,* ed. by R. L. Rosnow and E. J. Robinson (New York: Academic Press, 1967), pp. 71–97.

4. G. C. Chu, "Prior Familiarity, Perceived Bias, and One-Sided Versus Two-Sided Communications," *Journal of Experimental Social Psychology,* III (1967), 243–254.

5. A. A. Lumsdaine and I. L. Janis, "Resistance to Counter-Propaganda Produced by a One-Sided versus a Two-Sided Propaganda Presentation," *Public Opinion Quarterly,* XVII (1953), 311–318.

6. C. A. Insko, "One-Sided versus Two-Sided Communications and Counter Communications," *Journal of Abnormal and Social Psychology,* LXV (1962), 203–206.

7. I. L. Janis and R. L. Fierbend, "Effects of Alternative Ways of Ordering Pro and Con Arguments in Persuasive Communications," in *The Order of Presentation in Persuasion,* ed. by C. I. Hovland, *et. al.* (New Haven: Yale University Press, 1957), pp. 115–128.

8. W. J. McGuire, "Order of Presentation as a Factor in 'Conditioning' Persuasiveness," in *The Order of Presentation in Persuasion,* ed. by C. I. Hovland, *et. al.* (New Haven: Yale University Press, 1957), pp. 98–114.

9. A. R. Cohen, "Need for Cognition and Order of Communication as Determinants of Opinion Change," in *The Order of Presentation in Persuasion,* ed. by C. I. Hovland, *et. al.* (New Haven: Yale University Press, 1957), pp. 79–97.

10. D. L. Thistlethwaite, J. Kamenetsky, and H. Schmidt, "Factors Influencing Attitude Change Through Refutation Communication," *Speech Monographs,* XXIII (1956), 14–25.

11. R. F. Holz and R. L. Rosnow, "Awareness of Expectation in Attitude Research," *Psychological Reports,* XX (1967), 642–649.

12. R. L. Rosnow, "'Conditioning' the Direction of Opinion Change in Persuasive Communication," *Journal of Social Psychology,* LXXIII (1966), 291–303.

13. D. P. Schultz, "Time, Awareness, and Order of Presentation in Opinion Change," *Journal of Applied Psychology,* XLVII (1963), 280–283.

14. H. Sponberg, "A Study of the Relative Effectivenss of Climax and Anti-Climax Order in an Argumentative Speech," *Speech Monographs,* XVIII (1951), 292–300.

15. H. Cromwell, "The Persistency of the Effect on Audience Attitude of the First Versus the Second Argumentative Speech of a Series," *Speech Monographs,* XXI (1954), 280–284.

16. H. Gilkinson, S. Paulson, and D. Sikkink, "Effects of Order and Authority in an Argumentative Speech," *Quarterly Journal of Speech,* XL (1954), 183–192; D. Sikkink, "An Experimental Study of the Effects on the Listener of Anti-Climax Order and Authority in an Argumentative Speech," *Southern Speech Journal,* XXII (1956), 73–78; and D. L. Thistlethwaite, J. Kamenetsky, and H. Schmidt, "Factors Influencing Attitude Change Through Refutative Communication," *Speech Monographs,* XXIII (1956), 14–25.

17. H. E. Gulley and D. K. Berlo, "Effects of Intercellular and Intracellular Speech Structure on Attitude Change and Listening," *Speech Monographs,* XXIII (1956), 288–297.

18. F. H. Lund, "The Psychology of Belief: A Study of its Emotional and Volitional Determinants," *Journal of Abnormal and Social Psychology,* XX (1925), 174–196.

19. A. T. Jersild, "Primacy, Recency, Frequency and Vividness," *Journal of Experimental Psychology,* XII (1929), 58–70.

20. F. H. Knower, "Experimental Studies of Changes in Attitudes: II. A Study of the Effect of Printed Arguments on Changes in Attitude," *Journal of Abnormal and Social Psychology,* XXX (1936), 522–532.

21. J. W. Doob, "Effects of Initial Serial Position and Attitude Upon Recall Under Conditions of Low Motivation," *Journal of Abnormal and Social Psychology,* XLIV (1953), 199–205.

22. H. Cromwell, "The Persistency of the Effect of the First versus the Second Argumentative Speech of a Series," *Speech Monographs,* XXI (1954), 280–284.

23. R. Ehrensberger, "An Experimental Study of the Relative Effectiveness of Certain Forms of Emphasis in Public Speaking," *Speech Monographs,* XII (1945), 94–111.

24. P. H. Tannenbaum, "Effect of Social Position on Recall of Radio News Stories," *Journalism Quarterly,* XXXI (1954), 319–323.

25. C. I. Hovland and W. Mandell, "Is There a 'Law of Primacy' in Persuasion?," in *The Order of Presentation in Persuasion,* pp. 13–22.

26. R. E. Lana, "Existing Familiarity and Order of Presentation of Persuasive Communications," *Psychological Reports,* XV (1964), 607–610; R. E. Lana, "Familiarity and the Order of Presentation of Persuasive Communication," *Journal of Abnormal and Social Psychology,* LXII (1961), 573–577; R. L. Rosnow and J. H. Goldstein, "Familiarity, Salience and the Order of Presentation in Communication," *Journal of Social Psychology,* LXXIII (1967), 97–110; R. L. Rosnow and R. E. Lana, "Complementary and Competing Order Effects in Opinion Change," *Journal of Social Psychology,* LXVI (1965), 201–207; and E. J. Thomas, S. Webb, and J. Tweedie, "Effects of Familiarity with a Controversial Issue on Acceptance of Successive Persuasive Communications," *Journal of Abnormal and Social Psychology,* LXIII (1961), 656–659.

27. S. E. Asch, "Forming Impressions of Personality," *Journal of Abnormal and Social Psychology,* XLI (1946), 258–290;

A. S. Luchins, "Definitiveness of Impression and Primacy-Recency in Communications," *Journal of Social Psychology,* XLVIII (1958), 275–290; A. S. Luchins, "Experimental Attempts to Minimize the Impact of First Impressions," in *The Order of Presentation in Persuasion,* pp. 62–75; and A. S. Luchins, "Primacy-Recency in Impression Formation," in *The Order of Presentation in Persuasion,* pp. 33–61.

28. R. E. Lana, "Controversy of the Topic and the Order of Presentation in Persuasive Communication," *Psychological Reports,* XII (1963), 163–170; and R. E. Lana and R. L. Rosnow, "Subject Awareness and Order Effects in Persuasive Communications," *Psychological Reports,* XII (1963), 523–529.

29. R. E. Lana, "Interest, Media and Order Effects in Persuasive Communications," *Journal of Psychology,* LVI (1963), 9–13.

30. C. I. Hovland, E. H. Campbell, and T. Brock, "The Effects of Commitment on Opinion Change Following Communication," in *The Order of Presentation in Persuasion,* pp. 23–32.

31. Hovland and Mandell, "Is There a 'Law of Primacy' in Persuasion?"

32. R. L. Rosnow, "A Delay-of-Reinforcement Effect in Persuasive Communication?," *Journal of Social Psychology,* LXVII (1965), 39–43; R. L. Rosnow, "'Conditioning' the Direction of Opinion Change in Persuasive Communication," *Journal of Social Psychology,* LXIX (1966), 291–303; and R. L. Rosnow and G. Russel, "Spread of Effect of Reinforcement in Persuasive Communication," *Psychological Reports,* XII (1963), 731–735.

33. R. L. Rosnow and E. J. Robinson eds., *Experiments in Persuasion* (New York: Academic Press, 1967), pp. 101–102.

SUGGESTED FURTHER READING

Cohen, Arthur R., *Attitude Change and Social Influence.* New York: Basic Books, Inc., 1964. (See also footnote 9 above.)

Hovland, C. I., *et. al.* ed., *The Order of Presentation in Persuasion.* New Haven: Yale University Press, 1957. (See also footnotes 3, 8, 9, 25, 27, 30, 31 above.)

Insko, C. A., "One-Sided versus Two-Sided Communications and Counter Communications," *Journal of Abnormal and Social Psychology,* LXV (1962), 203–206. (See footnote 6 above.)

Rosnow, R. L. and E. J. Robinson, eds., *Experiments in Persuasion.* New York: Academic Press, 1967. (See also footnote 32 above.)

Sharp, H., Jr. and T. McClung, "Effects of Organization on the Speaker's Ethos," *Speech Monographs,* XXXIII (1966), 182–183. (See footnote 2 above.)

The Concept of Ethos and The Structure of Persuasion

Paul I. Rosenthal

During an effort to study its function in the presidential television debates of 1960, it became evident to this writer that *ethos,* as an explanatory theoretical concept, was one of the great "poverty pockets" of rhetorical theory.[1] The investigation became stalled in its preliminary stages because several critical questions about the operation of the speaker's personality in the persuasive process could not be resolved by the existing body of thought accumulated under the heading of *ethos.* A re-examination of *ethos* theory in light of more recent thinking in the general field of human communication was therefore undertaken. The result of that inquiry was an enlarged and modified conception of *ethos* that departs from the notions traditionally associated with the term. This theoretical exposition is the subject of the present paper.[2]

The textbooks, theses, and monograph literature of contemporary rhetorical scholarship reveal that current pedagogy, theory, and criticism are dominated by what we shall term the "classical view" of *ethos.* The influence of this tradition in rhetorical criticism has been described by Edwin Black who calls it "neo-Aristotelianism."[3] Though the taproot of this influ-

Note: [At the time of this article's first appearance in June, 1966,] Dr. Rosenthal [was] Assistant Professor of Speech, University of California, Los Angeles. This article is based on a dissertation completed at UCLA under the direction of Professor Charles W. Lomas.

[1] Paul I. Rosenthal, "Ethos in the Presidential Campaign of 1960: A Study of the Basic Persuasive Process of the Kennedy-Nixon Television Debates," unpubl. diss. (University of California, Los Angeles, 1963).

[2] As developed here, *ethos* is presented as an active persuasive process operative in actual speaking situations; however, applicability of the theory to communications in which personal impressions are derived from sources antecedent or peripheral to the speech itself is not precluded.

[3] Edwin Black, *Rhetorical Criticism* (New York, 1965), pp. 27–35. Black's term "neo-Aristotelianism" and our "classical view" refer to the same mode of rhetorical criticism, except that our focus is more limited. We are particularly concerned with that aspect of "neo-Aristotelianism" that is manifested in critical works by "the classification of 'proofs' or 'means of persuasion' as logical, pathetic, and ethical"; p. 31.

ence is Aristotle's *Rhetoric,* the looser phrase "classical view" is preferred in this inquiry since no questions of historical authenticity or legitimacy are to be raised. It seems a convenient and not unfair expression by which to designate the notions used by contemporary rhetorical scholars, characterized by terminology and principles said to be derived from Greek and Roman theory.

The core of this system holds that rhetoric is the faculty of discovering in a given situation the "available means of persuasion" and that the "available means" are to be found in the speaker's total personality[4] (*ethos*), in the state of emotion produced in the audience (*pathos*), and in the credibility of the argument proper.[5] These "means" or "modes" of persuasion (depending upon the translation being used) have come to be regarded as the basic elements of the rhetorical process. In pedagogical volumes the speaker is typically counseled to use logic and reason, to appeal to emotion, and to demonstrate the right character, intelligence, and goodwill if he would persuade. In critical works, particularly at the thesis level, one too often finds the heart of the rhetorical analysis composed of excerpts from speeches catalogued under the headings of logical, emotional, and ethical appeals. This static conception of persuasion has retarded theory and confined criticism, and it is in reaction to such difficulties that this inquiry proceeds.

The immediate question that arises is one of definition and classification. Are the classical "means of persuasion" genuinely discrete and distinguishable elements of the persuasive process or has habitual and uncritical usage of the terms suggested differences that do not exist, while perhaps masking some that do? In short, is our nomenclature accurate?

THE PHYSIOLOGICAL BASES OF PERSUASION

Oral persuasion involves the generation of symbolic stimuli by a speaker and a reaction to these stimuli by a listener. This is a communicative act; thus any realistic standard for distinguishing among its elemental processes must be derived from the nature of the listener's response to the presentation of

[4]We use the term "total personality" to encompass any and all aspects of the speaker's character, intellect, temperament, or other personal traits including physical appearance, that may function in the communication. The meaning is not confined to the colloquial interpretation: charm, vivacity, or similar notions.

[5] *The Rhetoric of Aristotle,* trans. Lane Cooper (New York, 1932), 1.2, pp. 8, 9.

symbolic cues. The advances of modern physiological psychology afford increased knowledge of the human organism's reactions to external stimuli, and we turn to these data for this phase of our inquiry.

The foundation for this analysis is the fact that, within the listener's total physiological response to speaker-generated symbolic stimuli, there are certain differentiable subclasses. Thus, the intellectual processes—thinking, learning, reasoning—have their physiological base in the Central Nervous System—specifically, in a highly complex system of cortical dynamics or neural activity in the brain.[6] In the persuasive communication such activity is stimulated by certain combinations of visual and aural symbols issued by the speaker, and the totality of these stimuli and the cortically centered response is conventionally designated as the *logical* element of the communication.[7]

the logical element of a communication

Distinguishable by psychometric techniques is the more diffuse type of physiological activity generally termed the emotional response. In addition to the action of the Central Nervous System, emotion involves the acceleration of numerous other mechanisms of bodily response—the "activity and reactivity of the tissues and organs innervated by the autonomic nervous system."[8] Emotion may be described as visceral action of an extremely complex nature, and though criteria for thresholds of emotional and nonemotional states are not universally agreed upon, the general physiology of the reaction has been recorded.[9] In persuasion this type of response is activated by certain uses of visual and aural symbols, and the totality of these stimuli and the viscerally centered response is conventionally designated as the *emotional* element of the communication.

the emotional element of a communication

There are, then, determinable differences in the nature of the response evoked from the listener, but these reactions are not mutually exclusive. Let us consider this excerpt from General Douglas MacArthur's address to Congress in April 1951: "I have just left your fighting sons in Korea . . . and I can report to you without reservation that they are splendid in every way."

logical and emotional elements not mutually exclusive

[6]M. A. Wenger, F. N. Jones, and M. H. Jones, *Physiological Psychology* (New York, 1956), ch. 19.

[7]Contemporary experimental psychologists classify these responses under the term *cognition*. See Egon Brunswik, Leon Festinger, Charles E. Osgood, *et al.*, *Contemporary Approaches to Cognition: The Colorado Symposium* (Cambridge, 1957).

[8]Wenger, p. 343.

[9]*Ibid.*, ch. 21.

Colleagues asked to classify it in traditional terms labeled it an emotional or an ethical appeal or a combination of both. None called it a logical appeal. But suppose the passage had been uttered, "Sons your Korea I fighting left splendid just are have reservation every in can in without report you to that I they way and." This scrambling makes obvious the fact that an orderly presentation of linguistic items is necessary for basic comprehension and therefore preliminary to any visceral effect the statement may evoke other than confused irritation. What is required is a pattern of word arrangement that will elicit a cognitive response from the auditor—a response comprised within the concept of *logic* as applied to the persuasive process.

But it is also true that when the proper linguistic pattern is employed, a complex visceral reaction may result from these cues. The auditor's reaction may be emotional or may be only a preliminary condition which can be accelerated into emotion by further stimulation.[10] A cortically centered response, therefore, in no way precludes the operation of a visceral response, but in order to perform its function in a persuasive communication, the latter must be preceded by some logical decoding of the source stimuli.[11] That these responses occur simultaneously in a fusion of unitary physiological reaction does not alter the fact that it is possible to distinguish them by their physiological differences, and these may serve as the defining characteristics of logic and emotion.

[10] There is no practical method for calculating how extensive a set of symbols is necessary to produce the physiological condition of emotion in a listener. In some instances considerable development of a theme is required to do so; in other cases the use of single words or gestures of high connotative value is sufficient. Whether or not an emotional reaction is effected depends upon the meanings the symbols have for the listener in the context in which they are used. Thus, the passage from the MacArthur speech as it actually occurred in the total context of the communication perhaps intensified an already existing emotional condition for some listeners, pushed others across the threshold into a state of emotion, and had no effect on the rest. Because of the pluralistic nature and the fluid variation of audience response in the course of a speech, one can make only speculative judgments about the effect of any given passage or phrase in itself. This is why the classification of "appeals" is an artificial form of criticism. Since the impact varies from person to person according to his particular values, attitudes, and sensitivity, one can never be sure of the differential effect of any given part of a speech.

In any case, it is unnecessary for our purposes that we be able to delineate exactly where the nonemotional state ceases and the emotional response begins. What is important is the recognition that the total reaction is a fusion of these two basic subtypes and that these are the only discernible elements of the speaker-listener interaction.

[11] Charles Henry Woolbert, "The Place of Logic in a System of Persuasion," *Quarterly Journal of Speech,* IV (January 1918), 19–39.

Our concern, however, is with the concept of *ethos*. If the term is to be commonly used as a counterpart of logic and emotion, possessing the same elemental status, then it should also be distinguishable by the same standard. In other words, one should be able to discern a substantially distinct form of physiological activity that can be approximately related to the "ethical" appeal. Put directly, the question is whether or not the personal involvement of the speaker in the substance of the message evokes a pattern of physiological response comparable to but distinguishable from those already designated as logical and emotional. While such a pattern may exist, there is no evidence of it at present. Accordingly, it is inappropriate and misleading to speak of *ethos* as we speak of logic and emotion—as a basic element of the communicative interaction—until such time as an "ethical" physiological base can be established.

If the presence of a distinct pattern of physiological response corresponding to ethical proof cannot be demonstrated, then what hitherto has been termed an ethical appeal can be classified as logical or emotional or a combination of both, and our inquiry could end. However, there is a real difference between the phenomenon denoted by the broad concept of *ethos* and the casually used classification, "ethical appeal." The latter can be easily disposed of within the system set forth above; the former, however, is a much more meaningful and complex idea and cannot be dismissed by a simple process of reclassification.

The human factor in oral communication is an empirical reality. In varying degrees, it permeates every kind of speaking situation and is especially significant in persuasive communications, where one human being deliberately seeks to influence the conduct of others. To liquidate a concept which attempts to define the nature of this phenomenon is not the purpose of this analysis. On the contrary, the intent here is to amplify this notion in an effort to make its explanatory value more meaningful in the study of persuasive communications.

Thus far, we have propounded the view that there are two fundamental types of physiological response in the communicative interaction, to which the terms *logical* and *emotional* can be fairly applied, but that no such third type of response can be established that corresponds to the idea of *ethos*. The thesis we now advance is that *ethos,* properly considered, is not a basic element of the persuasive process but an end product of the combined logical and emotional responses— that is, a specific type of persuasion, *in toto.*

ethos: not an element but end product of combined logical, emotional responses

ETHOS AND THE PERSUASIVE PROCESS

The persuasive phenomenon involves a speaker generating visual and aural cues which evoke neural and chemical responses from the listener. Though these responses can be differentiated psychometrically, they normally occur in a fusion of unitary physiological reaction. Necessary to our discussion of *ethos* is an explication of the interplay of these logical and emotional responses in the overall process.

At the base of persuasion is emotion—a visceral response generally producing a positive or negative feeling state in the listener. As a result of his total life experience, the auditor comes to attach emotional valences to objects of belief or attitude; that is, he develops certain *values* or *disvalues* regarding things, conditions, or ideas. The term *value* designates not an emotion but an abstract concept which has formed an emotional association, appeal to which can generate an emotional state in the listener.[12] Emotion may be thought of as the motive force for the persuasive effect and the value as the activating mechanism. Properly galvanized, the value triggers the emotional response that motivates the behavior sought by the speaker, or in Woolbert's phrase, "touch[es] off the hearer's acting nature."[13] *Value terms* are linguistic expressions which have acquired emotional valences and may be used in persuasive discourse with greater or lesser specificity, e.g., Hitler, Nazi, evil.

persuasion: dominated by value responses activated by life experience

We should re-emphasize that the listener acquires his value structures by virtue of his total life experience; consequently, they are subject to change as experience accumulates. Similarly, a listener holds values and disvalues of varying degrees of intensity, i.e., of varying degrees of emotional involvement, some of which may be in direct conflict. On this theory, therefore, the ultimate persuasive effect will depend upon the actuation of those values in the listener's hierarchy that are controlling for a given situation. Additionally, the total impact will be affected by the intrinsic rhetorical skill of the speaker, i.e., the extent of his ability to exact the optimum response from the values activated.

What we have characterized as the logical element of the

[12] For a discussion of the emotive theory of values, see Alfred Jules Ayer, *Language, Truth and Logic* (New York, 1952), ch. VI. The emotional content of values is also emphasized by Edward D. Steele, "Social Values in Public Address," *Western Speech*, XXII (Winter 1958), 38–42.

[13] Charles Henry Woolbert, "Persuasion: Principles and Method, Part III," *Quarterly Journal of Speech*, V (May 1919), p. 215.

communication—the cognitive processes of thinking, learning, and reasoning—serves an instrumental function in creating the persuasive effect. Its purpose is dual: (1) to advance systematically the listener's thought processes toward the value or emotional base of a given proposition and (2) to activate a value response sufficient to achieve the desired effect.[14]

The interrelationship of logic and emotion in the persuasive process can be briefly illustrated by reference to a specific set of communication stimuli—Lincoln's First Inaugural Address. In this example we are, of course, only inferring the rhetorical strategy of the speaker from the communication content, but this will be sufficient for our purposes here. Lincoln's central proposition was that the doctrine of secession by individual states would, in practice, bring about a state of anarchy in the country. Inherent in the proposition are both the logical and emotional elements, the former being demonstrable by reason and the latter being an expression of value demanding a sympathetic response from the listener for its effectiveness.[15]

logic and emotion interrelated in total persuasive process

The logical function of Lincoln's rhetoric was to demonstrate the probability that the secession of individual states would lead to the eventual disintegration of the Federal Union as a viable form of government and that there would be certain inevitable consequences following from this disintegration. These assertions were made credible by the use of an accepted system of linguistic inferences that was meaningful to those who heard it.[16]

The emotional component of the proposition is embodied in the value term, *anarchy.* In the chain of reasoning Lincoln developed, secession begins the process of disintegration that ends in total anarchy. Anarchy is then explicated as a series

[14] Although the terminology differs and the relationship is made more explicit here, this explanation of the function of logic and emotion is basic to Woolbert's system, which is set out in three parts in the *Quarterly Journal of Speech,* V (January, March, May 1919), 12–25, 101–119, 212–238, under the title "Persuasion: Principles and Method." See also Edward D. Steele, "Social Values, the Enthymeme, and Speech Criticism," *Western Speech,* XXVI (Spring 1962), 70–75; Edward D. Steele and W. Charles Redding, "The American Value System: Premises for Persuasion," *Western Speech,* XXVI (Spring 1962), 83–91.

[15] Ayer, pp. 108–111.

[16] The method of creating belief must be acceptable and meaningful to the listener. Beliefs fixed by the mode of authority or tradition may stand impervious to a contrary view advanced according to the logical method in argumentation. In Lincoln's speech the argument was believable to those who accepted his system of inferences as a legitimate method for establishing the validity of this type of proposition. For an exposition of the various ways in which people arrive at belief, see "The Fixation of Belief," in Charles S. Peirce, *Chance, Love, and Logic* (New York, 1923), pp. 7–31.

of specific forms of social and political chaos. Had the listeners not been emotionally committed against the empirical correlates of the linguistic symbol "anarchy," that is, had they been indifferent or had they viewed such conditions as desirable, there would have been no motivational force generated for the persuasive effect sought by the speaker.[17] This, then, is the functional interplay of logic and emotion in the rhetorical act. We now turn to the consideration of *ethos* as it relates to this process.

either message or image as agent of value activation

When a speaker delivers a speech with the intent of influencing the behavior of his auditors in a particular direction, we may conceive of the communication *per se* as presenting two distinct objects as potential foci of listener reaction: (1) the message—the subject matter, its development, and the policies entailed—and (2) the total personality of the speaker. That is, rather than concern himself with the policies or arguments propounded, the listener may focus upon personal factors such as appearance, intelligence, and sincerity. When this occurs, we say that he is responding to the image or, in traditional terminology, the *ethos* of the speaker.

We are not suggesting here that either the message or the image must become the *sole* object of the listener's total reaction, but we do hypothesize that the controlling value or values for a given persuasive effect will be actuated *primarily* by one or the other. In other words, either the image or the message will ultimately emerge as the dominating agent of value activation for the listener, and this will determine the basic character of the persuasive process. Accordingly, persuasion may be classified either as personal or nonpersonal, depending upon whether the speaker's personality or his message becomes the primary object of value response.[18] If the reaction to the content is direct, that is, if the message itself

[17] There were, of course, many who did view the disintegration of the Federal Union and the concomitant consequences thereof as desirable. Lincoln recognized this fact and polarized this value structure before making his appeal. Prior to enumerating the consequences of dissolution, he stated, "That there are persons in one section or another who seek to destroy the Union at all events, and are glad of any pretext to do it, I will neither affirm or [sic] deny; but if there be such, I need address no word to them. To those, however, who really love the Union, may I not speak?" "Lincoln's First Inaugural," in W. M. Parrish and Marie Hochmuth, *American Speeches* (New York, 1954), p. 38.

[18] For example, a listener concerned about his own physical safety may respond to a specific policy advocated in the speaker's message or, in the absence of any such statement, to the impression that the speaker is or is not the "kind of man" who might implement such a policy. There may be no difference in the value that motivates the listener's behavior, but there will be a difference in the source of the stimuli that activate it, and this will serve to classify the effect as personal or nonpersonal.

activates the dominant value response, the process may be designated *nonpersonal persuasion,* regardless of the source. However, if the message functions primarily as a medium by which the speaker's personality activates the dominant value response, the process may be categorized as *personal persuasion.*[19] We have, then, two basic genres of persuasive phenomena, the last of which we consider the proper referent for the term *ethos.*

> message activation (non-personal) *vs.* speaker's personality activation (personal)

Personal persuasion involves a complex pattern of reaction which needs further explication here. Clearly, some responses to the speaker's personality are of the direct variety, e.g., reactions to physical appearance, attire, voice, diction, and self-references in the speech—the traditional "ethical appeals." But of equal, if not greater, importance are the indirect responses to the speaker's personality created by the speech itself. In other words, the message is also a source of what is, in practical effect, an interpretation of the personality of the speaker. If the speech has actually been composed by the man who utters it, then the subject matter, the organization of the ideas and the degree to which they are developed, the nature and extent of the supporting materials, and the language in which the totality is expressed will be a reflection of the intelligence, character, and temperament of the personality that created it. The topics a speaker chooses to discuss or avoid, the precision with which he orders his thoughts and/or structures his argument, the accuracy and thoroughness of his support or the lack thereof, and his choice of words can reveal as much or more about his personality than any deliberate personal reference.[20] To single out only the speaker's references to himself or to another person as an indication of the extent to which the personality operates in the persuasive process and to ignore the whole rhetoric as the vehicle of the speaker's image is totally unrealistic.

> direct, indirect reaction to speaker's personality important in assessing ethos

To summarize, then, we can use the term *ethos* to refer to a communication in which (1) the persuasive effect is dominated by value response activated by the personality of the speaker as opposed to the content of the message and (2) the perception of the personality is derived from and conveyed by the whole rhetoric—the invention, arrangement, style, and delivery—the "man speaking."

We are brought, therefore, to our final consideration. If

[19] To avoid confusion, this term is preferred to the traditional "ethical persuasion."

[20] Indeed, the entirety of the rhetoric may well be a more authentic reflection of the speaker's personality than any personal reference he deliberately chooses to make.

the image is created both directly by the speaker and indirectly by the message, what determines whether the listener will be affected by the message as a basic cause of persuasion in itself or as a vehicle for the personality of the speaker? In short, what determines whether the dominant persuasive process will be of a personal or nonpersonal nature?

THE CONFIGURATION OF COMMUNICATION

Every act of communication occurs within a given period of time and involves a given human population; these constitute its temporal and spatial dimensions, its external boundaries. Within this framework are four basic elements: the listener, the speaker, the message, and the environment (the socio-political and cultural conditions surrounding the speaking situation), the totality constituting what we shall term the *configuration of communication*. The center of this structure is the listener. The nature of his relationships to the speaker, the environment, and the message determines the personal or nonpersonal orientation of the value response and thereby the character of the basic persuasive process.

listener relationship to speaker, message, environment will determine response orientation

The Speaker-Listener Relationship requires a determination of the actual as opposed to the ostensible purpose of the rhetoric. For example, in a campaign for elective office the ostensible purpose of a given speech may be to gain acceptance of a particular policy, whereas the actual purpose is to gain votes for the candidate. The relationship between the speaker and the listener is defined by the nature of the conduct the communicator seeks from him.

relationship determined by behavior sought

The Environment-Listener Relationship refers to the effect of the social, political, and cultural milieu on the psychological set of the listener for a given communication or series of communications. The environment itself consists of the actual conditions in the real world, past or present, that are external to the communication. The relationship, however, is expressed in terms of how and to what degree the listener experiences and internalizes the environment. One characteristic of this relationship, as it affects persuasive communications, we shall term *immediacy:* the extent of the listener's knowledge and concern about the external conditions that are relevant or perceived by him as relevant to the communication.

relationship determined by degree of listener internalization

The Message-Listener Relationship refers to the nature of the speech content and the degree of clarity and impact with which it is received by the listener. The message is the instrument by which the speaker attempts to delimit, specify, and/or intensify the listener's perception of the environment. In persuasive discourse this involves the presentation of a clear choice or *cleavage* between alternative policies. The degree of impact the message has upon the auditor varies with the extent to which it activates values favorable to the preferred policy. This depends upon the intrinsic rhetorical skill of the speaker.

relationship determined by degree of impact on listener

We are concerned, then, with a system of relationships, the collective nature of which determines the focus of the listener's reaction. If they coalesce in such a way as to orient value response directly to the subject matter of the message, the speaker's personality becomes a secondary consideration. If, however, the configuration is so structured as to impel the dominance of personality-oriented response, the message then serves as a vehicle for the speaker's image. These two patterns can be shown by two examples, intentionally simplified for the purposes of illustration:

> *Case #1:* Assume a situation in which a board of directors of a large, influential corporation is undecided whether to endorse or oppose a right-to-work measure that has been placed on the ballot for a statewide referendum. A week before the election, the board agrees to make public its decision after hearing the issue argued by two of the company's attorneys, one of whom favors while the other opposes the bill. Each speaker is given equal time to present his case, and each places primary emphasis on the economic implications of the bill.

In this example, the structure of the communicative configuration promotes the message as the primary agent of value activation, a situation created by the nature of the three listener-centered relationships.

The Speaker-Listener Relationship. The speaker's ultimate objective in this situation is inherently nonpersonal. The behavior he seeks from the listener is a vote for or against a particular policy—a proposition on a ballot—and this decision can be resolved upon the merits of the issue itself.

The Environment-Listener Relationship. By virtue of its close and constant association to his daily work, the sociopolitical context of the communication has immediate, significant meaning for the listener. A policy-making official of a firm that relies upon a large labor force must be sensitive to matters that can affect the stability of his industry, and such an individual comes to the communication with a pre-established knowledge and concern about the subject. The critical question, of course, is the extent of the listener's concern for the subject, and this will vary from person to person. In the kind of situation indicated in case #1, however, the probabilities militate toward an environment-listener relationship the immediacy of which creates a propensity for message-oriented response long before the speaker has uttered a word.

The Message-Listener Relationship. The predisposition for message-centered response engendered by the structures described above is further solidified by the nature of the message-listener relationship. The message content offers two alternative courses of action, i.e., to vote for or against the measure, and contains within it subject matter sufficient to provide a nonpersonal basis for value activation. That is, the economic emphasis of the message would be addressed directly to the question of profit and loss (which we shall assume to be the controlling value) and the question of endorsement or opposition resolved upon that basis alone. The critical significance here is that the message presents two distinct policy choices based upon arguments keyed to the mutual value systems of the auditors. The message-, speaker-, and environment-listener relationships combine to make case #1 a paradigm configuration for nonpersonal persuasion.

Consider now a second illustration which is structured to promote not the message but the personality as the primary agent of value activation.

> *Case #2:* Assume that two speakers contesting for a national elective office debate before a large group of nonpartisan, undecided voters. They discuss several subjects about which the listeners have little knowledge or concern. Though they debate for several hours and each has equal time, the candidates fail to demonstrate any significant differences between their respective policies or approaches to the issues.

The Speaker-Listener Relationship. In this situation, the purpose of the rhetoric is to elect a man to an office and not, as in the previous example, to gain endorsement for a legislative proposition. The nature of the desired persuasive effect is pre-eminently personal—each speaker's aim being to influence the listener to vote for him or against his opponent. Though the debate is conducted on the issue level, the true purpose of the dialogue is achieved when the listener votes for or against a name on a ballot.

The Environment-Listener Relationship. The personal orientation of the speaker-listener polarity is augmented by the character of the relationship between the listener and his environment. Unlike the executive in the first illustration, in this instance the listener lacks knowledge of and concern for the sociopolitical milieu that relates to the subjects under discussion. In other words, he perceives little or no immediacy or significance between the topics discussed and their relationship to conditions in the real world and to himself, and therefore he comes to the communication with little or no propensity to respond to the content of the message. In this context the personality of the speaker emerges as the only other potential source of value activation.

The Message-Listener Relationship. For the moment, let us suppose that the environment-listener relationship is the opposite of what we have described—that actually the listeners possess a high degree of knowledge and concern about the issues and their empirical implications, as in case #1. Would this be sufficient to shift the focus of response to the message?

While such a condition would predispose the listener in this direction, any such inclination would be nullified by the nature of the relationship between the listener and the message content of the speeches. If the voting decision were to pivot on nonpersonal grounds, there would have to be clearly established policy differences, a cleavage, on the controlling issue or issues. The failure of the two candidates to present perceptibly distinct and cogent policy alternatives means that the potential voter is afforded no basis for choosing between them on the issue level, no matter how strong his concern for an issue *per se.* Accordingly, if he is to reach an electoral decision at all, the motivation must shift to the personal level. The tendency toward or away from personal considerations is proportionate to the degree of cleavage exhibited in the message; that is, as the differences become more subtle, the propensity for personality-oriented response increases. Regardless of the immediacy of the environment to the listener, the failure of the message to specify alternative policies or approaches precludes its functioning as a basis for choosing one candidate over the other. When this relationship augments those we have previously described, a communicative configuration is structured in which the primacy of personal persuasion is assured.[21]

[21] It is fully recognized that the formation of an electoral decision in a political campaign may be affected by myriad influences other than direct exposure to the candidate in a speaking situation. We do not discount these factors, but we are not concerned with them here. What we are concerned with is the impact of the speaking itself, and our thesis is that, to the degree that the speaker's rhetoric has a persuasive effect, its nature will be determined by the structure of the communicative configuration.

when speaker is for
personal support,
listener decides
based on speaker as
a person

We have described two paradigm cases. The first example demonstrated a nonpersonal relationship between the speaker and the listener; the second example, a personal relationship. The polarity between the listener and the environment was strong and immediate in the former, weak and remote in the latter. The message provided a clear choice between the policies advocated by the speakers in the original case, but no such cleavage existed in the second example. It is clear, then, that when the speaker's purpose is essentially the seeking of personal support and when there is an absence of any issue meaningful to the listener and a concomitant lack of clear-cut policy alternatives by the candidates, the listener's voting decision will be motivated by an assessment of the speaker as a person. It is clear, also, that the relationships of the listener to the speaker, the message, and the environment are the elemental structures of the communicative configuration which determine the focal point of the listener's response and, therefore, the basic source of value activation.

these three
relationships are
necessarily
interdependent

Moreover, it is most important to recognize the interdependence of these three relationships. As we noted, even if the environment-listener relationship had been very strong in the second case, the primary focal point of reaction would not have been changed, because the speaker-listener relationship was still personal in nature and the message-listener relationship did not provide a clear division on the issues. Similarly, a clear division of policy in the message would have had little effect on the object of reaction unless the listener was already strongly concerned about the subject or was made concerned by the message itself, in which case a change in the environment-listener relationship could be said to have been effected. Though a speaker's purpose may be of a personal nature, the persuasion may emerge as nonpersonal if the environment and the message exhibit the proper relationship with the audience. In the final analysis the determination of these relationships must be made on the basis of the actual communication being studied

The second example is not hypothetical. It is, in broad terms, a description of the communicative configuration of the presidential campaign of 1960.[22] By their very nature, campaigns for elective office begin as natural configurations for personal persuasion. However, frequently an issue or issue-complex begins to agitate public emotion as the campaign progresses and eventually becomes of such great concern to

[22] Rosenthal, ch. III.

the electorate that, given a basic cleavage between the candidates' policies, the issue eclipses the personality as the object of listeners' value responses. The position he takes on the issue is virtually superimposed on the candidate, and the persuasion becomes nonpersonal; the speaker, in practical effect, is perceived as the embodiment of the policy.[23]

Election campaigns, however, are usually of considerable duration, which permits the structure of the configuration to be modified according to the increase or decrease of voters' concern for the issues. In the 1960 campaign, for example, the issue of the United States' policy toward the offshore Chinese islands, Quemoy and Matsu, caught the public's attention during the first week in October and, for a while at least, appeared to be a stronger persuasive force than the candidates' images because the electorate was perceiving it as a not-too-remote question of peace or war. By the end of the month, however, with no empirical corroboration of their fears, the voters' concern for the issue had almost completely abated. By this time, also, the candidates' policy statements in regard to the islands—which seemed to be markedly divergent when the question first arose—had become so similar as to be virtually indistinguishable. Therefore, though a change in the structure of the communicative configuration produced a temporary period of issue-oriented persuasion, it was but a brief interlude that terminated when the configuration reverted to its original structure, which prevailed thereafter.[24] Thus, in the presidential campaign of 1960, the reaction centered primarily on the personalities of the candidates and produced personal persuasion—the phenomenon denoted by the concept of *ethos.*

the 1960 presidential campaign ultimately a contest in ethos

IMPLICATIONS FOR RHETORICAL CRITICISM

Speeches may be and are studied for a variety of purposes: as manifestations of the intellectual and cultural climate of the

[23] For example, probably any reputable Republican running against William Jennings Bryan in 1896 would have won the election, regardless of the strength or weakness of his image. The widespread and intense public hostility to the free coinage of silver—a policy with which the name of Bryan was synonymous—virtually preordained his defeat at the polls. This is not to say that Bryan's personality was totally ineffectual in attracting and alienating some voters; rather, the issue of free silver emerged so broadly and with such vitality that personal considerations were relegated to a minimal influence while nonpersonal, issue-oriented response was thrust into a controlling status.

[24] Rosenthal, ch. III.

times, as models for learning to speak well in public, as a kind of literature or an unusual combination of stylistic devices, or as an assembly of parts which are presumably in need of identification, to name but a few. All of these, seemingly, are legitimate objects of inquiry. However, if the corpus of speech as an academic discipline is the process of human, spoken communication, then the closer our studies come to explaining that process—what "goes on" between the speaker and his audience—the more significant they become as vehicles of knowledge. To achieve their optimum usefulness, therefore, strategies of rhetorical criticism should aim toward some visible relationship to the totality of the communicative act. It is hoped that the conceptual system of *ethos* described above may provide a frame of reference for the development of such critical approaches.

Though the purpose of this analysis has been to create an enlarged theoretical base for the concept of *ethos* rather than to translate the descriptive formulations of this theory into an integrated critical system, some possible applications of these notions to the evaluation of public address may be briefly mentioned. As a conceptual framework for rhetorical criticism, this system could be most advantageously employed in studies where the critic is able to acquire data on all aspects of the communication, and especially data indicating the character of the audience reaction. It has been successfully used for the study of contemporary political speaking and conceivably could be applied to historical investigations if the necessary information were obtainable.

More specifically, we suggest that the study of campaign speaking, particularly campaigns for national elective offices, could be enhanced by the use of critical procedures built on this theory of *ethos.* In the decades since World War II, the average citizen of the civilized world has come to realize the harrowing fact that it is within the official power of three or four men to unleash a violence from which there is no sanctuary. The natural consequence of this constant threat to individual safety is that the character, intelligence, and temperament of the men who hold this power become the pre-eminent concerns of those who place them in office. The opportunity to make appraisals of these personal attributes has been enormously widened by the postwar development of the mass media in general and, in particular, the medium of television, which has given the once-distant personalities of high state officials an almost daily household exposure. In the United States the gradual disappearance of the ideological cleavage between the two major political parties has also contributed to the emergence of personality dominance in election campaigns. Even in nations where party differences are more marked and party loyalty more rigid, the personality of the national leader has, in recent years, become a much more significant factor in the electoral decision.[25]

It may be, as we have suggested, that these developments are of post-World War II origin or that actually they have been occurring for a much longer period of time and have simply escaped our notice. The 1948 presidential election in the United States, for example, upset a revered maxim of political folklore known as "Farley's Law,"[26] and while the notion possibly had some validity during the Roosevelt years and was rendered obsolete by the social changes effected by the war, it is also possible that it was never more than a myth in the first place. The study of political campaign speaking using approaches suggested by the theory advanced here might serve to illuminate such questions.

The conceptual system we have described might be useful as a basis for experimental research in *ethos.* As we have indicated, the actual content of the message is only one aspect of the totality, and if one wishes to measure the effect of a speaker's image, he should construct a configuration in which personality-oriented value response dominates the persuasive effect. It is unrealistic to try to calculate the impact of the personality by inserting or deleting "ethical appeals," as is done with so many experimental studies of artistic *ethos.* This is attested to by the high incidence of inconclusiveness among investigations of the latter type. On the other hand,

[25] There is evidence that the impact of the personality of the national party leader has become an increasingly significant factor in the British elections, despite the complicating system of local constituencies and a rigid party structure. Upon his return from England where he spent the fall of 1964 studying the campaigning, Professor Charles W. Lomas of the University of California, Los Angeles, affirmed the emergence of this trend. A similar observation was made by columnist Anthony Howard of the *New Statesman* writing in the *Sunday Times,* September 6, 1964: "In 1959 one could scan the billboards in vain for any poster showing a picture of Hugh Gaitskell; today there is scarcely a hoarding [sic] that does not carry a huge portrait of Mr. Wilson surrounded by microphones. Behind the change lies a revolution in Labour's approach to electioneering. For the first time in its history the party is prepared—indeed eager—to fight a personality rather than a policy election. Almost everything has been staked on the party leader's success as a national, presidential candidate."

[26] "Farley's Law" is attributed to James A. Farley, Franklin D. Roosevelt's campaign manager and later Postmaster-General of the United States. The "law" asserted that presidential elections are decided by the time the conventions are over—that campaigning wins few, if any, votes and that these are of insufficient number to affect the final outcome.

efforts to measure nonartistic *ethos* (source credibility, prestige suggestion, etc.) have enjoyed a greater measure of success.[27] One possible explanation for this is that, in experiments dealing with nonartistic *ethos,* the character of the source is made a salient fact of the environment-listener relationship just before exposure to the communication, which suggests, at least as an immediate effect, a configuration strongly colored by personal considerations. It would also be predictable that without continued reinforcement, this personality-oriented configuration would reassume a message or nonpersonal orientation, which might explain why measurements of the delayed reaction (one to several weeks after the initial communication) have revealed a regressive effect.

SUMMARY

This analysis has been an explication of the concept of *ethos* as a theoretical category. We noted at the outset that the long-enduring triadic association of logic, emotion, and *ethos,* as presented in the "classical view" of rhetorical theory, has fostered the unwarranted implication that these concepts are coordinate in class and elemental in nature. We have attempted to demonstrate that this trichotomy is misclassified and misleading; that *ethos* does not properly belong to that conceptual system; that it more accurately designates a distinct type of communicative act and, as such, should be conceived on a different level or plane of classification. Adhering to the interactive view of persuasion, we have limited the elements of the persuasive process to the phenomena designated by the concepts of logic and emotion in communication and have based this classification on the differentiable characteristics of the physiological responses evoked by the communicative stimuli.

We have removed *ethos* from its habitual partnership in the triad and have classified it as a complete and distinct type of persuasion—one of two basic genres—which we have termed *personal* as opposed to nonpersonal persuasion. We have distinguished these two forms by the agent of value activation, that is, by which of two objects, the speaker or the message, becomes the focus of the listener's reaction. If the response centers upon the message of the communication

---

[27] For a brief survey of experimental research in *ethos,* see Kenneth Andersen and Theodore Clevenger, Jr., "A Summary of Experimental Research in Ethos," *Speech Monographs,* XXX (June 1963), pp. 59–78.

and the value activation derives primarily from that source, the persuasion is designated as *nonpersonal.* If, however, the personality of the speaker becomes the focal point of the re-action and the activation of the controlling value response is derived from that source, either directly or indirectly, the per-suasion is termed *personal.* Whether the speaker or the message becomes the object of the primary value response is determined by the *configuration of the communication:* the relationship between the listener and (1) the speaker, (2) the environment, and (3) the message, at a given period of time and in a given place. We have indicated how the nature of these relationships structures a context that impels to domi-nance either the message or the speaker as the agent of value activation and thereby determines the type of persuasion that will prevail.

As we have already stated, the purpose of this analysis was the development of theoretical and not critical princi-ples. Accordingly, we have concluded with only brief sugges-tions as to the possible applications of this theory and the hope that it may prove a serviceable frame of reference for the study and criticism of public address.

SUGGESTED FURTHER READING

Anderson, Kenneth and Theodore Clevenger Jr., "A Summary of Experimental Research in Ethos," *Speech Monographs,* XXX (June, 1963), 59–78. (See footnote 27 above.)

Ayer, Alfred Jules, *Language, Truth, and Logic.* New York: Dover Publishers, 1952, Chapter VI. (See footnotes 12 and 15 above.)

Black, Edwin, *Rhetorical Criticism.* New York: The Macmillan Company (1965), 27–35. (See footnote 3 above.)

Cooper, Lane, translator, *The Rhetoric of Aristotle.* New York: Appleton-Century Crofts (1932), 8–9.

Steele, Edward D., "Social Values, the Ethymene, and Speech Criticism," *Western Speech,* XXVI (Spring, 1962), 70–75. (See footnotes 12, 14 above.)

Steele, Edward D. and Charles Redding, "The American Value System: Premises for Persuasion," *Western Speech,* XXVI (Spring, 1962), 83–91. (See footnote 14 above.)

Woolbert, Charles H., "Persuasion: Principles and Method," *Quarterly Journal of Speech,* V (January, March, May, 1919). (See also footnotes 11 and 13 above.)

The Impact of Evidence
on Decision Making

William R. Dresser

Common sense tells us that as a rule a speaker who uses factual information to support his assertions will be more likely to influence his listeners than one who does not. It seems obvious that a speaker who seeks to change a listener's mind about something, but who does not bother to give the listener any facts about it, is engaged in a hazardous enterprise: a speaker should use sound evidence.

However, a number of recent experimental studies throw doubt on this obvious, common-sense notion. Different investigators have discovered that the amount of evidence in their experimental speeches, the quality of the evidence in the speeches, or the identification of the evidence as evidence instead of assertion simply did not make any significant difference to their listeners.[1] It would appear from these experiments that, while one would like to assume that listeners are rational, they are not. They seem to react to a speaker's personality, or to his delivery, but not to any significant extent to the information that he presents.[2] One is tempted to conclude from these studies that common sense is wrong—that in theory evidence should be important, but that in actuality it has no impact on decision making.

At the same time, one might well wonder if a conclusion

Note: [when this article first appeared in May, 1966,] William R. Dresser (Ph.D., Northwestern, 1962) [was] Assistant Professor of Speech at Denison University. This article is adapted from a paper presented at the sectional meeting on Argumentation and Evidence at the 1965 S.A.A. convention.

[1]For a summary of these studies see William R. Dresser, "Studies of the Effects of Evidence: Implications for Forensics," *The Register,* X (Fall, 1962), 14–19. A condensed summary is also included in Glen E. Mills, *Reason in Controversy* (Boston: Allyn and Bacon, 1964), pp. 115–117.

[2]See, for example, the results reported by Erwin P. Bettinghaus in "The Operation of Congruity in an Oral Communication Situation," *Speech Monographs,* XXVIII (August, 1961), 131–142.

of this kind would necessarily hold true for all speeches given by all speakers to all audiences in all circumstances. One of the first principles discussed in a beginning public speaking course is that speech is an act that takes place in a physical and social context—that what is highly effective speaking in one situation may prove to be totally ineffective in a different situation. The conditions under which experiments testing the impact of evidence are conducted—with an audience of pre-tested college freshmen and sophomores listening in a class-room to a speech by an unknown speaker appearing under the sponsorship of the college instructor in a rather dramatic departure from the normal class routine—obviously represent a special type of speech situation. What would happen in speech situations involving other audiences, other settings, other speakers?

It is the purpose of this paper to consider some of the elements present in any speech situation that might be ex-pected to interact with a speaker's evidence to affect its im-pact on the listener, and then to speculate for a moment as to the conditions that might have to be met for evidence to affect decision making. The purpose is not to offer a definitive treatment of the subject complete from theoretical genesis to empirical verification, but merely to see what types of hypothe-ses might be generated.

prior knowledge affects impact of speaker's evidence

One element in a speech situation which quite obviously will interact with the speaker's evidence is *the view of the speaker's subject brought to the speech by the listener:* the listener's existing knowledge of the subject, his beliefs and prejudices about it, etc. Asch and others have pointed out that there seems to be a negative correlation between knowledge about something and persuasibility with regard to it.[3] If audi-tors already possess a large quantity of information about a subject—say, federal policies with regard to commercial fish-ing in Alaska—the evidence offered by a speaker talking about these policies is not going to add very much to their store of information and probably will not change their view of the policies very significantly. But if all that they know about these policies is what the speaker tells them, then the facts pre-sented by the speaker may well have an impact.

existing beliefs affect impact of evidence

In the same way, it is fairly obvious that the listener's existing beliefs about a subject can affect the impact of the speaker's evidence. In describing a lecture tour made by the

[3]S. E. Asch, Helen Block, and Max Hertzman, "Studies in the Principles of Judg-ments and Attitudes: I. Two Basic Principles of Judgment," *Journal of Psychology,* V (April, 1938), 251.

novelist Jack London in 1905 and 1906, Glancy pointed out that London used a great deal of evidence pertaining to the deplorable conditions under which the poor were struggling to survive in American cities at that time. The evidence had no impact at all—primarily because London's listeners simply could not believe it. Their existing beliefs about the poor made the evidence presented by London incredible.[4]

A second element in the speech situation that can quite obviously affect the impact of the speaker's evidence is *the listener's perception of the importance of the decision to be made.* Crocker has suggested that deliberation—which would include the weighing of evidence—is suited to "important matters;"[5] Hayakawa has expressed the perhaps unduly optimistic opinion that people are more likely to act rationally when making important purchases than they are when making trivial purchases.[6] It takes energy to assimilate a speaker's evidence and to try to figure out its implications, and expending that energy is unpleasant. If the pain to be suffered by making a foolish decision is less than the pain involved in making the decision wisely, then listeners will probably pay little attention to evidence regarding the decision: they will go ahead and make it, and, if it is foolish, take the consequences. If the listener views the decision to be made as unimportant, the speaker's evidence will probably have little impact.

perceiving the importance of the question affects impact of evidence

At the same time, Sherif, Sherif, and Nebergall in their recent book *Attitude and Attitude Change* point out that attitudes that are a part of a person's view of himself cannot be changed very readily.[7] A man is who he is partly because of the beliefs and attitudes that he holds; in his mind these beliefs and attitudes are a part of himself. A speaker who asks him to change them is in a sense asking him to change his identity—to become a different person. Instead of undertaking this painful transformation, in all probability the listener will simply reject the speaker's message—including any evidence in it. If the listener sees the decision to be made as so important that

---

[4] Donald R. Glancy, "Socialist With a Valet: Jack London's 'First, Last, and Only' Lecture Tour," *Quarterly Journal of Speech,* XLIX (February, 1963), 31–39.

[5] Lionel Crocker and Herbert W. Hildebrandt, *Public Speaking for College Students,* 4th ed. (New York: American Book Co., 1965), p. 434.

[6] S. I. Hayakawa, "Why the Edsel Laid an Egg: Motivational Research vs. the Reality Principle," in S. I. Hayakawa (ed.), *The Use and Misuse of Language* (Greenwich, Conn.: Fawcett Publications, Inc., 1962), p. 173.

[7] Carolyn W. Sherif, Muzafer Sherif, and Roger E. Nebergall, *Attitude and Attitude Change: The Social Judgment-Involvement Approach* (Philadelphia: W. B. Saunders, 1965). The variable mentioned is a free translation of the term *involvement* as it is used in this book. For a succinct discussion of it, see the preface, p. vi

it involves his identity as a person, the speaker's evidence again will probably have little impact.

habit patterns developed by experience affect impact of evidence

Another element in the speech situation that can quite obviously affect the impact of evidence is *the set of habit patterns formed by the listener in previous speech situations.* In his recent discussion of nineteenth century political speaking in Hawaii, Ching pointed out that in that particular culture voters became used to reacting to political speeches that stressed the integrity of the speaker and appeals to various desires. He concluded that as a result of this learning process listeners "responded best to the kind of address that they were used to traditionally—speeches based on emotional and ethical appeals rather than on logical ones."[8] As a result of their experiences with previous campaign speeches, these listeners saw the presentation of a political speech as a kind of ceremonial occasion, and responded appropriately—emotionally—not with a reflective, critical consideration of the speaker's message. The habit pattern developed through experience affected the impact of the speaker's evidence. If a listener has developed a habit of reacting to speeches in an unreflective way, the speaker's evidence will probably not affect him very significantly.

ethos of the speaker affects impact of evidence

A fourth element in the speech situation that might be expected to affect the impact of evidence is *the ethos of the speaker.* Many studies have established the importance of ethos in persuasive speaking: a speaker who appears to be an unbiased authority is more likely to influence his listeners than one who seems biased or incompetent.[9] But how might the speaker's ethos interact with his evidence? An answer to this question might be suggested by raising two additional questions. When a rational person goes to the doctor, receives a prescription, and is told to have it filled and to take one spoonful every four hours, to what extent does the doctor's presentation of evidence affect that person's decision? Secondly, just how much serious consideration is given to the "evidence" offered by the smiling actor in the television commercial who offers "positive proof" that his product is the best on the market? A reasonable hypothesis might be that if a speaker's ethos is neither extremely good—like the doctor's—nor extremely bad—like the television actor's—then his evidence might have an impact. If the speaker's ethos is either

---

[8] James C. Ching, "Campaign Speaking in the Hawaiian Kingdom: 1874–1891," *Quarterly Journal of Speech,* XLIX (December, 1963), 402.

[9] For a review of these studies see Kenneth Andersen and Theodore Clevenger, Jr., "A Summary of Experimental Research in Ethos," *Speech Monographs,* XXX (June, 1963), 59–78.

very strong or very weak, the evidence probably will not make much difference. Ethos interacts with evidence.

An element in the speech situation closely related to the speaker's ethos is suggested by B. J. Diggs in his recent discussion of persuasion and ethics.[10] Diggs suggests that *the social "role" or "position" of the persuader in relation to the person he is trying to persuade* has an important bearing on what is ethical in persuasion. A teacher, for example, cannot ethically seek to persuade his students to do certain things. If he were a used car salesman, an evangelist, or a political worker, he could. What he can properly set out to do is governed in part by his social role. A listener who senses that a speaker is stepping beyond the limitations imposed by his social role may well be inclined to react negatively to the speaker's message, including the evidence in it.

social "role" of the speaker affects the impact of his message

There are obviously many additional elements in a speech situation that could affect the listener's reaction to the speaker's message—the perceived reactions of other listeners, the physical setting, the time of day, etc. It seems reasonable to suppose that at least some of these might interact with the speaker's evidence to influence its impact.[11] Elements in the speech situation are important.

What conditions might have to be met, then, for evidence to influence a listener? One might start by simple addition and subtraction—by considering a situation in which none of the adverse conditions discussed above is present. Thus if a listener has little knowledge and few beliefs about the speaker's subject; if he considers the decision to be made neither unimportant nor so important that it involves his identity as an individual; if he has learned to react thoughtfully to speeches; if the speaker's ethos is neither extremely good nor extremely bad; and if the social role of the speaker in relation to the listener makes advocacy appropriate—then evidence might have an impact on decision making. If any of these conditions is not met, it probably will not.

But to stop this analysis here would be to overlook the nature of the evidence itself, and its relation to other elements in the speaker's message. There are three observations that might be made about these things.

[10] B. J. Diggs, "Persuasion and Ethics," *Quarterly Journal of Speech,* XL (December, 1964), 359–373.

[11] By the same token, it should be noted that the five aspects of the speech situation discussed might be expected to affect the impact of the speaker's argument *per se,* as well as the impact of his evidence—the raw material of the argument. They would presumably affect the impact of the evidence by virtue of the fact that the evidence is part of an appeal to "rationality." We might expect that other parts of such an appeal would be similarly influenced.

First, it seems reasonable to assume that such qualities as the vividness of the evidence, its clarity, and its relationship to the listener's needs and wants will have an effect on its impact.

Secondly, a consideration of the way in which the evidence and the other materials in the speech are each related to the listener suggests certain requisites.

conditions to be met
for evidence have an
impact

Evidence is used to support an assertion. Its function is to give the listener some ground for believing the assertion. Since this is true, it would appear that at least three conditions will have to be met for evidence to have an impact. The assertion to be supported must be one that the listener would doubt if evidence were not offered. The evidence must *not* be doubted by the listener. And the relationship existing between the evidence and the assertion must seem both clear and valid to the listener once it is pointed out.

A moment's reflection suggests that in order for these conditions to be met one of two situations must exist. Either the evidence itself must be "news" to the listener, or the relationship existing between the evidence and the assertion it supports must be one that had not occurred to the listener before the speech. For if the listener already knows the information presented by the speaker, and is already aware of its relationship to the speaker's assertion, then one of the conditions will not have been met: either the listener will believe both the evidence and the assertion, or he will doubt them both, or he will have rejected the validity of the speaker's reasoning.

Finally, it might be interesting to raise the question as to why evidence—facts and opinions found by the speaker—might be expected to influence a listener at all when an assertion by the speaker that vividly says the same thing would not. When evidence has an impact it would appear that the listener doubts the speaker when he himself asserts something, but does not doubt his willingness to present without distortion evidence that says the same thing. This suggests a refinement of the conclusion reached with regard to the speaker's ethos. If evidence is to have an impact, apparently the listener must have some faith in the speaker, but not very much.[12] When

[12] In any given situation, of course, how much faith in the speaker is "not very much" can be seen as relative to such factors as the importance of the decision to the listener, the listener's view of his own competence with regard to the matter, etc. A listener who has great faith in a speaker's expertise and probity may still feel that this is "not very much" when it comes to providing a basis for a decision regarding a life and death matter.

evidence affects decision making it is apparently in part because of the existence of a rather special speaker-listener relationship.

Does evidence have an impact on decision making? It would appear that the only adequate answer to this question is: "It depends." It depends on at least five variables in the speech situation, on the nature of the evidence, on the relation of the evidence and the assertion it supports to the listener, and on how much faith the listener has in the speaker. One might be inclined to wonder if all the conditions necessary for evidence to influence decision making could ever possibly be met in any actual speech situation. It would not be unreasonable to assume that meeting them might well be easier than this discussion has made it sound. At the same time, it should be fairly obvious that a number of these conditions were not met in the experiments that found that evidence did not affect listener attitudes. It is hardly surprising that these experiments turned out the way they did: considering the conditions under which they were conducted, what would have been startling would have been a finding that evidence did make a difference. Future experimental investigations of the impact of evidence must take into account a number of variables that so far have remained uncontrolled. Only then can we see how experimental findings are related to common sense.

Impact varies with speech situations, nature of evidence, relations of evidence to listener, and faith in speakers

SUGGESTED FURTHER READING

Cathcart, Robert S., "An Experimental Study of the Relative Effectiveness of Four Methods of Presenting Evidence," *Speech Monographs,* XXII (August, 1955), 227–233.

Diggs, B. J., "Persuasion and Ethics," *Quarterly Journal of Speech,* XL (December, 1964), 359–373.

Dresser, William R., "Studies of the Effects of Evidence: Implications for Forensics," *AFA Register,* X (Fall, 1962), 14–19. (See footnote 1 above.)

————, "Effects of 'Satisfactory' and 'Unsatisfactory' Evidence in a Speech of Advocacy," *Speech Monographs,* XX (August, 1963), 302–306.

McCroskey, James C., "The Effects of Evidence in Persuasive Communication," *Western Speech,* XXXI (Summer, 1967), 189–199.

Miller, Gerald R., "Evidence and Argument," in *Perspectives on Argumentation,* eds., Gerald R. Miller and Thomas R. Nilsen. Chicago: Scott, Foresman and Co., 1966.

Mills, Glen E., *Reason in Controversy.* Boston: Allyn and Bacon, Inc., 1964. See Chapters 3 and 7. (See footnote 1 above.)

Wheelwright, Philip, *Valid Thinking.* New York: The Odyssey Press, 1962, See Chapters 8 and 9.

A Summary of Experimental Research on the Effects of Evidence in Persuasive Communication

James C. McCroskey

Traditional theories of rhetoric, person-to-group persuasive communication, stress the value of documented supporting materials, commonly called evidence, in the production of attitude change. Contemporary theorists for the most part concur with traditional theorists in this regard. However, because of the conflicting findings of the few reported experimental studies of the effect of evidence on attitude change, some writers have questioned whether evidence actually has much, if any, impact in persuasion. After reviewing some of these studies, for example, Gregg concluded that "the audience reaction to an argument may have little or nothing to do with whether the argument includes fully documented or completely undocumented evidence, relevant or irrelevant evidence, weak or strong evidence or any evidence at all."[1]

The purpose of this paper is to examine the results of several studies of the effects of evidence, most of which have been conducted by the present writer, and to suggest when and how evidence may function in persuasive communication. The studies conducted by the writer that underlie this paper are reported in detail elsewhere.[2]

Note: [At the time of this article's first appearance in April, 1969,] Mr. McCroskey [was] Assistant Professor of Communication, Michigan State University. The early phases of the research discussed in this paper were the basis of Mr. McCroskey's doctoral dissertation at Pennsylvania State University (1966) under the direction of Dr. Robert E. Dunham.

[1] Richard E. Gregg, "Some Hypotheses for the Study of the Psychology of Evidence," paper read at the 1964 SAA Convention.

[2] An extensive report of these studies is available in James C. McCroskey, *Studies of the Effects of Evidence in Persuasive Communication,* Report SCRL, 4–67, Speech Communication Research Laboratory, Michigan State University, 1967. Copies of this report are available from the writer upon request.

STUDIES REPORTED BY OTHER RESEARCHERS

Nine studies have been reported by other investigators that involved research on the effect of evidence on attitude change in persuasive communication. Two of these found that inclusion of evidence increased the amount of attitude change produced by the message; two found a trend in this direction; and five observed no significant effect on attitude change attributable to evidence.

The two earliest reported studies, those reported by Cathcart[3] and Bettinghaus,[4] were the only ones to produce statistically significant results favoring inclusion of evidence in a speech designed to achieve attitude change. Studies reported by Gilkinson, Paulson, and Sikkink[5] and Ostermeier[6] demonstrated trends favoring inclusion of evidence that did not meet normal criterion levels for statistical significance. Anderson,[7] Costley,[8] Dresser,[9] Gardner,[10] and Wagner[11] found no sig-

[3] Robert S. Cathcart, "An Experimental Study of the Relative Effectiveness of Selected Means of Handling Evidence in Speeches of Advocacy" (unpublished Ph.D. dissertation, Northwestern University, 1953). See also "An Experimental Study of the Relative Effectiveness of Four Methods of Presenting Evidence," *Speech Monographs,* XXII (August 1955), 227–233.

[4] Erwin P. Bettinghaus, Jr., "The Relative Effect of the Use of Testimony in a Persuasive Speech upon the Attitudes of Listeners" (unpublished M.A. thesis, Bradley University, 1953).

[5] Howard Gilkinson, Stanley F. Paulson, and Donald E. Sikkink, "Effects of Order and Authority in an Argumentative Speech," *QJS,* XL (April 1954), 183–192.

[6] Terry H. Ostermeier, "An Experimental Study on the Type and Frequency of Reference as Used by an Unfamiliar Source in a Message and Its Effect upon Perceived Credibility and Attitude Change" (unpublished Ph.D. dissertation, Michigan State University, 1966).

[7] Delmar C. Anderson, "The Effect of Various Uses of Authoritative Testimony in Persuasive Speaking" (unpublished M.A. thesis, Ohio State University, 1958).

[8] Dan L. Costley, "An Experimental Study of the Effectiveness of Quantitative Evidence in Speeches of Advocacy" (unpublished M.A. thesis, University of Oklahoma, 1958).

[9] William R. Dresser, "Studies of the Effects of Satisfactory and Unsatisfactory Evidence in a Speech of Advocacy" (unpublished Ph.D. dissertation, Northwestern University, 1962). See also "Studies of the Effects of Evidence: Implications for Forensics," *AFA Register,* X, No. 3 (1962), 14–19; "Effects of 'Satisfactory' and 'Unsatisfactory' Evidence in a Speech of Advocacy," *Speech Monographs,* XX (August 1963), 302–306; and "The Impact of Evidence on Decision Making," paper read at the 1965 SAA Convention.

[10] James C. Gardner, "An Experimental Study of the Use of Selected Forms of Evidence in Effecting Attitude Change" (unpublished M.A. thesis, University of Nebraska, 1966).

[11] Gerard A. Wagner, "An Experimental Study of the Relative Effectiveness of Varying Amounts of Evidence in a Persuasive Communication" (unpublished M.A. thesis, Mississippi Southern University, 1958).

nificant superiority in the production of attitude change for a speech including high quality evidence over a speech including either no evidence or low quality evidence.

In the only reported study of the effects of evidence on perceived source credibility conducted by an individual other than the writer, Ostermeier found that including a form of evidence significantly increased perceived credibility.[12]

From these studies no firm generalization can be drawn concerning the effect of evidence on attitude change and one can only tentatively conclude that evidence has an impact on source credibility.

no firm generalization on effects of evidence on attitude change

In an attempt to provide data upon which meaningful generalizations concerning the effect of evidence in persuasive communication could be based, the writer has conducted twelve studies. The following discussion is organized around the variables that were suspected as interacting with evidence in producing either attitude change or perceived source credibility. In each section there is presented a theoretic rationale for the hypothesized relationship between evidence and the other variable and a discussion of studies investigating this relationship. Since all of these studies have been reported in considerable detail elsewhere, the discussion in the following sections will stress results rather than procedures. The reader may find information on procedural details in previous reports that are cited.

A consideration of relationships between evidence and other communication variables require several operational definitions to avoid confusion in interpreting the material that follows.

The meaning of the term "evidence" as used by various authors of articles and books on persuasive communication is not always the same. The definition of "evidence" employed by the researchers involved in the studies discussed in this paper is compatible with that of the majority of writers. "Evidence" is taken to mean *factual statements originating from a source other than the speaker, objects not created by the speaker, and opinions of persons other than the speaker that are offered in support of the speaker's claims.* Only opinions and factual statements clearly identified with a source other than the speaker have been used in most of the studies; the use of audio-tape as the medium of transmission in most of the experiments precluded the use of tangible objects as evidence.

operational definitions: evidence, ethos, and attitude change

[12]See note 6.

Source credibility or ethos was operationally defined in this series of studies as perceived "authoritativeness" and "character" as measured by either Likert or semantic differential instruments designed for this purpose.[13] Attitude change was operationally defined as the difference between attitude prior to exposure to the experimental stimuli and attitude subsequent to exposure as measured by Likert or semantic differential instruments designed for this purpose.[14]

EVIDENCE AND SOURCE CREDIBILITY

The first variable suspected of interacting with evidence in the production of attitude change was source credibility. Specifically it was hypothesized that a speech including evidence would be more successful in producing attitude change than a speech not including evidence when the speech was presented by a moderate-to-low-credible source but that inclusion of evidence would have no effect when the speech was presented by a high-credible source. The rationale behind this hypothesis is twofold. First, the use of opinions or facts attested to by a source other than the speaker is a direct attempt to employ the credibility of the cited source as a persuasive tool. When the speaker's credibility is initially high, bringing even more credibility to bear on the case may be unnecessary. In short, there may be a point beyond which increasing credibility does not increase attitude change. Second, consistency theory suggests that, within limits, the greater the inconsistency between attitude toward source and attitude toward concept the greater the pressure to change attitude. When the speaker's credibility is initially high, the fact that other high-credible sources agree with him is consistent and thus unlikely to have much effect on the speaker's credibility. The initially low-credible source, on the other hand, has much to gain in credibility by demonstrating that high-credible sources agree with him. As his credibility increases the inconsistency between the audience's attitude toward him and toward the concept he favors is increased. Thus, while the initially high-credible source has little to gain from evidence, the low-credible source may increase his credibility by citing evi-

[13] James C. McCroskey, "Scales for the Measurement of Ethos," *Speech Monographs,* XXXIII (March 1966), 65–72.

[14] James C. McCroskey, "Experimental Studies of the Effects of Ethos and Evidence in Persuasive Communication" (unpublished D.Ed. dissertation, Pennsylvania State University, 1966).

dence and, in turn, increase the amount of attitude change produced in his audience.

The previously cited study by Ostermeier found that evidence did increase a source's credibility. For the most part, my studies have produced similar results, but only when the source was perceived by the audience initially as moderate-to-low-credible. My first study involved an unknown, unidentified, tape-recorded speaker. The subjects were college students participating in an experiment outside their normal classroom in the evening with only an unknown experimenter present. The results of this study indicated that inclusion of evidence increased both perceived credibility and attitude change.[15] A partial replication of this study employed subjects who were high school students participating in an experiment under classroom conditions with two known and respected teacher-experimenters present.[16] The results of this study indicated no effect of evidence on either credibility or attitude change. These conflicting results led to the speculation that the initial credibility of the unknown, unidentified, tape-recorded speaker was artificially increased in the second study by the presence and tacit sponsorship of the known and respected teacher-experimenters.[17] This speculation was borne out by the results of a study reported by Holtzman that employed the same instruments included in the previous studies under more controlled conditions.[18]

The combined findings of these three studies provide support for the hypothesis that inclusion of evidence can increase the credibility of and the attitude change produced by an initially moderate-to-low-credible source but has no effect when the source is initially high-credible.

evidence increases credibility and attitude change for low-credible but not high-credible sources

Six subsequent studies have provided additional support for this hypothesis.[19] In no case was evidence observed to increase the attitude change produced by an initially high-credible source while, in most cases, inclusion of evidence by an initially moderate-to-low-credible source was observed to increase attitude change. Similarly, inclusion of evidence

[15]*Ibid.* See also "The Effects of Evidence in Persuasive Communication," *Western Speech,* XXXI (Summer 1967), 189–199.

[16]McCroskey, "Studies of the Effects. . . ."

[17]James C. McCroskey and Robert E. Dunham, "Ethos: A Confounding Element in Communication Research," *Speech Monographs,* XXXIII (November 1966), 456–463.

[18]Paul D. Holtzman, "Confirmation of Ethos as a Confounding Element in Communication Research," *Speech Monographs,* XXXIII (November 1966), 464–466.

[19]McCroskey, "Studies of the Effects. . . ."

rarely was observed to increase the perceived credibility of initially high-credible sources but, in most cases, was observed to increase perceived credibility of initially moderate-to-low-credible sources.

Taken as a whole, these nine studies provide substantial justification for the generalization that initial credibility and evidence usage interact to produce attitude change and perceived credibility. Briefly stated, the initially high-credible source gains little from including evidence but the initially moderate-to-low-credible source can substantially increase his perceived credibility and the attitude change he produces in his audience by including evidence to support his position. This generalization, however, will be somewhat tempered by the results concerning evidence and other communication variables discussed below.

initial credibility and evidence interact to produce attitude change and credibility

CREDIBILITY OF SOURCES OF EVIDENCE

Traditional theory insists that for evidence to have a favorable impact on an audience it must come from sources the audience accepts as credible. Because of conflicting results across topics in two studies[20] it was suspected that evidence included in the experimental messages employed may not have been the "best" evidence. Most of the evidence included was of the "unbiased" type. Several writers have asserted that, while unbiased evidence is better than biased evidence, reluctant evidence (a biased source testifying against what appears to be his best interests) is the best of all. Two studies by Arnold and McCroskey[21] and two by McCroskey and Wenburg[22] found no support for this theory. In each study biased sources were perceived to be less credible than unbiased or reluctant sources, but unbiased sources were found regularly to be more credible than reluctant sources. While these four studies do not provide definitive answers to questions concerning the credibility of sources of evidence, their results provide ample support for the contention that the evidence included in the other evidence studies was of sufficiently high quality so that the results of the studies were not contaminated by audiences perceiving the evidence as emanating from low-

unbiased sources more credible than reluctant or biased; reluctant more credible than biased

[20] *Ibid.*

[21] William E. Arnold and James C. McCroskey, "The Credibility of Reluctant Testimony," *Central States Speech Journal,* XVIII (May 1967), 97–103.

[22] McCroskey, "Studies of the Effects. . . ."

credible sources. Additional support for this contention was provided by ratings on evidence quality obtained from subjects in several of the studies. In each case where such ratings were requested, subjects rated speeches including evidence much higher on "evidence usage" than speeches not including evidence.

EVIDENCE, DELIVERY, AND MEDIA OF MESSAGE PRESENTATION

In two experiments results relating to the effects of evidence on attitude change and perceived credibility were conflicting across topics when the message was attributed to a moderate-to-low-credible source.[23] In both studies evidence had its predicted effect when the speech topic was federal control of education, but in neither study did evidence have its predicted effect when the speech topic was capital punishment. Post-experiment interviews with selected subjects indicated that they perceived the delivery of the speaker on federal control of education to be very good but the delivery of the speaker on capital punishment to be dull and monotonous. Therefore the quality of presentation of a message was suspected as a variable that could interact with evidence usage and, in turn, could produce the conflicting findings across topics.

Delivery long has been thought to be a significant variable in oral communication. Poor delivery theoretically distracts from the content of the message by drawing attention of the audience to poor delivery characteristics and by reducing the clarity of the verbal message. Because poor delivery might cause an audience to miss evidence as it is presented by causing them to attend to something else and because it might prevent the audience from clearly understanding evidence which they do hear, poor delivery could interact with evidence usage in persuasive communication.

Two studies were designed and conducted to test the following hypothesis: Inclusion of evidence in a persuasive speech increases attitude change and perceived credibility when the speech is well delivered but has no effect on either attitude change or credibility when the speech is poorly delivered. The results of both studies provided partial support for this hypothesis.

[23] *Ibid.*

Arnold and McCroskey employed a live speaker to present an "evidence speech" and a "no-evidence speech" under conditions of both good delivery and very poor delivery.[24] Greater attitude change and higher perceived credibility were produced by the condition including evidence and good delivery than any of the other three conditions. The other three conditions did not differ in amount of attitude change produced. However, even in the poor delivery condition, the speech including evidence produced higher perceived credibility than the speech with no evidence, though not as high as in the condition including evidence and good delivery.

In a subsequent and much broader study, the results were consistent with those of the Arnold and McCroskey study. In this study four main variables were manipulated—evidence, delivery, initial credibility, and media of transmission.[25] The results indicated that inclusion of evidence increased immediate attitude change only under conditions of good delivery accompanied by initial low credibility. The results were consistent across transmission media—audio-tape and video-tape. Although poor delivery was found significantly to reduce perceived credibility, again, as in the Arnold and McCroskey study, the speech including evidence consistently produced higher perceived credibility than the speech not including evidence.

poor delivery inhibits effect of evidence on attitude change, not on credibility

The results of these studies, taken together, support the conclusion that poor delivery can inhibit the effect of evidence on immediate attitude change but does not inhibit its effect on credibility. Because the results of these studies were consistent for live, audio-taped, and video-taped speakers, one has no reason to believe that media of presentation is related to the effect of evidence in persuasive communication.

EVIDENCE AND PRIOR KNOWLEDGE OF AUDIENCE

Although the findings discussed in the previous section indicate that evidence and delivery are related in the production of attitude change, this does not provide a full explanation of the conflicting results across topics in the two studies previously noted. In those studies the results on credibility also conflicted. As a result of post-experiment interviews with sub-

[24] *Ibid.*

[25] *Ibid.*

jects involved in the studies in which conflicting results were obtained, another variable was suspected to be related to evidence in the production of attitude change and perceived source credibility. This is the variable of prior familiarity of the audience with evidence cited by a speaker.

In the post-experiment interviews the almost universal reaction from the subjects was that the evidence cited in the capital punishment speech was "old hat." On the federal control of education topic, on the other hand, the most frequent comment was one of interest and surprise at what was described by several subjects as the "shocking facts" presented.

If evidence must be "new" to have an effect, the inconsistent results become explainable. Such an assumption is highly consistent with some information theories. It is also consistent with dissonance theory. Old evidence has already entered the cognitive domain of the subject. If it created dissonance, that dissonance would have already been resolved or defense mechanisms constructed to avoid the recurrence of dissonance as a result of that evidence. Thus the presentation of that evidence to the subject would have no effect.

On the basis of this theory it was hypothesized that presenting evidence to people who previously have been exposed to that evidence will have no effect on either attitude change or credibility, but presenting the same evidence to people who are not familiar with it will significantly increase attitude change and credibility if the source of the message is initially moderate-to-low-credible.

The study designed to test this hypothesis involved the manipulation of three variables—evidence, initial credibility, and degree of prior familiarity with the evidence on the part of the subjects.[26] Evidence and credibility were manipulated as in previous studies. The speeches on the topic of federal control of education were selected as experimental stimuli because it was assumed that the subjects were not familiar with the evidence included in these speeches. Half of the subjects, therefore, were systematically exposed to this evidence under appropriate cover conditions prior to being exposed to the experimental speeches.

The results of this study were precisely predicted by the hypothesis. Evidence increased attitude change and credibility only in the condition including low initial credibility and no prior familiarization with the evidence. These results seem to provide an explanation of the conflicting results of the earlier

[26] *Ibid.*

only "new" evidence
effects attitude change
or credibility

studies. But more importantly, the results indicate that evidence must be "new" to the audience before it can have an impact on their immediate attitude change or their perception of the message source.

THE EFFECTS OF EVIDENCE ON SUSTAINED ATTITUDE CHANGE

The previous sections of this paper have been concerned only with the effects of evidence on credibility and attitude change measured *immediately* subsequent to exposure to persuasive messages. Evidence has an impact on these important variables only under relatively limited circumstances. In several of these studies the effects of evidence on sustained attitude change for periods up to seven weeks were measured.[27] In four of the five cases in which the effect of evidence on sustained attitude change was measured, inclusion of evidence was found significantly to increase the amount of attitude change retained over time. In the fifth case the difference was in the same direction although not statistically significant. Further, no interactions between evidence usage and other communication variables were found relating to sustained attitude change.

evidence may increase
sustained attitude
change

Precisely why evidence has an effect on sustained attitude change even when it has no effect on immediate attitude change is not at all clear. Since all speeches produced significant immediate attitude change, one possible explanation is that evidence may interfere with the process of selective recall. The evidence included in the experimental messages in the studies that measured sustained effect was, for the most part, quite vivid and memorable. Such material may have been more memorable than other elements of the messages. Whether less striking evidence would have a similar impact is unknown.

CONCLUSIONS

Some twenty-two studies concerned with the functioning of evidence in persuasive communication have now been reported in the literature. The purpose of this paper has been to examine these studies to determine what generalizations

[27] *Ibid.*

of value to the practicing communicator or communication researcher tentatively may be drawn at this point in time. The following are generalizations which seem appropriate:

generalizations on the functioning of evidence in persuasion

(1) Including good evidence has little, if any, impact on immediate audience attitude change or source credibility if the source of the message is initially perceived to be high-credible.

(2) Including good evidence has little, if any, impact on immediate audience attitude change if the message is delivered poorly.

(3) Including good evidence has little, if any, impact on immediate audience attitude change or source credibility if the audience is familiar with the evidence prior to exposure to the source's message.

(4) Including good evidence may significantly increase immediate audience attitude change and source credibility when the source is initially perceived to be moderate-to-low-credible, when the message is well delivered, and when the audience has little or no prior familiarity with the evidence included or similar evidence.

(5) Including good evidence may significantly increase sustained audience attitude change regardless of the source's initial credibility, the quality of the delivery of the message, or the medium by which the message is transmitted.

(6) The medium of transmission of a message has little, if any, effect on the functioning of evidence in persuasive communication.

NEED FOR FUTURE RESEARCH

Although the number of studies concerning the functioning of evidence in persuasive communication has increased sharply in recent years and several studies not discussed in this paper are in progress, there is a major need for more, and more imaginative, research in this area. Only a few very tentative generalizations about the place of evidence in persuasive communication are available. What are some of the questions that remain to be answered? The following are some that seem worthy of consideration: (1) What is the effect of evidence on overt behavior change? All the studies to date have been concerned with attitude. (2) Can evidence from non-credible sources serve as well as evidence from credible sources? Dresser's results suggest they can, but in his study credibility of the speaker was not manipulated.[28] (3) What type

[28] Dresser, "Studies of the Effects of Satisfactory. . . ."

of evidence (opinion, statistics, examples) produces the most favorable impact? Some researchers have investigated this area, but too many uncontrolled factors were in their designs to make interpretation of the results possible. (4) Are there factors that interact with evidence in producing sustained attitude change? The studies to date have found none, but they have been very limited in scope. (5) What factors other than delivery, source credibility, and prior knowledge interact with or inhibit the effects of evidence? Some that might are structure of the message, intelligence of the audience, and salience of the topic. (6) Do non-students respond to evidence the same way as students? Most of the subjects in the studies to date have been college students. Have we merely contributed one more "tidbit" to the rhetoric of the college sophomore? (7) Does evidence function the same way in inter-personal or group communication as it does in person-to-group communication? This area has received no previous attention. (8) Does evidence function in the written media the same way it does with live, audio-taped, and video-taped speakers? There is no previous research here either. (9) Can evidence enhance a communicator's efforts to inoculate his audience against counterpersuasion? The consistent effects favoring evidence on sustaining attitude change suggest that it might. (10) Does evidence function the same way in various cultures? The response may be very different if one studies evidence in something other than the U.S. middle-class culture in which the previous studies have been conducted.

The above questions are included in this paper to make clear that, while considerable information has accumulated upon which generalizations may be formed about the place of evidence in persuasive communication the surface of this problem area has barely been scratched. If we as communication researchers are to continue to focus our attention on message variables within the communication process, evidence should continue to be one of the major variables we study.

SUGGESTED FURTHER READING

Arnold, William E. and James C. McCroskey, "The Creditibility of Reluctant Testimony," *Central State Speech Journal,* XVIII (May, 1967), 97–103. (See footnote 21 above.)

Holtzman, Paul D., "Confirmation of Ethos as a Confounding Element in Communication Research," *Speech Monographs,* XXXIII (November, 1966). 464–466. (See footnote 18 above.)

McCroskey, James C., "The Effects of Evidence in Persuasive Communication," *Western Speech,* XXXI (Summer, 1967), 189–199. (See footnote 15 above.)

McCroskey, James C. and Robert E. Dunham, "Ethos: A Confounding Element in Communication Research," *Speech Monographs,* XXXIII (November, 1966), 456–463. (See footnote 17 above.)

McCroskey, James C., *An Introduction to Rhetorical Communication.* Englewood Cliffs, New Jersey: Prentice Hall, 1968.

———, *An Introduction to Interpersonal Communication.* Englewood Cliffs, New Jersey: Prentice Hall, Inc., 1971, See Chapter 8.

Toulmin, Stephen E., *The Uses of Argument.* New York: 1958.

ACTIVITIES

1. Select five advertisements from current magazines and bring them to class. Be prepared to discuss these advertisements in terms of specific appeals the advertiser intended to achieve. How has he attempted to appeal to the dominant values—or what he considers to be the dominant values? Does he present "good reasons" for buying his product?

2. Using your class members as subjects, attempt to determine the dominant values in the class. Prepare a short speech in which you specifically address yourself to ideas which violate or support those values.

3. As a class, determine ten values you accept and arrange them in a hierarchy. Encourage each class member to take this list and poll six other people (2 college students, 2 professors, and 2 members of the non-university community) and ask them to rank these same ten values. Discuss the differences and similarities in the value orientation found in the surveys. Think of adjustments in communication behavior which are suggested by the differences.

4. Give a speech on a controversial subject and experiment with one-sided versus two-sided arguments. Using a shift-of-opinion ballot, let each member of your audience record his opinion before and after the speech. After you collect the ballots, determine if your audience was more influenced by one or two-sided arguments. Explain your results in terms of the research presented by Anderson.

5. Prepare a one-page essay in which you take a definite stand on a controversial subject. The first time you write the paper use as much evidence (statistics, examples, analogies, comparisons, and expert testimonials) as you can find to support your argument. Using the same subject, write another one-page essay in which you consciously try to support your arguments by building your own ethos or credibility. Exchange these papers with other members of your class to determine which is more effective in terms of obtaining belief for your proposition. Try to explain your results by referring to the concepts of ethos and evidence presented by Dresser, Rosenthal, and McCroskey.

6. Consider Rosenthal's discussion of ethos as it relates to the speaker-listener relationship. Find a copy of or listen to a speech of a candidate running for elective office. Record the methods used by the speaker to gain acceptance of his policy and himself. Did he emphasize what Rosenthal's theory suggests he should have?

7. Remembering Carpenter's statement that "style is personal and reflective of a man's singular condition," write an advertisement in which you attempt to write in the style that would persuade an "average" businessman to take his wife on a trip to the Caribbean.

8. Find a copy of the Gettysburg Address and re-write it in the style in which it might have been written by
   (a) an active member of the Peace Movement of the late 1960's and early 1970's;
   (b) a rock and roll star;
   (c) a superpatriot.

Part 3.

Concepts
of
Communication
Criticism

3.

Introduction (by Jimmie D. Trent). Part One provided a general view of speech-communication. Part Two presented the theoretical conclusions derived from various types of research by speech-communication scholars. Now we turn to suggestions of ways you can continue on your own to learn about speech-communication as it has been practiced by others.

What can you learn by criticizing speakers? The word "you" is important in answering that question because your choice of speech-communication situation and your choice of method for study will determine the type of information you will find. Whether it be negotiation, interviewing, or public speaking, the type of communication situation will affect the findings which can be expected. And whether you study the situation as an historian, a psychologist, a sociologist, an anthropologist, or a rhetorician will determine what you believe to be relevant. And your methodology, whether it observes major trends or counts minute reactions will determine the nature of your findings.

You can learn what others have found successful in the past. You can learn to evaluate others' efforts in the situations in which they attempted communication. You can make judgments about others' motivations and methods and thereby, if you are careful not to generalize too far, make judgments of personality, ability, and character. You can gain understanding of situations as you study the communication components which were interacting to create meaning.

What you will not learn is equally important. You will not learn techniques of communication behavior which will be effective without application to the specific situation in which you must speak. As emphasized previously, successful communication depends on achieving the combination of variables which are effective in a particular situation.

But systematic observation of the methods used by successful speakers will give you an opportunity to expand your repertoire of communication tools. And you will have an opportunity to examine concrete applications of theoretical concepts and generalizations from research. In so doing, you can increase the choices available to you when you must decide what communication path to follow through the situation salient to your goals.

Part Three contains two types of articles. The first three discuss the applications, importance, and methods of criticism. Each of the last three presents an application of a method which, if you study it carefully, will give you information about a specific speech communication event and a methodology that you can use to examine other events.

In "Evaluative and Formulative Functions in Speech Criticism," Professor Jon M. Ericson argues that students can benefit from learning to criticize speeches. Among the many reasons he gives is the fact that students will have to criticize speeches more frequently than they will have to give them. Ericson also suggests types of elementary criticism which are well suited to the student who lacks sophistication or motivation.

Professor Anthony Hillbruner suggests three interdisciplinary approaches to criticism in his article, "Speech Criticism and American Culture." In addition to the rhetorical criticism suggested by Ericson, Hilbruner explains the benefits and general concepts of sociological, psychological, and anthropological criticism of speech-communication. He suggests that interdisciplinary approaches should be used much more extensively than they have been in past criticism.

Where Hillbruner suggests approaching criticism from the knowledge of different disciplines, Dean Henry E. McGuckin, Jr. suggests a different methodology. In "The Experimentalist as Critic," McGuckin suggests that experimentalists and traditionalists each heed the contributions of both to achieving knowledge about speech-communication behavior. In answering the experimentalists' critics, McGuckin describes the experimentalist as a rhetorical critic "with some promising new tools for refining some portions of an ancient inquiry."

Although Ericson, Hillbruner, and McGuckin all seem to be referring primarily to the criticism of public speaking situations, their ideas apply to the criticism of any speech-communication behavior. The major components, source, message, and receiver, are present in all speech-communication acts. While the behavior varies with the nature of the act, it also varies between two attempts at communication where the general type, such as public speaking, discussion, or interviewing, is the same. It is from such variance that we learn about factors which change the requirements of communication.

As you criticize speech-communication events, you will discover subtleties of situation for which no set of rules will account adequately. The suggestions of Ericson, Hillbruner, and McGuckin are not intended to be complete guides to speech criticism. Each methodology assumes some knowledge and assumes that you can interpret events in terms of that knowledge. Types of knowledge (psychological, rhetorical, experimental) which contain possible bases for analysis are presented. Recipe-type directions are avoided. If you follow the implication of most of these articles, you will find yourself learning more from devising your *own* methods—utilizing your knowledge, interests, awareness of possibilities, and situational demands—than you would learn from following any narrow set of rules.

Each of the concepts presented in this book can add to your understanding of speech-communication. Thus each article presents variables which can be studied in any speech-communication situation. An illustration of utilizing such concepts in criticism is contained in an original article by Professors Judith S. Trent and Jimmie D. Trent. Using the information provided in the articles by McCroskey and Rosenthal (See Part Two) as a basis for interpreting the results of an empirical study, the Trents suggest possible explanations for differences in Richard Nixon's use of evidence in his 1960 and 1968 campaigns for president. The importance of this article is that you should be able to follow the same methodology in interpreting speech-communications events for which you already have a description.

The fifth article in this section, Professor I. W. Rosenfield's "A Case Study in Criticism: The Nixon-Truman Analog," presents an additional method of criticism while describing and evaluating historical speech-communication events. The analog method of criticism involves comparison of two speech-communication events. Rosenfield examines and compares the situations, messages, and effects of two cases of apology on mass media. Harry Truman's speech, which followed a charge that he had given important responsibility to a Communist agent, is compared with Richard Nixon's successful "Checkers" speech.

Professors Stephen Kosokoff and Carl W. Carmichael use experimental methodology to determine effect in the final article in this section. "The Rhetoric of Protest: Song, Speech, and Attitude Change" reports an experiment on the relative effectiveness of protest songs and protest speeches used alone and in combination. In addition to providing useful conclusions and interesting examples of songs, this article illustrates how experiments can contribute to rhetorical criticism.

Each of the six articles in this section are included in order to help you find your own way of criticizing speech-communication events. Your method can be expected to vary according to your interests at the time you begin each subject. Your early study will probably be limited to elementary methods, but, as you gain sophistication in the concepts of speech communication, you will be able to make more comprehensive studies of more complicated speech-communication situations, acts, and effects. Whether your studies are elementary or complex, remember that you are searching for variables of speech-communication which will enhance your ability as speaker and critic.

Evaluative and Formulative Functions in Speech Criticism

Jon M. Ericson

The principle aims of an elementary course in public speaking are to introduce a student systematically to the rhetorical world and to develop his ability to function in that world. Speech criticism is exceptionally useful in achieving both of these objectives because the comprehension and application of rhetorical theory is the beginning of purposeful speech-making and criticism is at once the beginning and the end of rhetorical theory.

speech criticism: useful way to learn about speechmaking

While rhetoric itself is a formal study leading to the development and understanding of principles, the learning process for the student, by being something more than the repeated application of prescriptive advice, can be both analytical and creative. To illustrate: at the same time Demosthenes was delivering speeches to the public assembly, his contemporary, Aristotle, was privately writing that successful speakers could be studied and their craftsmanship reduced to a method. The circumstance suggests the text for the study of rhetoric: In the beginning was the word. But, just following the word, there is the critic who observes, analyzes, describes, and evaluates. Principles are then formulated by the critic-rhetorician. They are useful principles if they later serve to give effectiveness to another speaker. The process begins and ends with a speaker. Consequently, a student's involvement in the process of criticism makes him a participant both in the act of the speaker and in the act of the rhetorician.

role of the critic: observe, analyze, describe, evaluate

A student, acting as a critic, participates in the act of a speaker because the process of criticism closely parallels the process of speech composition. As he observes, analyzes, describes, and evaluates, he is in effect reviewing the speak-

Note: [At the time of this article's first appearance in summer of 1968,] Mr. Ericson [was] Department Chairman and Professor of Speech, Central Washington State College.

er's process of preparation. In this sense he has an important concern with results, for he views the speech itself as an end product; he describes and appraises the various rhetorical choices which combine to make up the speech. The focus is on the speaker's method, his employment of rhetorical form to effect his intended purpose.

critic uses results of criticism to formulate principles or confirm, revise existing theory

The student-critic functions as a rhetorician, as one who codifies principles, when he uses the results of his criticism to formulate new principles or to confirm or revise existing theory. Indeed, there has been enough (perhaps too much) emphasis on the purely evaluative function of criticism. If it is accepted that the scene changes, that each time and society has its own rhetoric, then it ought to be emphasized that a new rhetoric may require a reformulation of rhetorical theory. Criticism, whatever its brand, functions to observe, analyze, describe, evaluate, and then formulate. Evaluation uses the body of rhetorical theory but should not be bound by it. Formulation adds to the body of theory. Each function is necessary and gives purpose to the other. Empirical studies, too, may result in the formulation of new theory by which to evaluate current practice. At its roots, all criticism serves to evaluate: one either evaluates against a standard of judgment, or one evaluates the standard of judgment.

student as critic tests principles in his own speechmaking

As critic-rhetorician, the student finally tests principles in his own speechmaking. He has thus made the full circle: observation, analysis, description, evaluation, formulation, and application.

At this point, one might ask: Why involve a student in criticism? The application of principles can proceed with his being involved neither in evaluating speeches nor in formulating principles. Four reasons support the student's use of criticism:

1. After his classroom experience, he will function more as a critic than as a speaker. Therefore, the student ought to learn a *method* of observation, analysis and evaluation.
2. Speech criticism involves the student in the total rhetorical phenomenon and thus serves to sharpen his rhetorical consciousness.
3. Rhetorical theory by itself is made up of abstracted principles; speech criticism, followed by formulation and revision of principles, gives them concreteness and vitality.
4. Criticism allows the student to treat rhetoric as a whole. Observation, analysis, and description lead to *evaluation;* evaluation leads naturally enough to *formulation;* formula-

tion results in *conscious application.* The conscious application of principles is the end in view. It emerges from
a rhetorical awareness and is an ingredient of effective
speaking.

Since speech criticism is a useful means to learn about
speechmaking, the question then arises as to what the most
useful method may be. To answer that question, however, one
needs to understand certain problems which arise regardless
of methodology.

potential problems for
the student as critic

In the first place, because the form and substance of a
speech must be evaluated in a historical context, there is a
tendency to become involved in historical, rather than rhetorical investigation. While the mature critic should contribute
special insights to historical scholarship, it is suggested here
that the beginning student might be supplied the historical
context so that he can get on with his *rhetorical* work.

Another problem is that any design for criticism will modify
the result of the critical act. That is to say, any critical method
may be potentially complex in itself, but it is, nevertheless, a
simplification whose very structure influences the critic's end
result. Rhetorical acts must be viewed from some perspective,
and one's method modifies his perspective to the extent that
the methodological structure functions as a formal cause.

Finally, any critical method is complex because the rhetorical act is complex. Any critical method may present to the
beginning student more problems than he can cope with.
Nevertheless, criticism can proceed one step at a time.
Although criticism is least useful when it only describes,
learning to observe and analyze (in order to describe accurately) is a significant first step. Emphasis may properly be
placed on description. Overcomplicating criticism, moreover,
takes the joy out of it for the student. A part of its appeal is
that in criticism a student can begin where he is and, as he
matures, move on to more sophisticated levels. Burke's design, for example, begins with five uncomplicated questions
about the rhetorical act: What was done? When or where was
it done? Who did it? How did he do it? Why was it done?
Students can understand that. They can also understand appeals to reason and to emotion, and the appeal of form and
symbol, because these appeals are in the very substance of
human experience. The complexity of any method of criticism
is not in the points of analysis, but in the complex relationships
which appear as one learns more about them. In effect, a
teacher can help his students toward maturity by literally tak-

ing advantage of their rhetorical innocence. Rhetoric seems very uncomplicated to those who know nothing about it.

possible methods of analysis

Various methods of analyzing the rhetorical act have striking similarities among themselves and each is similar to Aristotle's four metaphysical causes. One may, for example, relate Aristotle's analysis of cause to Burke's pentad: the material cause may be regarded as the *scene,* the efficient cause the *agent,* the final cause the *purpose,* and the formal cause the *agency.* Each element is, as in Aristotle's analysis, subordinate to the ACT.

Another type of analysis might use as its points of focus the speaker, his purpose, his audience and occasion, the issues, and the kinds of identification or appeal made through proofs, arrangement, and language. Whatever the design of the analysis, emphasis at this level should focus on the agency—the method of appeal. In understanding the nature of formal appeal, the student will understand the nature of rhetoric.

useful forms of critical analysis: whatever turns out most useful

Any critical method must focus on the uses of appeal and must regard language as symbolic action. The most useful form of critical analysis may be whatever happens to be most usable. The result of the critical act depends less on the particular method of analysis than on the particular critic's ability to synthesize the result of his analysis into a meaningful whole. Both the truth and beauty of Burke's method is that it naturally leads to synthesis. And we are not as interested in putting Humpty Dumpty back together again as in finding out what he was before he fell.

SUGGESTED FURTHER READING

Auer, J. Jeffery, ed., *The Rhetoric of Our Times.* New York: Appleton-Century-Crofts, 1969.

Brandes, Paul D., *The Rhetoric of Revolt.* Englewood Cliffs, New Jersey: Prentice Hall, Inc., 1971.

Croft, Albert J., "The Functions of Rhetorical Criticism," *Quarterly Journal of Speech,* XLII (October, 1956), 283–291.

Holland, Virginia, "Rhetorical Criticism: A Burkian Method," *Quarterly Journal of Speech,* XXXIX (December, 1953), 444–450.

Holtzman, Paul D., "Speech Criticism and Evaluation as Communication," *Speech Teacher,* IX (January, 1960), 1–7.

Nilsen, Thomas R., "Criticism and Social Consequence," *Quarterly Journal of Speech,* XLI (April, 1951), 173–178.

Simons, Herbert W., "Requirements, Problems, and Strategies: A Theory of Persuasion for Social Movements," *Quarterly Journal of Speech,* LVI (February, 1970), 1–11.

Speech Criticism and American Culture

Anthony Hillbruner

In *The Liberal Imagination,* Lionel Trilling says, "a culture is not a flow, nor even a confluence; the form of its existence is struggle, or at least debate—it is nothing if not a dialectic."[1] This statement suggests the basis of what contribution speech criticism can make to American society. If one accepts the idea that a culture always struggles with itself, that it is in a state of flux as a result of the struggle, and that struggle in a civilized society manifests itself largely through debate or dialectic, then the function of speech criticism becomes rather obvious.

Speechmaking is a continuing part of the cultural debate. A culture can be defined in this context as a social heritage; in advanced governments such as the United States, it is synonymous with civilization. "Culture," says Bronislaw Malinowski, "comprises inherited artifacts, goods, technical processes, ideas, habits and values."[2]

critic's role: help form ideas, habits, and values of society by criticizing its important speeches

My concern here is with the latter three: ideas, habits and values. The true role of the speech critic is to help form these significant aspects of the culture by engaging in the debates that develop them. He engages in the debate by criticizing the speeches of those who actively participate in the formulations: the politicians, the statesmen, the agitators, the social and intellectual reformers, the theologians and the speculators.

The discipline of American studies looks at, explains, and criticizes the culture, not from one simplistic point of view—be it literary, sociological, rhetorical or any other—but rather from

Note. [when this article first appeared in summer, 1968,] Mr. Hillbruner [was] Professor of Speech and Coordinator of the American Studies Program, California State College, Los Angeles.

[1] Garden City, N.Y., 1957, p. 7.

[2] "Culture," *Encyclopedia of the Social Sciences,* ed. Edwin R. A. Seligman (New York, 1962), IV, 621.

an interdisciplinary approach. American studies scholars like to say that a more comprehensive understanding of our civilization can be found if we travel via the broad road of American studies. It is characterized by the cross-fertilization which comes from various areas of study rather than from using the narrow path of only *one* of these areas.

The speech critic's commitment to the cross breeding of American studies will put on this broad highway and away from the country lane. From this highway he can view the culture in broader and perhaps more significant perspectives than when he is restricted to the narrower horizons of the country lane.

to enter contemporary dialogue, critics need a broad interdisciplinary approach

It is true, of course, that the country lane has a charm and function of its own. A critic concerned with purely rhetorical criteria can be concerned with the language, for example, as an integral part of the culture. He can contribute his bit by focusing on this facet. This is, in fact, what most contemporary rhetorical critics do. Not all have focused on language, of course, but most of them have been pleased to saunter on the familiar ground of the country lane. They have engaged themselves with elements formal rather than substantive. The broad horizon of the distant highway, while it may seem fascinating to a few, since they see some of the important ideas, has not been intriguing enough for critics in general to make the effort to get to it and use it. On the broad highway are found the rules, laws and customs sanctioned in the culture. Here also are found the moral values by which man is driven to definite behavior. All these, if they are part of the speaking of a time, need to be examined and evaluated. Today's culture, moreover, is replete with problems which demand such consideration: Vietnam, the civil rights debates, open housing, police brutality allegations, urban problems, the unionizing of the clergy, not to say that of college professors, to name a few. All are part of the culture, the form of whose existence, if not struggle, is at least dialectic or debate. Standing on the country lane, the rhetorical critic can see these only dimly. He neglects to engage himself with these problems because he prefers the formal aspects of his own discipline.

"Culture consists of the body of commodities and instruments as well as of customs and bodily or mental habits which work directly or indirectly for the satisfaction of human needs. All the elements of culture, if this conception be true, must be at work, functioning, active, efficient," says Malinowski.[3]

some interdisciplinary approaches to rhetorical criticism

[3] "Culture," 625.

If this indeed is true, then the essentially dynamic character of cultural elements and of their relations one to another is at the root of invention. Moreover, if this is so, it is at base the task of the speech critic to enter this significant dialogue of his time. But how is he to enter it, how is he to move from the country lane to the broad highway? Several avenues lead from the country lane to the highway. These are the several routes of criticism which, added to the formal rhetorical one, will enable him to accomplish this task more effectively: the psychological route, the sociological route and the anthropological route.

psychological approach

The psychological route is one with which rhetoricians and rhetorical critics are already somewhat familiar.[4] It could be used more effectively, however, if two aspects of it were given more emphasis. The first of these two is the use of a more precise language with which to discuss the creative rhetorical process. This is part of what I. A. Richards means when he discusses art "as conductive to synaesthetic equilibrium."[5] Applied to rhetoric, Richards' notion suggests that an instance of communication such as a speech or a lecture serves as a stimulus to bring about a particular and harmonious type of response in the audience. It is along the psychological route that the critic approaches an examination and analysis of the unconscious relations between speaker and listener.

The second use of the psychological approach goes back to rhetorical biography—as differentiated from other kinds: literary biography (of Emerson for example), political biography (of John F. Kennedy, for instance), theological biography (of Reinhold Niebuhr), to name a few. The psychological approach enables rhetorical biographers to speculate upon the interior parts of a speaker's life. In using it, the critic becomes a lay analyst who takes the speechmaking to be a symptom of unconscious repressions and drives in the speaker. These interpretations may lead toward a better understanding of his rhetoric.[6]

Of course, the use of these two facets may be dangerous

[4] See Robert T. Oliver, *Psychology of Persuasive Speech* (New York, 1957).

[5] See I. A. Richards, *Principles of Literary Criticism* (London, 1928).

[6] A recently published work by Sigmund Freud in collaboration with William C. Bullitt, *Thomas Woodrow Wilson* (New York, 1966), is a case in point. According to Freud, Wilson submitted first to his father, then to God, with whom he believed himself to be in direct communication. This accounts for Wilson's conviction that he was a savior, who through his speeches dictated the terms which would ensure world peace. It also accounts for his "pedantic" style.

if they are applied injudiciously by critics with only a superficial knowledge of psychology. But if they are used well, the light cast upon rhetoric by psychology can be substantial. Elements of modern psychology from Sigmund Freud and Alfred Adler applied to rhetorical criticism can add new dimensions to an understanding of the culture. According to Harold D. Laswell, it is "no exaggeration to say that we have learned more about human beings in the last fifty years than in the previous history of mankind . . . ."[7] If we utilize this knowledge, it will help us get onto the broad highway of American studies.

The sociological route to the broad highway starts with the conviction that the relationship of speech to society is vitally important. It continues by asserting that an investigation of these relationships may deepen one's response to a work of rhetoric. The rhetorical critic who makes use of sociological criticism is primarily interested in the social milieu and the manner in which the speaker responds to it. This, to some degree, rhetorians attempt to do. They have for a long time been interested in the relationships among the speech, the speaker and the social milieu. Determining these relationships is not a simple task, because the ties between rhetoric and society are reciprocal. Speechmaking is not only the effect of social causes; it is also the cause of social effects as anyone can see who examines the speaking of a statesman, in the first instance, and of an agitator, in the second. Thus an objective juxtaposition of the work of rhetoric and social theory, be it capitalism, socialism or communism, can strike sparks that are genuinely illuminating. The best example of this kind of criticism is Vernon L. Parrington's *Main Currents in American Thought,* although F. O. Matthiessen's *American Renaissance* also ably illustrates the approach. There are articles in speech journals as well which attempt this type of study.

sociological approach

Anthropological criticism serves also as an avenue to making the rhetorical critic inter-disciplinary and thus more useful to American civilization. In it the many characteristics of culture and acculturation are significant elements. Unlike the psychological and the sociological routes, the anthropological approach has not been widely used by rhetoricians. Kenneth Burke, however, in his study of Hitler's *Mein Kampf,* analyzes the myths used by Hitler to seduce the German people into Nazism.[8] The method can be delineated as the

anthropological approach

[7] *Power and Personality* (New York, 1962), p. 104.

[8] *The Philosophy of Literary Form* (New York, 1957).

utilization of some kind of basic cultural pattern which has not only great meaning but also a great appeal for a particular group. The myth of the purity of the blood of the Aryan had such an appeal for post World War I Germany.

The impetus for the anthropological avenues of myths came originally from James G. Frazier's *The Golden Bough* (1890–1915) as well as Edward Tyler's *Primitive Cultures* (1871). These are concerned with magic and religion. But Carl G. Jung is also a seminal figure in archetypal criticism with his chief contribution, the theory of the collective unconscious. Civilized man, according to this theory, unconsciously retains those prehistorical areas of knowledge which originally and obliquely have been articulated in myth.

But archetypal criticism need not use specific myths. It may discover cultural patterns which can assume a mythic quality because they have been so permanent within a culture.[9] Malinowski suggests that not only has myth been important in culture, but so also have such ideas as religion and cooperation. "Religion . . . can be shown to be intrinsically although indirectly connected with man's fundamental, that is, biological needs."[10] And "cooperation means sacrifice, effort, subordination of private interests and inclinations to the joint ends of the community, the existence of social restraint."[11] Both ideas are used constantly in speechmaking.

Malinowski says that myth "is a statement of primeval reality which lives in the institutions and pursuits of a community. It justifies by precedent the existing order and it supplies a restrospective pattern of moral values, of sociological discriminations and burdens and of magical belief. In this consists its main cultural function."[12] When Winston Churchill said in his *History of the English-speaking Peoples* that all the happenings of the Anglo-Saxons were true, or should have been, he recognized the probative power of myth. An archetypic analysis of Lincoln's "Gettysburg Address" has shown it to contain a large measure of myth as do ethical characteristics of other prominent statesmen (Washington's cherry tree incident).

some interdisciplinary criticism exists, more is needed

Rhetorical criticism has made use of some facets of all three of the avenues discussed. In this use lies its contribution to the struggle involving the dialectic and debate in American

[9] See Thurman W. Arnold, *The Folklore of Capitalism* (New Haven, 1937).

[10] "Culture," 640.

[11] "Culture," 633.

[12] "Culture," 641.

culture. Much more can be done, however, if speech critics were less committed to the critical monism of formal rhetoric than they are and if they were to use whatever aspects of these three adjuncts to formal criticism would give them insights into the American character and psyche. If their own scholarly perambulations used these approaches to a greater degree, their contributions to history, to American studies and to American culture would be even greater than they have been thus far.

SUGGESTED FURTHER READING

Black, Edwin, *Rhetorical Criticism.* New York: The Macmillan Company, 1965.

Burke, Kenneth, *The Philosophy of Literary Form.* New York: Random House Publishing Company, 1957.

Hockmuth, Marie, "I. A. Richards and the New Rhetoric," *Quarterly Journal of Speech,* XLIV (February, 1958), 1–16.

Hoffer, Eric, *The True Believer.* New York: Harper & Row Publishers, 1951.

Laswell, Harold D., *Power and Personality.* New York, 1962.

Murphy, Richard, "The Speech as Literary Genre," *Quarterly Journal of Speech,* XLIV (April, 1958), 117–123.

Nichols, Marie Hochmuth, *Rhetoric and Criticism.* Baton Rouge, Louisiana: Louisiana State University Press, 1963.

The Experimentalist as Critic

Henry E. McGuckin, Jr.

In 1959, Sir Charles Percy Snow introduced his thesis of the "two cultures" in contemporary Western intellectual life— "literary intellectuals at one pole—at the other the scientists . . . Between the two a gulf of mutual incomprehension— sometimes . . . hostility and dislike, but most of all," he said, "lack of understanding."[1]

Snow's thesis was the subject of such abuse, especially in America, that in 1964 he published a "Second Look" wherein he attempted to refute his critics.[2] Had he but known, he might have turned with advantage to American rhetorical studies and found a microcosm of his thesis. For that same gulf of mutual incomprehension, sometimes hostility and dislike, but most of all, misunderstanding, slashes across the field of rhetorical studies between traditional critics who conceive rhetoric as a humane discipline and experimentalists who conceive rhetoric as a behavioral science.

mutual incomprehension between traditional critics, experimentalists

Experimentalists tend to view traditionalists as stodgy reactionaries, resting where they have rested for 2,000 years, unmoving and unmovable, squarely on Aristotle's laurels and crushing the life out of them in the process. Traditionalists tend to view experimentalists as pseudo-scientific opportunists riding a cultural crest of scientism, reducing complex human impulse to simplistic numerical equations.

Nathan Maccoby, for example, an experimental psychologist and a self-styled "new rhetorician," implies an obvious degree of contempt when he writes:

> The new scientific rhetoricians, far from confining themselves to repeated discussions of the sophists—Socrates, Plato,

Note: [when this article was published in summer, 1968,] Mr. McGuckin [was] Associate Dean of Humanities, San Francisco State College.

[1] *The Two Cultures and the Scientific Revolution* (New York, 1959), p. 4.

[2] *The Two Cultures and a Second Look* (Cambridge, 1964).

Aristotle, and Quintilian—are finding, through the inventive formulation of theory and . . . the impersonal fire of experimental tests . . . an ever widening scope of inquiry.[3]

Eric Kahier, on the other hand, a concerned and literate humanist, expresses in *The Tower and the Abyss* the usual traditionalist critique of such claims:

> Systematic research in its limitless expansion sets out to ascertain everything scientifically, even facts which any person with common sense and a little bit of observation has been aware of in his day-to-day life. . . . What was known as human wisdom is on the wane.[4]

Perhaps conflict between these opposing forces is inevitable. Perhaps the gulf between the two rhetorical cultures is simply too wide to bridge. One can hardly infer that inevitability, however, from traditionalist and experimentalist statements of *purpose.*

Traditionalists Thonssen and Baird, for example, define rhetorical criticism as "comparative study in which standards of judgment deriving from the social interaction of a speech situation are applied to public address to determine the immediate or delayed effect of the speeches upon specific audiences, and, ultimately, upon society."[5]

"New rhetoricians" Hovland, Janis, and Kelley similarly, though more succinctly, assert the concern of their inquiry to be ". . . understanding the ways in which words and symbols influence people."[6]

the conflict may be a difference in methodology

Surely Thonssen, Baird, Hovland, Janis, and Kelley are all talking about the same thing. Surely, traditionalist or experimentalist, all are engaged in the same endeavor; surely, all are rhetorical critics in the broadest and best sense of that term. Is it not methodology alone which finally divides? And if methodology is the single point of division, does that sole difference warrant the gulf?

traditionalists have two common indictments of experimental methods

The roots of traditionalist suspicion probably lie fundamentally in two common indictments of the experimental methodology. The first indictment is that the method quantifies what cannot be quantified. It sums, for example, numerical

---

[3]"The New Scientific Rhetoric," *The Voice of America Forum Lectures,* Mass Communication Series, no. 4 (n.d.), p. 9.

[4]New York, 1957, pp. 19–21.

[5]*Speech Criticism* (New York, 1948), p. 16.

[6]Carl J. Hovland, Irving L. Janis, and Harold H. Kelley, *Communication and Persuasion* (New Haven, 1957), p. 147.

representations of discrete individual reactions to communication and generalizes upon these sums. But these generalizations are inherently invalid, it is suggested, because the sums are, finally, artifices without objective reality. The second indictment charges that the method never moves beyond belaboring the obvious, anyway.

The first indictment possess a certain surface credibility, but it is ultimately a thoughtless criticism—the debunker, to paraphrase Kenneth Burke, suffers with the debunked.[7] If discrete reactions *cannot* be summed and generalized, what is to be done with a traditional critic's speculations on the "effects" of, say, the Kennedy-Nixon debates? The traditional critic, after all, gathers whatever discrete reactions he can and generalizes upon them, and if the focus of his study is far removed in time, if his sources are newspaper accounts, personal journals and so forth, his evidence is likely to be already generalized, so that he sums old sums, as it were.

first indictment: experimental method quantifies what cannot be quantified

The experimentalist, in contrast, can claim that his is the first order of generalization, including a numerical approximation of *all* the discrete reactions and that, furthermore, his control of the stimulus and audience variables places him in a relatively secure position from which to infer what was *cause* and what was *effect.* He can claim, finally, that the bulk of his statistical manipulation, the bulk of his "quantification," is designed simply to specify the likelihood of at least some of his potential error—a likelihood seldom even discussed in traditional criticism.

The second indictment, that experimentalists inevitably belabor the obvious, is, to a degree of course, quite true, but nonsignificant work is simply nonsignificant work, and no methodology, including traditional methodology, is inherently immune from that disease. Have experimentalists, however, been especially susceptible? Have experimentalists, in fact, contributed little beyond common sense to an understanding of rhetorical processes?

second indictment: experimentalists belabor the obvious, contributing little to the field

A battery of recent studies might be cited as significant contributions. Consider, instead, some old ones, studies which have been around for over a decade and which are common knowledge to the most fledgling experimentalist and which have, nonetheless, had little impact in traditional circles. A group of experiments on the effects of fear-arousing communications, for example, has indicated a point of diminishing

---

[7] "Virtues and Limitations of Debunking" in *The Philosophy of Literary Form* (New York, 1957), p. 147.

returns in the rhetorical effect of fear. The results of these experiments suggest that when one is sufficiently threatened personally, defense mechanisms come into play, and one dissociates himself from the dangers threatened. Thus moderate or mild fear appeals seem to be most efficacious in changing behavior.[8] An experience of the California Highway Patrol dramatically demonstrates the fact that not everyone's common sense would lead him to that conclusion. For over twenty years, that agency has shown to senior high school classes a film depicting the results of highway carelessness. Year after year, bleeding, smashed, decapitated victims of highway accidents are graphically displayed to swooning students, a number of whom become ill or unconscious with monotonous regularity; yet teen-age accident rates remain tragically high. It may be that the California Highway Patrol, led astray by its common sense, has been obviating its own best efforts in driver education.

Another group of older studies, on one-sided and two-sided persuasive appeals, has demonstrated some of the conditions under which one is more effective than the other. One important condition is the presence or absence of "counter-propaganda," the two-sided strategy being most effective for long-term persuasion when the audience is likely to confront counter argument.[9] Not everyone's common sense would lead him to that conclusion, either. In California, again, a Superintendent of Public Education launched a crusade to "bring patriotism back to the public schools." His plan of attack includes expurgation of even the mildest critical social commentary from California's textbooks. Among the variety of reasons for resisting his position is the fact that it is probably self-defeating; his one-sided approach is destined to create the lushest of targets for the very counter-propaganda which so disturbs him—unless, of course, he can throttle that, too. In an open society, it seems, one-sided indoctrination programs are relatively ineffective, the common sense of indoctrinators notwithstanding.

It may be argued that when traditionalists charge experimentalists with belaboring common sense, they are not speak-

[8] Hovland, et al., Chapter 3. See also Sidney Kraus, Elaine El-Assal, and Melvin L. DeFleur, "Fear-Threat Appeals in Mass Communication: An Apparent Contradiction," *Speech Monographs,* XXXIII (March 1966), 23–29, for a recent amplification and qualification.

[9] Hovland, et al., Chapter 4. See also Stanley F. Paulson, "The Effects of Prestige of the Speaker and Acknowledgment of Opposing Arguments on Audience Retention and Shift of Opinion," *Speech Monographs,* XXI (1954), 267–271.

ing to quite that level of common sense characteristic of Highway Patrolmen or Superintendents of Public Education; rather, they speak to a much less common level of common sense: to wit, their own. The fact remains, however, that if the California Highway Patrol or California's Superintendent of Public Education were to turn to the great bulk of traditional texts in rhetoric, basic or sophisticated, they would find little to direct them from their errors. Traditional rhetoric would not tell them what they really need to know about, of all things, the available means of persuasion.

But if traditionalists fail to note important experimental contributions to the field, the view from the other side of the gulf is not much better. Experimentalists tend to ignore or discount the vast rhetorical tradition from which their efforts spring. As a result, great numbers of relevant experimental studies accumulate in a variety of behavioral journals but few attempt seriously to relate their findings to a body of principle or theory. Kenneth Burke has described this general condition in behavioral research as "a cult of 'fact-finding' with no order of facts considered too lowly for the collector. In itself the attitude has much to recommend it. It is scientific humility in the best sense. But it should not be allowed to give specious justification for inquiries where the sheer *absence of intrinsic value* is assumed to imply the *presence of pragmatic value.*"[10]

experimentalists ignore or discount rhetorical tradition

This problem is not totally unrecognized by experimentalists. Most attempts to relate, however, are directed toward recent behavioral formulations. The obvious body of integrating principle and theory, 2,000 years of the rhetorical tradition, remains largely untapped by our "new scientific rhetoricians."[11] Furthermore, as Otis Walter has pointed out, there are important questions which are simply not experimental—philosophical questions, esthetic questions, ethical questions.[12] A rhetoric, however "scientific," which ignores such questions is ultimately proverty-stricken, is *inhumane* in the ultimate sense of that term.

experimentalists seldom relate results to general principle or theory

many important questions to be answered are not experimental

C. P. Snow was charged with overstating the case for his "two cultures." It should not be overstated here. There have been gentle moves toward integration of the humane and

[10] *A Grammar of Motives and A Rhetoric of Motives* (Cleveland, 1962), p. 387

[11] See Gerald K. Miller, "Theory in Quantitative Speech Research," *Western Speech,* XXVIII (Winter 1964), 15–22.

[12] "On Views of Rhetoric, Whether Conservative or Progressive," *QJS,* XLIX (December 1963), 367–382. For an experimentalist view, see also Wayne M. Thompson, "A Conservative View of a Progressive Rhetoric," *QJS,* XLIX (February 1963), 1–7.

behavioral approaches within the field of rhetoric and out of it. A few integrating volumes have been published in speech: Minnick's *Persuasion*[13] and that of Brembeck and Howell[14] are early steps in that direction. A joint speech-psychology major planned at San Francisco State College indicates mutual perception of the need for integration. A variety of recent dissertations in speech have been purposeful attempts to relate behavioral methodology and humane tradition—experimental tests or Aristotelian or Burkean principles, for example.[15] The major journals in speech publish both traditional and experimental studies. But the bridges which span the gulf between humanists and behaviorists generally—between traditionalists and experimentalists in rhetoric—are yet of pretty flimsy stuff. They will not support the discipline as they must.

critics must work with all resources to chart the rhetorical process

It is probably meaningless to suggest that all experimentalists *become* traditionalists, that all traditionalists *become* experimentalists. All ought to do what they do best. But certainly it is time that all heed with real conviction one another's contributions to what is ultimately a single purpose. Perhaps a reconstruction of self-image is the starting point. Perhaps the needed bridges cannot be built until experimentalists conceive themselves with more humility as what they are, as rhetorical critics with some promising new *tools* for refining some portions of an ancient inquiry; until traditionalists conceive themselves with more grace as what they are, as rhetorical critics with some timeless questions and some proven responses from an *uncompleted* inquiry; until all are willing to use all there is to use in charting the rhetorical process in the human condition. That, finally, is the use of speech criticism. To that endeavor each one must welcome every other, humanist or scientist, traditionalist or experimentalist, not (to borrow a final image from C. P. Snow) as stranger, but as brother.

[13] Wayne C. Minnick, *The Art of Persuasion* (Boston, 1957).

[14] Winston Lamont Brembeck and William Smiley Howell, *Persuasion: A Means of Social Control* (New York, 1952).

[15] See, for example, the unpubl. diss. (University of Illinois, 1961) by Dennis Day, "An Exploration of the Theory of Identification with an Experimental Investigation of Its Operation in Oral Communication."

SUGGESTED FURTHER READING

Berlo, David K., "Problems in Communication Research," *Central States Speech Journal,* VII (Fall, 1955), 3–7.

Bitzer, Lloyd F. and Edwin Black, eds., *The Prospect of Rhetoric.* Englewood Cliffs, New Jersey: Prentice-Hall, Inc., 1971.

Geiger, Don, "Rhetoric and Science Notes for a Distinction," *Speech Teacher,* VII (January, 1958), 54–60.

Maccoby, Nathan, "The New Scientific Rhetoric," *The Voice of America Forum Lectures,* Mass Communication Series, No. 4. (See footnote 3 above.)

Miller, Gerald K., "Theory in Quantitative Speech Research," *Western Speech,* XXVIII (Winter, 1968), 15–22. (See footnote 11 above.)

Thonnsen, Lester and A. Craig Baird, *Speech Criticism.* New York: The Ronald Press, 1948. (See footnote 5 above.)

Trent, Judith S., "The New Nixon: A Comparison of the Types of Sentences Used in His 1960 and 1968 Campaigns," *Michigan Speech Association Journal,* VI (1971), 12–24.

Trent, Judith S., "Content Analysis of Nixon's 1960 and 1968 Campaigns," *Today's Speech,* XIX (Fall, 1971), 23–30.

An Experimentally Based Rhetorical Analysis: Richard Nixon's Use of Ethos and Evidence

Judith S. Trent and Jimmie D. Trent

A content analysis study of Richard Nixon's methods of support in his speeches of the 1960 and 1968 campaigns for the presidency disclosed that the primary emphasis shifted from building personal ethos in the first campaign to a discussion of issues in 1968.[1] This essay explores the nature of Nixon's shift and attempts to explain it in terms of the theoretical and empirical conclusions of Rosenthal[2] on ethos and of McCroskey[3] on evidence. As such, it utilizes theoretical and empirical findings in the criticism of public address events.

both theoretical and empirical findings used for criticism

The research of Judith Trent indicates that Richard Nixon's use of ethos and evidence as means of support differed significantly between his two campaigns for president. Nixon's use of ethos as support was measured through coding of two categories: *personal expertise* (defined as "references to the speaker's education, traveling he has done, experiences he has had, and training he has undergone to make him qualified for the office he is seeking") and *expertise by association* (defined as "references to generally perceived high credibility sources—the speaker's acquaintance and relationship to high prestige persons, virtue by association").

ethos appeal: personal expertise

expertise by association

The frequency of Nixon's use of personal expertise and expertise by association was reduced significantly in 1968. Six percent of Nixon's statements in 1960 were attempts to establish his personal expertise through such assertions as "I have had experience dealing with Khrushchev," "I have sat with the President," "I have seen America," "I have been in the Communist world," and "I have seen the world." In 1968, only four tenths of one percent of Nixon's statements asserted his personal expertise. Nixon attempted to establish his personal

ethos as a means of support reduced (1968)

expertise by association with prestige sources in two percent of his statements in 1960 but used this device in only one tenth of one percent of his statements in the 1968 campaign.

In every speech in the 1960 campaign sample, Nixon promoted his ethos through prestige association with statements such as:

> When a President speaks, when he acts, he can't take it back. I have been there when a President makes a decision. I was there the day we went into Lebanon. I remember the President on a Monday morning very early pacing the floor in the oval office of the White House, finally making up his mind, turning to me and saying, "Well, we've got to send the boys in . . ."[4]

Such statements occurred rarely in the 1968 campaign. Thus, the emphasis in the 1968 campaign was shifted away from attempts to enhance Nixon's prestige through direct means. Where one statement in nine was directly focused on Nixon's personal ethos in 1960, fewer than one in a hundred had that purpose in 1968.

Significant increases in the use of reasoning and evidence in 1968 indicate that Nixon had shifted his emphasis to issue development. Reasoning, defined as "any statement (normally of a specific position) which is supported by reasons or a discussion of consequences," was the least used means of support in 1960 but the most frequent method of support in 1968. Evidence, which included statistics, testimony, example, comparison, and analogy, was in eleven percent of Nixon's statements in 1960 but in twenty-three percent in 1968. The shift to emphasis on issues was also indicated by the concentration of each speech in the 1968 campaign to a thorough development of a single issue as contrasted with mentioning from five to seven issues in each speech in 1960.

reasoning and evidence increased to stress issue development (1968)

Thus it it apparent that Nixon's emphasis shifted from an attempt to concentrate attention on himself and his ethos in 1960 to an attempt to concentrate attention on the issues in 1968.

concentrated attention on himself (1960) vs. stress on issues (1968)

Rosenthal, in *Speech Monographs* in 1966, explained the conditions which centered the 1960 campaign on the personal relationship between the speaker and the audience—that is, on the ethos of the speaker. Rosenthal suggested that the nature of the listener's relationships to the speaker, the environment, and the message will determine whether the listener responds to the speaker's ethos or to his message.

"The speaker-listener relationship requires a determination of the actual as opposed to the ostensible purpose of the

speaker-listener relationship in politics

rhetoric."[5] Obviously, in a political campaign, the speaker is more interested in obtaining a vote than he is in gaining agreement on an issue.

environment-listener relationship possibilities

The environment-listener relationship "is expressed in terms of how and to what degree the listener experiences and internalizes the environment," defined by Rosenthal as "the actual conditions in the real world . . . that are external to the communication."[6] If the listener does not perceive the environment as salient, the emphasis will be on the speaker's ethos rather than on the message. But the contradictory is not necessarily true; a listener can perceive the environment as being salient without shifting emphasis to the message. The message-listener relationship must offer a choice between alternatives before the message will affect the decision more than ethos.

If we can accept the premise that Nixon and his advisors were attempting to adapt to prevailing conditions, Rosenthal's theories offer some explanation for the shifts of emphasis.

Rosenthal theory supports the finding on ethos in 1960 campaign

In the 1960 campaign, the speaker-listener relationship encouraged what Rosenthal classified as a personal campaign—a campaign based on ethos. Nixon was not seeking agreement on issues so much as he was seeking votes for himself as a man. And perhaps the vote was not his only personal motivation. White described Nixon as a "friend seeker, almost pathetic in his eagerness to be liked. He wanted to identify with people and have a connection with them."[7] An office seeker who needed a connection with people would be expected to emphasize his personal characteristics if other conditions were right for doing so.

Rosenthal argued that the speaker-environment relationship in 1960 also contributed to a personal approach, but Trent's research does not support this. Since the saliency of the environment does not dictate a nonpersonal or issue approach if there is no opportunity to choose between alternate solutions, it makes little difference in our analysis of the 1960 campaign. The proposals of Nixon and Kennedy differed so little that the listener was forced to select between the speakers on the basis of personal characteristics.[8] Since Nixon was vice president, he was forced to defend the Eisenhower administration; it was up to Kennedy to propose alternate solutions. When Kennedy's proposals approximated the administration's, Nixon was given free rein to, if he was not forced to, emphasize his personal characteristics.

Rosenthal's concepts also offer a plausible explanation for the 1968 campaign.

In 1968, the speaker-listener relationship was still one of a candidate seeking a vote. But the candidate had changed. Nixon was reported to have lost his need for public adulation; he was more confident of his own abilities. He had become wealthy in private law practice and he wanted only respect.[9]

Rosenthal wrote that even "though a speaker's purpose may be of a personal nature, the persuasion may emerge as nonpersonal if the environment and message exhibit the proper relationship with the audience."[10] With Nixon's basic psychological need for direct ethos statements assuaged, he could attempt nonpersonal persuasion based on emphasizing issues if the environment and message relationships were correct.

Listeners must be aware of problems in the environment if issue persuasion is to result in transference of votes for an individual. In 1968, the listeners had already shown their concern about conditions. Concern over the Viet Nam War had caused Johnson to retire. The crime rate was at an all time high. And millions of viewers had watched television coverage of the police riots at the Democratic National Convention. The speaker-listener relationship was conducive to an issue orientation because listeners were aware of problems in the environment.

In 1968, Nixon could control the message-listener relationship. This time Humphrey had to support the administration and Nixon was free to select the issues and create alternatives which would allow the decision between candidates to become embodied in a policy choice. Nixon aligned himself with the people who wanted changes in foreign policy, with people who said the courts were too lenient on criminals, and with people who believed the problems of poverty and welfare could be alleviated by volunteer programs and private industry working in conjunction with the cities and states. He presented alternatives and freed himself from an ethos contest with an experienced Humphrey with his traditionally more trustworthy ethos image.

Nixon's shift away from ethos in 1968 was accompanied by a significant increase in the use of evidence and this reliance on evidence may have meaning beyond a mere shift to issue orientation. McCroskey's conclusions from twenty-two experimental studies concerned with the functioning of evidence suggest some possible explanations.[11]

McCroskey indicated that "including good evidence has little, if any, impact on immediate audience attitude change or source credibility if the source of the message is initially perceived to be high-credible."[12] Nixon's increased use of evidence suggests that he and/or his strategists believed that his credibility was not high with a significant number of voters. If he and his staff had considered his credibility to be high, his significant increase in the use of reasoning would have been sufficient to shift the emphasis to issues. It does not seem necessary to labor this point; the familiarity of the "buy a used car" slogan and the "tricky Dicky" label combine with the perennial declaration of "this is a New Nixon" to indicate that there was less than total confidence in his image. The increased use of evidence appears to be part of a strategy to overcome the low credibility rating that some voters gave Nixon.

increased evidence in strategy to overcome low credibility

Whether the exact strategy was to gain belief on specific issues, to dramatize issues as a means of detracting attention from the man, to create a new image for the candidate, or a combination of these strategies is not so apparent. Mc-Croskey's report suggests that evidence would have the effect of gaining support for specific issues and that may have been the total purpose perceived by the speaker and his staff.

vivid unusual evidence recognizes limited value of the familiar

But Nixon's evidence was more vivid in 1968; his statistics, examples and comparisons were such that they would attract attention. This may have been an attempt to dramatize the arguments as a means of attracting attention away from the man. But another of McCroskey's conclusions would describe this phenomenon equally well. McCroskey determined that "including good evidence has little, if any, impact on immediate audience attitude change or source credibility if the audience is familiar with the evidence prior to exposure to the source's message."[13] The use of vivid unusual evidence may be nothing more than a recognition of the limited value of the familiar.

use of evidence to create presidential image (1968)

A third possible explanation for an increase in the use of evidence by a low-credible source is that it is part of an attempt to increase credibility. Nixon may have been creating the image of an informed, qualified, and reasonable man, a man who should be president.

McCroskey's findings also support this explanation. Three studies are cited by McCroskey which combine to indicate that the "inclusion of evidence can increase the credibility of a moderate-to-low-credible source."[14]

Regardless of the exact strategy, it is apparent that Nixon did not give up on establishing his credibility in 1968. His shift away from directing attention to his personal characteristics and his increased emphasis on evidence, reasoning and issues represented an attempt to associate himself with credibility.

In summary, content analysis of Nixon's methods of support in his 1960 and 1968 campaign speeches reveals that the number of direct attempts to build personal ethos was significantly reduced in 1968 and the use of reasoning and evidence was significantly increased. The theoretical framework that Rosenthal derived from his research was found to offer a plausible explanation for the conditions which made this shift of emphasis at least possible if not necessary. The experimentally based conclusions of McCroskey suggest that the shift to evidence was simply another method of improving the image of a low-credible source.

One more comment seems in order. This essay explains the results of descriptive research of a public address event by utilizing the conclusions from other empirical research as a theoretical framework. In the authors' opinions, this methodology led to conclusions which would not have been derived from more traditional critical methods. Experimental research has often been proposed as a method for testing the results of critical research in a laboratory situation. This essay has found that laboratory research is also useful for creating a framework for criticism of public speaking events.

all methodologies needed in criticism to provide maximum insight

But in another place, the same findings of Nixon's shift from ethos to evidence were explained using the historical-critical method.[15] While the results were not identical for the two methodologies, they were consistent, and each methodology provided some insights not found in the other. Experimental research provides a useful supplement to the critic's traditional methodology but not a replacement. An eclectic approach is needed for obtaining maximum insight.

REFERENCES AND FOOTNOTES

1. Judith S. Trent, "An Examination And Comparison Of The Rhetorical Style Of Richard Milhous Nixon In The Presidential Campaigns Of 1960 And 1968: A Content Analysis," (unpublished Ph.D. dissertation, University of Michigan, 1970).

2. Paul I. Rosenthal, "The Concept of Ethos and the Structure of Persuasion," *Speech Monographs,* XXXIII (June, 1966), 114–126.

3. James C. McCroskey, "A Summary of Experimental Research On The Effects Of Evidence In Persuasive Commu-

nication," *Quarterly Journal of Speech,* LV (April, 1969), 169–176.

4. Partial transcript of the speech of Vice President Richard M. Nixon, Muhlenburg College Gymnasium, Allentown, Pennsylvania, October 22, 1960. The text of the speech is from U.S. Congress, Senate. Committee on Commerce. *Freedom of Communications: The Speeches, Remarks, Press Conferences, and Study Papers of Vice-President Richard M. Nixon, August 1 Through November 7, 1960* (S. Rept. 994, Part II, 87th Cong., 1st sess., 1961), pp. 706–714.

5. Rosenthal, 120.

6. *Ibid.*

7. Theodore H. White, *The Making of the President 1960* (New York: Atheneum Publishers, 1961), p. 300.

8. Rosenthal, 124.

9. Theodore H. White, *The Making of the President 1968* (New York: Atheneum Publishers, 1969), p. 166.

10. Rosenthal, 123.

11. McCroskey, 169–176.

12. *Ibid.,* 175.

13. *Ibid.*

14. *Ibid.,* 172.

15. Trent, 69–93.

SUGGESTED FURTHER READING

Chester, Lewis and Godfrey Hodgson and Bruce Page, *An American Melodrama: The Presidential Campaign of 1968.* New York: Dell Publishing Co., Inc., 1969.

Lane, Robert E. and David O. Sears, *Public Opinion.* Englewood Cliffs, New Jersey: Prentice-Hall, Inc., 1964.

McCroskey, James C., "A Summary of Experimental Research on the Effects of Evidence in Persuasive Communication," *Quarterly Journal of Speech, IV* (April 1969), 169–176. (See article in this text, and also footnotes 3, 11–14 above.)

McGinniss, Joe, *The Selling of the President 1968.* New York: Trident Press, 1969.

Rosenthal, Paul I., "The Concept of Ethos and the Structure of Persuasion," *Speech Monographs,* XXXIII (June, 1966), 114–126. (See article in this text and also footnotes 2, 5, 6, 8, 10 above.)

Weisbord, Marvin R., *Campaigning For President.* New York: Washington Square Press, Inc., 1966.

White, Theodore, *The Making of the President 1960.* New York: Atheneum Publishers, 1961. (See footnote 7 above.)

―――, *The Making of the President 1968.* New York: Atheneum Publishers, 1969. (See footnote 9 above.)

A Case Study in Speech Criticism: The Nixon-Truman Analog

L. W. Rosenfield

two examples of mass media apologia

One of the most controversial public addresses of modern American history is also one on which rhetorical scholars have remained strangely mute. I refer to the radio-television broadcast by the then vice presidential candidate Richard Nixon on September 23, 1952, the famous "Checkers" speech in which Nixon explained to the American public his use of a special campaign fund.[1] There also exists a remarkably similar address, a broadcast by ex-President Harry S. Truman on November 16, 1953 in which Truman answered charges that while president he had allowed a Communist agent, Harry Dexter White, to hold high governmental office. The generic resemblance of the two speeches (both may be classified as mass-media apologia) invites what may be called analog criticism—comparing the speeches in such ways that each address serves as a reference standard for the other. The objective of such a method of comparison and contrast is two-fold: to specify the fundamental anatomical features which relate the two speeches (engage in a *factorial* analysis of the category of apologetic discourse exemplified by the messages) and to assess the relative artistic merit of each speech, compared to the other.[2]

analog critic compares speeches so one serves as reference for another

Comparison of these particular speeches is fruitful on several counts. First, an element of objectivity (especially im-

Note: [In November, 1968, when this article appeared,] Dr. Rosenfield [was] Associate Professor of Speech, University of Wisconsin, Madison.

[1] The only formal scholarly reference to it is Professor Baskerville's sketch of the "Nixon affair" in F. W. Haberman (ed.), "The Election of 1952: A Symposium," *Quarterly Journal of Speech,* XXXVIII (December 1952), 406–408.

[2] For further discussion of the analog method as a tool for speech criticism see Rosenfield "The Logic of the Critical Act" in *Rhetorical Criticism,* ed. D. Burks and J. Cleary (in press).

portant when discussing contemporary partisans like Nixon and Truman) is introduced when the speeches are played off against each other in the critic's analysis. Second, the identification of similar qualities in the two messages suggests to the critic certain constants operating in an otherwise undefined form—use of instantaneous electronic media to answer accusations. In these two instances we have cases of relatively early efforts by public officials to cope with the rhetorical problems raised by the demands of apologiae nationally broadcast. Where we discover similarities in the messages, we have grounds for attributing those qualities to the situation or the genre rather than to the individual speaker. And should we at some future date find modified tactics in apologetic speeches, we would be in a position to determine whether an evolution occurred in the form itself. Finally, because the surface conditions of these two speeches are so similar, the critic will be alert to the distinctive qualities of each. And having recognized those differences, he will be justified in evaluating the configuration of unique features in each speech as evidence of the individual speaker's artistry in responding to the exigencies of the situation.

three reasons for comparing Nixon and Truman speeches

The remainder of this paper is divided into five sections. A brief sketch of the incidents surrounding the two speeches is followed by discussion of similarities in the rhetorical contexts which gave rise to the speeches, by specification of the common elements in the two addresses, by consideration of their divergent features, and by discussion of the critical and theoretical implications of the entire rhetorical analysis.

The Nixon fund affair occurred during the 1952 Eisenhower-Stevenson presidential race. On Thursday, September 18, the *New York Post* featured a story headlined "Secret Nixon Fund." It opened as follows:

> The existence of a "millionaire's club" devoted exclusively to the financial comfort of Senator Nixon, GOP Vice Presidential candidate, was revealed today.[3]

Democratic National Chairman Mitchell, in a "great show of indignation over corruption," promptly demanded that all details of the fund, including contributors and expenditures, be made public, and he called on candidate Eisenhower to remove Nixon from the Republican ticket. The next morning the battle was joined when Nixon responded to the charges in a

[3] Richard M. Nixon, *Six Crises* (Garden City, 1962), pp. 80–81.

whistle-stop speech in Marysville, California, characterizing them as a smear by Communists and crooks.[4]

This puerile exchange might have been muffled in the campaign cacophony had not the Republicans been touchy on matters ethical. They had pinned their election hopes on a "crusade to clean up the corruption mess in Washington." Hence, they felt themselves being hoisted on their own petard as the charges against Nixon spread and as several prominent newspapers began to give editorial support to the proposal that Nixon be dropped from the ticket. Should they retain Nixon the "crusade" might take on the shabby appearance of a huckstering attempt to horn in on the proceeds of corruption. But dropping him would imply a plea of "no contest" on the corruption charge and would open them to scorn for having nominated a rook. In either event they would forfeit the corruption issue. The Republicans chose to skirt these painful alternatives and to throw the question of Nixon's future open to a national plebiscite—they purchased a half hour of national broadcast time and instructed Nixon to clear himself of the charges with the electorate.[5]

Nixon three-part speech: denying charge: explaining finances; attacking opposition

Thus it was that on September 23, a bare five days after the charges were leveled, Richard Nixon addressed in his own defense the largest television audience to that time, sixty million people. The speech had three sections: a denial of unethical conduct in maintaining a campaign fund, a revelation of Nixon's personal financial history, and a partisan counterattack on the ethical qualifications of the Democrats' nominees. The response to the speech was immediate and fantastic: the public was virtually unanimous in its support of Nixon. Within hours the Republican panic had turned to glee; the "crusade" issue was more vital than ever, and Democrat Stevenson was straining to account for his own personal campaign fund. With a single speech Richard Nixon had won a decisive initiative for his party.[6]

Ex-President Harry S. Truman's ordeal smacked somewhat less of Armageddon and more of a joust; and the outcome was for several reasons less distinct than in Nixon's case. On November 6, 1953, Republican Attorney General Brownell charged in a Chicago speech (some claimed it was a smokescreen to draw attention away from recent Republican

[4] Nixon, pp. 83–84; *New York Times,* September 20, 1952, p. 9.

[5] Nixon, pp. 95–112.

[6] Nixon, p. 118; A. Hillbruner, *Critical Dimensions: The Art of Public Address Criticism* (New York, 1966), p. 60.

congressional election losses) that one Harry Dexter White, an alleged Communist spy now dead, had been promoted to a sensitive position with the International Monetary Fund during the Truman administration despite knowledge of his spying activities by "those who appointed him."[7] Truman at first denied ever having seen such reports on White. In the verbal sparring of the next few days both parties hedged. As bits of evidence came to public attention, Truman acknowledged that an unfavorable report had been received concerning White but claimed that at the proper time he had "fired" White. Later Truman shifted again to claim that he had "forced White's resignation." For his part, Brownell watered his accusation to one of "laxity" by the Truman administration in meeting Communist infiltration.

The immediate stimulus for Truman's national broadcast was a subpoena served on November 10 by Representative H. H. Velde (Illinois Republican) directing Truman to testify before the House Un-American Activities Committee regarding the White controversy.[8] Truman rejected the subpoena as his "duty under the Constitution" and chose instead to make his broadcast to fifty million people on Monday, November 16.

Like Nixon, Truman divided his remarks into three parts. He explained his refusal to testify before the H.U.A.C., justified his handling of Harry Dexter White's promotion, and attacked Brownell for having raised the issue. There were no immediate political stakes in the Brownell-Truman clash, so reaction to the speech was undramatic. In the ensuing week F.B.I. Director J. Edgar Hoover's testimony before the Senate Internal Security Committee cast some doubt on the interpretations Truman had offered in his speech. But, by November 18, Eisenhower signalled an end to the confrontation when he expressed hope that the whole issue concerning Communist internal subversion would be history by 1954. Within a week public interest had waned as congressional investigators turned from the White case to other allegations of espionage. Editorials tended to scold both Brownell and Truman for intemperate statements; then most newspapers dropped the matter. In retrospect Truman's can be considered a qualified

Truman's three sections: explaining no testimony; justifying his actions; attacking opposition

---

[7] *New York Times,* November 7, 1953, p. 1.

[8] Velde apparently acted in a fit of enthusiasm without consulting Republican congressional leaders. In any event the main effect of the subpoena, besides giving Truman an excuse to mount a national forum, was to embarrass the Eisenhower administration. During his November 11 press conference, President Eisenhower noted in typical fashion that he "personally wouldn't have issued a summons" to an ex-President. Cf. *New York Times,* November 12, p. 14.

victory. Though not as conclusive in its effects as Nixon's, his speech served to clear him of the main accusations and ended public interest in the circumstances of White's advancement.

These sketches of the two controversies provide sufficient background to enable the reader to consider the rhetorical context from which the two speeches grew.

both spoke to virtually the same audience

A prime resemblance between the two speaking situations can be found in the expectations of the two national broadcast audiences. The period 1952–1953 was not marked by any striking shifts in American public opinion on major political issues,[9] and virtually the same individuals comprised the bulk of the two audiences.

rhetorical reputations similar

The reputations of the two speakers were also such that the public would probably expect much the same rhetorical posture of each. With careers punctuated by flamboyant partisan utterance, there was little hint in the political biographies of Nixon and Truman that either was disposed to seek bipartisan consensus of the sort made popular by Dwight Eisenhower or Lyndon Johnson. Each stood in the public mind as a partisan "slugger," a staunch, uncompromising combatant for his party. As often as not it had been Truman's and Nixon's public remarks that had caused each to perform in the limelight of controversy. Richard Nixon was blessed with a kind of notoriety for pugnacious campaign tactics and for his role in the Alger Hiss investigations. "Irascible" is perhaps the most apt description of Harry Truman's prior public address. It was not without reason that the rallying cry of his 1948 presidential campaign had been, "Give 'em Hell, Harry!" And a public which remembered Mr. Truman's threat to punch the nose of a music critic who had panned daughter Margaret's singing would presumably expect the ex-President to deliver some pungent remarks in any address of self-defense.

overall rhetorical strategy the same

Subjected to a personal attack centering on charges of past misconduct in public office, each speaker was placed in a Demosthenic posture; he must go before the citizenry to clear himself of accusations leveled by political assailants. The appropriate argumentative strategy was clearly forensic. The listeners could expect arguments of accusation and defense relating primarily to the interpretation of past facts. To this extent one may say each speaker was propelled by the logic of his situation toward the same, overall rhetorical strategy.

[9] Cf. N.O.R.C. public opinion surveys 312, 315, 329, 334, 339, 348 for the period 1951–1953 (The Roper Public Opinion Research Center, Williamstown, Mass.); A. O. Hero, Jr., "The American Public and the United Nations, 1954–1966," *The Journal of Conflict Resolution,* X (December 1966), 436–475.

Though it was common practice in ancient Greece for the accused to speak directly to his judges, the use of electronic media for such a purpose was unorthodox in mid-century America. By their decisions to by-pass the customary medium of contemporary public dialog, the press, and to go instead directly to the people, Nixon and Truman tell us something about the intense character of their situations. Their choice may have been in part simply a symptom of things to come; we appear to rely more and more on the air waves for our contact with current affairs. But one cannot escape the feeling that in these two instances the central figures found the struggle so intense (if not climactic) that they felt it necessary to avoid the inevitable distortion of messages which results from the intervention of the newsprint channel.[10] At any rate, they chose to risk the outcome of their battles on single national broadcasts.

In retrospect a fourth similarity of context becomes apparent: both conflicts were short, sharp, and quickly resolved. The Nixon debate lasted from September 18 to September 24, the day Eisenhower announced that Nixon was vindicated. The Harry Dexter White affair merited headlines from November 7 to November 19. [11]

Finally, the broadcasts were in each case watersheds in the controversies. Nixon's speech caused the collapse of sniping at his campaign funds; Truman's speech was the last public mention of the possibility that a congressional committee might subpoena an ex-President. In view of their importance in each conflict, it is especially remarkable how brief the speeches were. Truman spoke for twenty-three minutes and Nixon's speech ran just under a half hour. One is reminded by contrast of the protracted, even leisurely paced, nineteenth-century oratorical struggles. These modern clashes seem abrupt in any such comparison.

> both speeches successful in ending the public controversies

> both speeches brief

We cannot with assurance attribute the differences between contemporary and former controversies either to qualities inherent in current issues or to the development of electronic media. The cost of air time limits the length of

[10] C. E. Swanson, J. Jenkins, and R. L. Jones, "President Truman Speaks: A Study of Ideas vs. Media," *Journalism Quarterly,* XXVII (Summer 1950), 251–262; J. Ericson, "The Reporting by the Prestige Press of Selected Speeches of Senator Goldwater in the 1964 Presidential Campaign," unpubl. diss. (University of Wisconsin, 1966).

[11] Although reverberations were felt afterward in connection with other congressional investigations, it is fair to say that Truman's role in it was a scant two weeks.

speeches, but it does not prevent continuance of debate by other means. But we can say that the contextual factors here mentioned—a forensic issue, use of broadcast facilities to carry a case directly to the public, relatively limited exposure time, and the sharp, decisive quality of the encounter—seem not coincidentally present in the two cases we are examining. If we as yet have no basis for determining which of the factors were antecedent and which were consequent, which were essential and which accidental, we can at least hypothesize that other contemporary apologiae are likely to display the same combination of attributes. The two speeches under investigation asked national audiences of roughly the same backgrounds to decide the guilt or innocence of two colorful political spokesmen. In choosing to risk defense on a single short speech transmitted directly to the public, the two speakers revealed something of the urgency they must have attached to their acts. What then, may we expect when men of such stripe find it necessary to speak as advocates in their own behalves under circumstances such as these? For a tentative answer we may turn to the messages actually presented by Nixon and Truman.

forensic arguments of motive and fact in Nixon denial

Both speeches adhered to classic forensic strategies, and both displayed martial overtones. In his denial of the charges, Nixon resorted to arguments of motive and fact (*quale sit* and *an sit*). At the outset he asserted that the appropriate standard for judging his acceptance of campaign contributions must be purity of motive:

> I say that it was morally wrong—if any of that $18,000 went to Senator Nixon, for my personal use. I say that it was morally wrong if it was secretly given and secretly handled.[12]

Having demonstrated that these moral precepts were not violated in his use of the funds, Nixon proceeded to a factual iteration of personal financial affairs. These considerations ranged from his need to work in the family grocery store as a boy through the current unpaid balance on his home mort-

---

[12] This and all following quotes from the Nixon speech are from an official speech transcript prepared by four National Broadcasting Company stenographers and printed in the *New York Times* of September 24, 1952, p. 22. The *Times* text was verified by comparison with a text appearing in *Vital Speeches of the Day*, XIX (October 15, 1952), 11–15. A variant text can be found in *U.S. News and World Report*, XXXIII (October 3, 1952), pp. 66–70. For a discussion of the problem of textual authenticity see E. G. Bormann, *Theory and Research in the Communicative Arts* (New York, 1965), 173–191.

gage. The point of the narrative was clear: there was no evidence of campaign funds diverted to personal use. Nixon denied the accusation with facts.

For Harry Truman, argument by fact was not an option. The public already had reason to believe that at the time he was promoted Harry Dexter White was at least suspected by authorities of subversive activities. Truman employed forensic arguments of motive and value (*quale sit* and *quid sit*) in his defense. He contended that White's promotion was engineered so as to minimize the security risk while at the same time keeping secret an ongoing F.B.I. investigation of subversion. Hence, the motives for Truman's past acts were honorable. He justified his refusal to appear before Representative Velde's committee by appealing to a higher value—such an appearance would represent a threat to the constitutional separation of the three branches of government because it would subject past executive decisions to Congressional review. Implicit in Truman's argument was the premise that constitutional prerogatives take precedence over investigations of national security breaches.

forensic arguments of motive and value in Truman defense

Forensic strategy normally entails accusation as well as defense. Whether from habit or because they perceived that their situations demanded such tactics, both Nixon and Truman chose invective as their mode of attack. It seems more than coincidental that their speeches abound in *ad hominem* innuendoes concerning the moral qualities of their accusers, that in each case roughly the last third of the speech is almost entirely devoted to this kind of forensic offensive.

ad hominem innuendoes in both attacks

According to Truman, the Eisenhower administration was guilty of "shameful demagoguery"; Mr. Brownell degraded his office by engaging in political trickery and skullduggery, by lying to the American people, by smearing a defenseless and patriotic American (Chief Justice Fred Vinson, now dead), and by displaying "mealy-mouthed" cowardice. Truman also drew a red herring across the issue when he slipped in a reference to Senator Joseph McCarthy:

> It is now evident that the present administration has fully embraced, for political advantage, McCarthyism. I'm not referring to the senator from Wisconsin—he's only important in that his name has taken on a dictionary meaning in the world. And that meaning is the corruption of truth, the abandonment of our historical devotion to fair play. It is the abandonment of the "due process" of law. It is the use of the big lie and the unfounded accusation against any citizen in the name of Ameri-

canism and security. It is the rise to power of the dema-
gogue. . . .[13]

The excerpt intrigues. Was Truman accusing the administration of merely aping McCarthy, or was he suggesting that
McCarthy exerted a substantial influence in the government?
His meaning was conveniently vague. What stands out in
Truman's attack is that it is unanswerable, for it substitutes
name-calling for an assessment of motive. Brownell, for instance, could only reply to the charge of being mealy-mouthed
by hurling a more insulting label at Truman; it was here, as
always, futile to treat such an accusation as a "charge" in
the traditional, legal sense.

Although not as explicit, Richard Nixon proved more adept
than Truman in his use of innuendo. The ex-President pinned
the label "liar" on Brownell outright; candidate Nixon was
content with a telling side-swipe at his opposition. Twice, as
if in tossing it off in passing, Nixon reminded the public
that his Democratic counterpart, vice-presidential candidate
Sparkman, had his wife on the Senate payroll. Nixon in both
instances hastened (almost too quickly, one might feel)[14] to
add, "I don't condemn him for that," "that's his business."
The critic detects the swish of a matador's cape here. Nixon's
nobility ("I'm for fair play") is deftly juxtaposed to the crass
conduct of Sparkman. Nixon doesn't plunge the sword—he is
content to draw blood. Standing aside, as it were, Nixon left
the audience to judge who was in fact honorable in the use
of Senate funds, but by means of the sharp contrast the auditor was offered only one option.

This distinctive habit of juxtaposing black and white dis-

[13]The Truman text is from the transcript in the November 17, 1953 *New York
Times,* p. 26. Variant texts can be found in *U.S. News and World Report,* XXXV
(November 27, 1953), 104–106 and the *Kansas City Times,* November 17, 1953,
pp. 1–2. The *New York Times* version gives internal evidence of being the most
accurate account of what Truman actually said except for its omission of the
bracketed words in the following sentence (spoken in reference to the late Chief
Justice Vinson): "But I deeply resent these cowardly in [sinuations against one
who is] dead." Philip C. Brooks, Director of the Harry S Truman Library of Independence, Missouri, agrees that the selected text is the most accurate one available (there being no reading copy of the text); but in a personal letter he refers
to the *New York Times* version as a "press release text," thus casting doubt on
its accuracy. Since no tape recording seems to exist, close stylistic analysis which
would demand the exact words uttered by Truman on the occasion has not been
attempted. See J. Thorp, "The Aesthetics of Textual Criticism," *PLMA,* LXXX
(December 1965), 465–482; R. W. Smith, "The 'Second' Inaugural Address of
Lyndon Baines Johnson: A Definitive Text," *SM,* XXXIV (March 1967), 102–108.

[14]Nixon documents his deliberate intent in his book. See *Six Crises,* p. 118.

tinguished Nixon's acrid invective from Truman's forthright smears. Consider the following passages:

> . . . I love my country. And I think my country is in danger. And I think that the only man that can save America at this time is the man that's running for President on my ticket, Dwight Eisenhower. You say, why do I think it's in danger? And I say, look at the record. Seven years of the Truman-Acheson Administration and what's happened? Six hundred million people lost to the Communists, and a war in Korea in which we have lost 117,000 American casualties.

> * * *

> You wouldn't trust a man who made the mess to clean it up. That's Truman. And . . . you can't trust the man who was picked by the man who made the mess to clean it up, and that's Stevenson.
> And so I say, Eisenhower, who owes nothing to Truman, nothing to the big-city bosses—he is the man that can clean up the mess in Washington.

> * * *

> I'm going to campaign up and down America until we drive the crooks and the Communists and those that defend them out of Washington, and remember, folks, Eisenhower is a great man. Believe me, he's a great man, and a vote for Eisenhower is a vote for what's good for America.

What is striking is Nixon's habit of joining off-handed insults of the opposition with knight-in-shining-armor depictions of him and his. By this uneasy combination of dropped lines and stereotypes a Nixon insult was made at once more provocative—and more suspect—than the ingenuous efforts of Mr. Truman. For listeners there was the satisfaction of discerning the *act* of attack often tinged, one may believe, with distaste at being told so bluntly and sweepingly that untarnished good imbued Republicans and unrelieved corruption permeated the Democratic Party.

In addition to common forensic strategies and *ad hominem* ploys, a third general similarity characterized the two speeches: the manner in which documentation was employed to support arguments. Had this been an oratorical contest between Nixon and Truman, one might be tempted to ask which speaker displayed the better looking set of facts. Nixon's speech is of course best remembered for the section which began:

documentation only in the middle of both speeches

> And I'd like to tell you this evening that just about an hour ago we received an independent audit of this entire fund . . . and I have that audit here in my hand. . . .

The section ended with the famous anecdote which caused the speech to receive the popular title "the Checkers Speech": the story of how Nixon had accepted only one personal gift while in public office—the cocker spaniel, Checkers.[15] The section occupied the entire middle third of the address and contained all of the documentation used in the speech.

Is it only coincidental that all of Harry Truman's documentation, such as it was, was also located in the middle third of his speech? Truman did not have any records in his hands. Instead he announced his presentation of inartistic data in this way:

> I have had my files examined and have consulted with some of my colleagues who worked with me on this matter during my term of office.

Truman then "reported" his findings as a narration interwoven with interpretation; his evidence tended to uphold the assertion that his decisions were the most expedient under the circumstances. He ended his narration with the death of White in 1948, after White's appearance before H.U.A.C.

Why both speakers should lump all documentation in the middles of their speeches, and why both should assign the same relative space to presentation of evidence I am not sure. The simple enumeration of quasi-documentary data found in both cases might be taken as proof of the contention that ours is an age which puts its faith in facts rather than reason, and that contemporary rhetorical strategies often reflect that trust.[16] It is in any case somewhat beside the point for the critic to test by the traditional logical criteria the soundness of conclusions drawn from such selective, factual data as Nixon and Truman presented.

It seems clear that in one sense it was less important that the materials these speakers presented should provide absolute corroboration of their assertions than that the core of each case should contain a disclosure of new data. These data constituted artifacts; their presence lent an air of scientific

---

[15] Nixon admits that he planted this anecdote as another barb at the Democrats. The inspiration for the ploy was F.D.R.'s "Fala" speech during the 1944 presidential campaign. *Six Crises,* p. 103.

[16] Cf. W. S. Howell, "The Declaration of Independence and Eighteenth-Century Logic," *William and Mary Quarterly,* XVIII (October 1961), 463–484; R. Weaver, *The Ethics of Rhetoric* (Chicago, 1953); Dwight Macdonald, "A Critique of the Warren Report," *Esquire,* LXIII (March 1965), 59ff.

proof (note the actuarial tone of Nixon's revelations) which could serve an important rhetorical end in and of itself. Professor Baskerville has argued that Senator Joseph McCarthy relied on an illusion of scientific proof to gain belief.[17] I suggest that if we leave aside matters of inferential soundness we can detect both Nixon and Truman benefitting from public acceptance of confirmation-by-a-heap-of-new-information.[18] And this interpretation gains plausibility when one recalls that the "charges" being answered alleged the *existence* of a fund and the motive of an act.

One final resemblance between the two apologiae is related to the use of documentation. Aside from the "good looking" new data presented, there were, strictly speaking, no new arguments in either speech. All the key ideas, and even the insults, can be found scattered in public statements made by the two speakers in the weeks prior to their television addresses. As early as September 19, for example, Nixon was claiming that the charges against him were a "smear by Communists and crooks" intended to make him relent in his campaign. On that same day Nixon also made references to Mrs. Sparkman's drawing a Senate salary.[19]

no new arguments in either speech

The finding that major speeches grew out of series of minor speeches, that the act of rhetorical invention was in fact an act of *selection* from previously used ideas is not unusual in rhetorical criticism. Studies of the major speeches of Grady, Bryan, Martin Luther King, and many others reveal the same thing: the oratorical masterpiece delivered at a crucial juncture in history reveals the orator not so much rising to heights of inspiration as choosing judiciously from a repertory of past ideas an appropriate mix of materials.[20] If our small sample is at all typical, the speech in the moment of crisis is most likely to represent a climax, a summing up, of those rhetorical

[17] B. Baskerville, "The Illusion of Proof," *Western Speech,* XXV (Fall 1961), 236–242.

[18] This "faith in the fact" hearkens back in the American rhetorical tradition at least as early as the age of Muckraker journalism. Cf. D. M. Chalmers, *The Social and Political Ideas of the Muckrakers* (New York, 1964); G. Ashenbrenner, "The Rhetoric of the Muckrakers," unpubl. thesis (University of Wisconsin, 1967).

[19] *New York Times,* September 20, 1952, p. 9.

[20] Cf. Baskerville, *Q.J.S.,* p. 407; T. D. Harrison, "The 'New South' Revisited," paper presented at "debut" session of S.A.A. National Convention, December, 1965; D. H. Smith, "Martin Luther King, Jr., Rhetorician of Revolt," unpubl. diss. (University of Wisconsin, 1964); R. T. Oliver, *History of Public Speaking in America* (Boston, 1965), pp. 484–485.

thrusts which seem to have been most effective with the public on previous dry runs.[21]

In the speeches under examination here, two possible implications seem to follow from the similar inventive processes. One is that under conditions of contemporary American public address little fresh adaptation of *content* is to be expected in a climactic message. Whether Nixon or Truman spoke to a whistle-stop crowd in Idaho, a group of reporters, or a national audience, the substance of the speaker's remarks remained the same. In either case adaptation was from the outset constantly directed to the American public as a whole rather than to the immediate audience.

The central place scholars have accorded speakers' adaptation of arguments to *specific* audiences may be somewhat less justified in explaining the characteristics of television apologiae than we might at first think. Indeed, the only original element in either of the speeches examined here was the inclusion of new facts. Disclosure of new information may be more significant as a rhetorical phenomenon in discourse prepared for a mass audience than are specific tactics of adaptation to the immediate audience.

To the extent that this implication holds, it suggests another. What distinguished Nixon's television apologia from Nixon's remarks to the press during the week prior to his speech was not the substance but the form. The *manner* in which Nixon chose to array for a national audience the ploys he had by trial and error found successful on more limited platforms cannot alone account for the potentialities of his broadcast address. The elements of rhetorical artistry unique to apologiae will be better seen if we turn from consideration of overall strategies to individual differences Nixon and Truman manifested in their tactics of array and emphasis.

three fundamental differences in the two speeches

Close reading confirms that there were indeed fundamental differences in the fabrics of the two speeches. Three formal qualities become prominent when one undertakes to depict the artistic genius of each discourse: the inferential patterns, the foci of attack, and the relative emphases on

[21] The critic may, if he chooses, examine the process whereby Nixon and Truman "discovered" the materials they eventually used—but only if he reckons with the clusters of earlier minor statements made by both men. In limiting the scope of the critical study to the television addresses themselves, the rhetorical critic must perforce adjust his notion of invention to one which emphasizes the means each speaker employed in selecting materials already available rather than broadening the concept of invention to include research procedures the speaker may originally have used.

public or personal affairs. These three elements seem to set Nixon apart from Truman as an apologist.

The first impression one draws on comparing the two speeches is that where Truman's message displays a kind of dynamic, structural progression, Nixon's is hortatory and reminds one of stone blocks cemented into an edifice. The instrument of Truman's kinetic coloration seems to be his tendency to fuse acceptable (from the point of view of the audience) universal principles and conditional propositions into short, direct, enthymematic inferences. In the following passage the first two sentences form the theoretical ground from which Truman, in the third sentence, drew the consequence. Let us assume that most auditors accepted the principle of maintaining the independence of the executive branch of government. By articulating that principle, Truman prepared them to accept the truth of his fourth and fifth sentences which extended the principle to cover his behavior as chief executive.

Truman's dynamic, structural progression of arguments

> The separation and balance of powers between the three independent branches of government is fundamental in our constitutional form of government. A congressional committee may not compel the attendance of a President of the United States, while he is in office, to inquire into matters pertaining to the performance of his official duties. If the constitutional principle were otherwise, the office of the president would not be independent. It is just as important to the independence of the executive that the actions of the President should not be subjected to questioning by the Congress after he has completed his term of office as that they should not be questioned while he is serving as President. In either case, the office of President would be dominated by Congress, and the Presidency might become a mere appendage of Congress.

There is a logical gap between premise and conclusion, but if we accept the notion of enthymematic inference it is not difficult to imagine that an auditor who fully granted the explicit major premise would be prepared to fill in for himself the implicit minor premise. Truman's "if" statement thus serves in this instance to intensify adherence to the basic principle and to prepare hearers to make the necessary logical leap.

A like inferential movement occurred in a section where Truman justified his disposal of the White case.

> But following receipt of the F.B.I. report and the consultations with members of my cabinet, it was decided that he would be limited to membership on the board of directors of the International Monetary Fund. With his duties thus restricted,

he would be subject to the supervision of the Secretary of the Treasury, and his position would be less important and much less sensitive—if it were sensitive at all—than the position then held by him as Assistant Secretary of the Treasury.

Tonight I want the American people to understand that the course we took protected the public interest and security and at the same time permitted the intensive F.B.I. investigation then in progress to go forward. No other course could have served both of these purposes.

Truman asked the audience to look to the consequences of his alternatives; he asked them to grant the worth of his dual objectives, and he devoted his verbal effort to convincing them (by mention of the F.B.I. report and cabinet consultations and by showing how the Secretary of the Treasury could better control White's activities) that the chosen policy was the most expedient.

Nixon organized by question and answer

It is no insult to Nixon to observe that his disposition suggests that of a catechism: he puts the question he wants the audience to consider and then he speaks to the question as if reading from a trial brief.

But then, some of you will say, and rightly, "Well, what did you use the fund for, Senator? Why did you have to have it?"

Let me tell you in just a word how a Senate office operates. . . .

* * *

But then the question arises, you say, "Well, how do you pay for these and how can you do it legally?"

And there are several ways that it can be done, incidentally, and it is done legally in the United States Senate and in the Congress. The first way is to be a rich man. I don't happen to be a rich man, so I couldn't use that.

And now I'm going to suggest some courses of conduct.

First of all, you have read in the papers about other funds, now. Mr. Stevenson apparently had a couple. . . .

These excerpts not only represent juncture points in Nixon's speech—they are also frames which shape the arguments. Given such overpowering lead-ins there is little room for an auditor's imagination to function. His mind remains riveted as the argument unfolds. Viewed as a performance-in-time, the inferences are pre-determined by the transitions, and the discourse stubbornly resists efforts by an auditor to participate independently in the communicative act. There are undoubted merits in such structure; but the organization does not permit enthymematic reasoning as did Truman's. It was perhaps this catechetical feature of Nixon's recital which lent that "harsh and boney" quality of pre-packaged argument, not fully digested by the speaker, which some respondents discerned in his address.

Opponents were for both men objects of scorn, but Nixon and Truman differed in the breadth with which they defined the enemy camp. For Truman the "enemy" was a single man—Herbert Brownell. At times, as in the opening words of the speech, he depicted Brownell as a tool of the administration, but for the most part his invective sought out Brownell alone.

primary source of Truman's attack was one person

> There can't be any doubt that Mr. Brownell was talking about me. Now let me talk about Mr. Brownell and this phony charge he has made.
> His charge is false, and Mr. Brownell must have known it was false at the very time he was making it.
> Mr. Brownell has made a great show of detail. . . . As Mr. Brownell should have learned by this time. . . .
>
>   *   *   *
>
> There is one aspect of this affair that should be clear to everyone. That is the obvious political motivations of this attack on me.
> In the launching of this attack on me, the Republican attorney general worked hand in glove with the Republican National Committee. The manner and the timing of what has been done made it perfectly clear that the powers of the attorney general have been prostituted for hopes of political gain.

In all cases Truman's tactic was to *accuse* Brownell, thus using consistently an overall forensic strategy. The cumulative impact of Truman's strategy would leave one who took the ex-President's words at face value with the feeling that the confrontation was between Truman and Brownell alone. Both the partial and the neutral auditor were given grounds for believing that Brownell unjustly maligned Mr. Truman. The entire force of Truman's argument was thus channeled to turn the attack back upon his accuser.

The clear focus of Truman's invective can be seen from these figures: of 15 accusatory references in the speech, 7 concern Brownell's personal behavior (he lied, fooled the public, is the source of malicious charges); 3 accuse Brownell of cheapening his office; 4 charge that the administration used Brownell as its tool in this affair; 1 places Brownell in conspiracy with the Republican National Committee. Again, where Truman stated the charges against him, he invariably coupled those statements with countercharges that Brownell lied in his accusation. Had he not been so consciously mounting an offensive against Brownell, Truman might have contented himself at those points with a simple denial of the charges, but roughly 45 percent of the Truman speech concentrated on the "sordid" role of Brownell. This is gross evidence of the sharp focus of Truman's invective.

sources of Nixon's attack were everywhere

The characteristics of Truman's attack are the more noteworthy because of the comparative diffusiveness of Nixon's invective. Where Truman carefully leveled his sights on a particular object of scorn, Nixon must appear to all but his most devoted listeners to be lashing out at a penumbral host of spectres. Consider the swath cut by the following excerpts.

> My fellow Americans: I come before you tonight as a candidate . . . and as a man whose honesty and integrity has been questioned.

By whom? Nixon never makes clear who is accusing him.

> I am sure that you have read the charge, and you've heard it. . . .

Again there is no recognition of a particular source for the charge.

> And the record will show that [he had not exerted influence on behalf of fund contributors] the records which are in the hands of the Administration.

Is the source of the charges somehow in league with the Administration?"

> . . . and let me say that I recognize that some will continue to smear, regardless of what the truth may be. . . .

Here again, the sources of attack are everywhere; perhaps reasonably, Nixon seemed to see himself in a state of siege. Yet, however justified such a belief may have been, its expression could not contribute to a well-focused counterattack.

> One other thing I probably should tell you, because if I don't they'll probably be saying this about me too. . . . [Nixon here employs the "Checkers" gambit.] And, you know, the kids love the dog, and I just want to say this, right now, that regardless of what they say about it, we're gonna keep it.
>
>   *   *   *
>
> . . . I remember, in the dark days of the Hiss case, some of the same columnists, some of the same radio commentators

who are attacking me now and misrepresenting my position, were violently opposing me at the time I was after Alger Hiss.

Is the squabble between Nixon and the press? Or is it the case that the unnamed columnists are joining forces with other sinister agents to destroy Nixon? No listener could tell *from the discourse,* for the last excerpt is as close as Nixon came to identifying his attackers.

Failure to name accusers would not be significant (it probably has certain redeeming features) were it not that a concomitant limitation must thereby be placed upon the impact of an apologia. Nixon could not thus control the vector of his counterattack as precisely as Truman. Hence the tone of Nixon's reply tended toward the petulant, as though the man were lashing out at unknown conspirators seeking to victimize him. A rough classification of approximately 20 attack-statements in Nixon's speech shows that one-third were references to unspecified opponents, another third were scattered digs at Mr. Sparkman, the State Department, Mr. Stevenson, etc., and the final third were epideictic magnifications of corruption in the Truman administration. There was, in short, no concerted effort on Nixon's part either to isolate the source of the accusations or to provide the audience an explanation for such attacks.

It may be objected that Nixon's two-fold goal of clearing himself and scoring election points would force him to employ this particular pattern in invective. But the pattern, it turns out, is a Nixon pattern, not one peculiar to the situation. As befits a campaigner, Nixon showed greater concern with the faults of his political opposition in 1952 than with the source and nature of accusations against him. But the consequences of this unfocused invective appear to have stretched beyond the political contest of 1952. Some years later Nixon was to refer to this apologia as the event which made possible his election as vice president and at the same time denied him the presidency in 1960.[22] It may be that the reputation for immaturity which attached itself to Nixon had its origins in the undisciplined, unfocused attacks found in this speech.

A third notable difference also distinguishes the two speeches. The tone of the public man doing public business pervades the Truman address, whereas Nixon offers a revelation of the personal morality of a private man. This difference in tone grew in part out of the exigencies of each speaker's

tone of the two speeches different

[22] Nixon, *Six Crises,* pp. 125–129.

self-defense; however, both men spoke as public officials, so the contrast may also be taken as in some degree an index to the habitual rhetorical postures of the men.

Truman's tone: a public man doing public business

As Harry Truman dealt with it, Brownell's accusation concerned the conduct of a public official in the execution of his office; the official happened to be named Truman.

> When I became President, I took an oath to preserve, protect and defend the Constitution of the United States. I am still bound by that oath and will be as long as I live. While I was in office, I lived up to that oath. . . . Now that I have laid down the heavy burdens of that office, I do not propose to take any step which would violate that oath or which would in any way lead to encroachments on the independence of that great office.

Was Truman using the office to shield himself from public scrutiny? Let us grant that he was not, that he was sincere in perceiving the demand that he testify as a genuine threat to the independence of chief executives. Corroboration for this interpretation is provided by Truman's other references to himself. Virtually all of the new data he provided, for example, were designed to show the calculated wisdom of the policy he eventually chose to follow. His mentions of himself served chiefly to enliven and personalize the image of an official struggling to arrive at a rational course of action. In the two instances where he mentioned himself as a person, it was to diminish his personal significance and to place the issue in the larger perspective of public affairs.

> First, I would like to tell you, the people of America, why I declined to appear before that committee. On the surface, it might seem to be an easy thing to do, and smart politics, for Harry Truman, now a private citizen of Independence, Missouri, to use the committee as a forum to answer the scurrilous charges which have been made against me. Many people urged me to do that. It was an attractive suggestion and appealed to me.
>
> But if I had done it, I would have been a party with the committee to an action which would have undermined the constitutional position of the office of President of the United States.
>
>   *   *   *
>
> If this were a matter which merely involved the name and reputation of Harry S. Truman, private citizen of Independence, Missouri, I would not be as concerned as I am. I can take care of myself. I believe that the American people know me well enough from my service as captain of Battery D in World War I to my service as President of the United States to know that

I have always acted with the best interests of my country at heart.

But Mr. Brownell knows that, in this matter, when the final decision was mine, I relied on my principal advisers. . . .

There is one aspect of this affair that should be clear to everyone. That is the obvious political motivations of this attack on me.

Clearly, Truman preferred the *persona* of the office, and he allowed it to slip for only the briefest, most stereotyped glimpses of the real man behind the mask.

Almost the reverse was the case with Richard Nixon. Let us grant to him, too, the sincerity of his utterance. It still remains that his self-references all highlight the human creature, Dick Nixon, not the United States Senator, a public figure seeking election to another office:

Nixon's tone: sketching one man's personal life

It was not a secret fund. As a matter of fact, when I was on "Meet the Press"—some of you may have seen it, last Sunday—Peter Edson came up to me, after the program, and he said, "Dick, what about this fund we hear about?" And I said. . . .

Nixon *could* have generalized his argument to a discussion of the dilemma faced by the public official who must avoid temptations to corruption even as he seeks campaign contributions. He began on this course when he briefly considered the difficulty of running a Senator's office on the meager funds allotted by Congress.[23] But in the main he chose to present an autobiographical recitation of The Life and Hard Times of Young Dick Nixon.

The baring of one's finances (Nixon called it baring his soul) is not lightly undertaken in our commercial society; it surely requires some self-sacrifice. Its spectacular quality leads one to wonder whether it was rhetorically essential to Nixon's apologia or whether it offers a special kind of reading on the speaker. A few, but only a few, public figures publicly report the full details of their finances. My own inclination is to believe that the prominence of creature-Nixon in this discourse served dual ends. It would seem unlikely, for instance, that a struggling young couple renting an eighty-dollar-a-month apartment in Fairfax, Virginia could be benefitting from graft. The material presented is persuasive, even for the doubter; and it is touching. But at the same time the informa-

[23] Professor Baskerville argues in the *Q.J.S.* symposium that Nixon *ought* to have taken this tack. I would not go so far, but would simply point out the ultimate rhetorical consequences of the path Nixon chose to follow.

tion offered is not entirely relevant, for it fails to address itself to the issue: "Was there a misuse of campaign funds?" Nixon had already treated that issue in his denial of dishonesty, in his description of the needs of a modern Senate office, and in his report of the audit. The impression remains that Nixon was more ready to display his personal self than is common among civic men.

This same impression is further confirmed when we notice that the homey tone pervaded Nixon's speech as thoroughly as the public tone colored Truman's address. In both cases there was, for example, the matter of justification for conduct. Nixon explained that he could have put his wife on his Senate payroll, as Sparkman had done:

> . . . but I have never done that for this reason: I have found that there are so many deserving stenographers and secretaries in Washington that need the work that I just didn't feel it was right to put my wife on the payroll.

Or consider Nixon's explanation of why he intended to continue to fight the smears:

> Because, you see, I love my country. And I think my country is in danger.

Nixon, it appears, persistently, as though habitually, accounted for his public behavior by reference to his personal sentiments. It seems reasonable to suggest that Harry Truman would probably have sought other, equally effective justifications and proofs had he been in Nixon's place. At any rate, his apologia was far less creature-centered than Nixon's.

It may be that this distinction between the image of a public figure and that of the private man accounts for the observer's subjective impression that Harry Truman's message all adds up to a public warning while Richard Nixon's message amounts to an extended claim: "They're out to get me." And this difference in the core of the messages may provide an additional clue as to why the "Checkers" speech, so effective with the immediate audience, could another day function as a barrier to Nixon's presidential ambitions.

The Nixon plea sacrificed the mystique of the public man. It displayed him as a living, breathing citizen—perhaps too suggestive of Dagwood Bumstead. News commentator, Eric Sevaried, may have expressed the long-range public judgment aptly when he tried to explain the defeat of homey though honest and capable candidates for office:

> We say in a democracy that we like the ordinary man. But
> we don't like him that much.[24]

When Nixon spoke to 60,000,000 people of his desire to help
one deserving steno rather than hire his wife, even his loyal
followers must have wondered whether he expected to be
believed totally and literally. With whatever sincerity, Nixon
ensnared himself by his rhetorical choices: he portrayed himself as at least a touch too simple for a complex age and too
insensitive to the demands of a national, public occasion. It
seems even fair to say that not every listener's smirk was one
of superiority, but some were smirks of embarrassment.
Nixon's response to attack, though emotionally appealing, was
not fully appropriate to the public man, at least in this century.

Let us now extrapolate from the foregoing analysis those
characteristics which appear to shed light on the two
speeches under investigation. Conceivably, these features
may represent parameters which will define other apologiae
presented via the mass media.

There are four similarities in the two discourses which I
take, at this time, to represent constants in the apologetic
equation. Recognizing that these similarities may be accidental, may reflect some underlying kinship of the two speakers,
or may be genuine symptoms of the demands of the apologetic
form, we may tentatively hypothesize that the broadcast apologia is likely to be a part of a short, intense, decisive clash of
views. We may further predict that a speaker who chooses
to argue in his own defense over the airwaves is unlikely to
limit himself to defensive remarks. In all probability he will take
the opportunity to engage in some form of invective. We may
perhaps be more than ordinarily aware of the invective in these
two addresses because of the speakers' reputations; therefore, future criticism ought to study the extent to which invective is a staple of the genre. A heaping of data without careful
attention to their artistic use may or may not be unique to
modern apologetics, but the lumping of facts in the middle
third of both speeches seems more than coincidental. It may
be that either the circumstances surrounding broadcasting or
the forensic demands of apologiae exert particular influences
in these connections. Finally, the apologists' tendency to re-
assemble previously used agruments for presentation from the
national rostrum (as evidenced in the fact that these two
speeches are simple composites of earlier remarks) may hold

*comparison: similarities
may represent four
basics of apologetic
speaking*

[24]Eric Sevareid, Columbia Broadcasting System election returns program,
November 8, 1966.

implications both for our conception of rhetorical invention and for the critic's selection of facets for interpretation.

Whether or not the similarities we have just reviewed represent constants in the apologetic equation, we may regard as variables the dimensions of individual difference which were observed. Here emerged three ways by which speakers may put their personal imprints on messages: the manner in which the inferential pattern controls the form of the address, the degree to which the speaker channels his attack and thereby directs his listeners' aggression, and the ratio of public-personal explanations which becomes prominent in messages employing otherwise intimate electronic media.[25] There may of course be other factors influencing the character of modern broadcast apologiae, and we cannot discount the probability that as men gain experience in the use of electronic media the forms and styles of apologiae will change. Be that as it may, the elements of form and style amplified here deserve further study in apologiae and other genres of rhetorical discouse.

Finally, we are in a position to draw some conclusions concerning specific qualities of the two speeches here analyzed. First, it seems patently unfair to hold either Mr. Nixon or Mr. Truman in contempt, as many have, because either "injected personalities" into his remarks. Even granting the mercurial nature of the two speakers, there is a possibility that resort to invective is virtually inevitable given the unique configuration of forces operating upon the apologist. Secondly, if we wish to judge the logical validity or weight of evidence in either speech, we shall need to distinguish formal standards (which are often drawn from the courtroom) from the relativistic norms inherent in apologetics or in the age. To accuse Mr. Nixon of inadequate support for his contentions is to overlook the impact of his evidence on his audience. If accusations are to be mounted in this connection they are better directed to a society which contents itself with piles of evidence in place of rigorous argument.[26]

Lastly, while recognizing the unfairness of many journalistic criticisms of Richard Nixon, it does seem reasonable to contend that the most curious shortcoming of his "Checkers" speech, when compared with Truman's address, was its en-

[25] Cf. J. M. Ripley, "Television and Recreational Patterns," *Television Quarterly*, II (Spring 1963), 31–36; M. McLuhan, *Understanding Media: The Extensions of Man* (New York, 1965), pp. 297–337.

[26] On this matter of loose standards of assessment in a given society see Aristotle, *Rhetoric,* 1354a 15–24.

durance in the public mind, its capacity to outlast the demands of the occasion. Whereas Harry Truman's discourse was totally relevant to specific rhetorical objectives, Nixon in a single stroke demolished both the opposition's case and injured his own standing as a public man. "Checkers" resulted in immediate victory for the campaigner; yet its traces admittedly continue to plague the political figure.[27]

[27] Cf. E. Black, *Rhetorical Criticism* (New York, 1965), pp. 162–164.

SUGGESTED FURTHER READING

Borman, Ernest G., *Theory and Research in the Communicative Arts.* New York: Holt, Rinehart, Co. (1965), 173–191.

Brockriede, Wayne and Robert L. Scott, *Moments in the Rhetoric of the Cold War.* New York: Random House, Inc., 1970.

Haberman, Frederick W., ed., "The Election of 1952: A Symposium," *Quarterly Journal of Speech,* XXXVIII (December, 1952), 406–408.

Hillbruner, Anthony, *Critical Dimensions: The Art of Public Address Criticism.* New York: Random House Company, 1966.

Swanson, C. E. and J. Jenkins and R. L. Jones, "President Truman Speaks: A Study of Ideas vs. Media," *Journalism Quarterly,* XXVII (Summer, 1950), 251–262. (See footnote 10)

Thompson, Wayne N., "Contemporary Public Address: A Problem in Criticism," *Quarterly Journal of Speech,* XL (February, 1954), 24–30.

Wallace, Karl, "Rhetoric and Politics," *Southern States Speech Journal,* XX (Spring, 1955), 195–203.

White, Eugene and Clair R. Henderlider, "What Harry S. Truman Told Us About Speaking," *Quarterly Journal of Speech,* XL (February, 1954), 37–42.

The Rhetoric of Protest: Song, Speech, and Attitude Change

Stephen Kosokoff and Carl W. Carmichael

Are Pete Seeger, Joan Baez, and Bob Dylan rhetoricians? An often overlooked rhetorical medium, the protest song, is introduced in this study which investigates the potential persuasiveness of this form of social-action rhetoric.

INTRODUCTION

Largely steeped in Aristotelian tradition, rhetorical scholarship is primarily concerned with the study of all available means of communicative persuasion. Until recently, the study of these means had been limited to those appearing in either written or spoken form. The essay and the speech were considered the most significant sources for rhetorical study. Attention is now being directed at the rhetorical elements in other communicative media such as radio, television, motion pictures, and creative press and poetry.

One may now ask whether all rhetorical media have been explored. Some contemporary rhetoricians suggest such far-ranging studies as the rhetoric of the uniform, the barbed-wire fence, and the comic strip. Others may argue that these items, although containing rhetorical elements, are extreme and inappropriate subjects for study by rhetorical scholars. Nevertheless, there is one obvious medium of persuasion through oral communication that has been largely ignored by those who profess to study persuasion in all its forms. That medium is the song, particularly the song of protest.[1]

protest song often ignored as medium for rhetorical study

Note: [When the article first appeared in summer, 1970,] Mr. Kosokoff, formerly Kaye, (Ph.D., University of Oregon, 1966) [was] Assistant Professor of Speech at Portland State College, and Mr. Carmichael, (Ph.D., University of Iowa, 1965) [was] Associate Professor of Speech at University of Oregon.

[1] The formal study of the rhetoric of protest, including a consideration of protest songs, is becoming more popular as is seen in college courses with this emphasis at such schools as University of California at Davis, Portland State College, and University of Kansas.

BACKGROUND

Man has created songs to express every human emotion. Although most of these songs have been primarily expressive rather than persuasive, man has often written and sung songs with the conscious intent of persuading those who hear them. Here we have a virgin field for the rhetorical scholar.

Careful study of American history indicates that song has been an integral part of many of the events studied for their significant spoken or written rhetorical activity. Such songs served much more than an entertaining function; many were written and sung for one general purpose—to persuade.

The study of the rhetoric of political campaigns usually includes an examination of speechs, pamphlets, editorials, and slogans. The significant songs of those campaigns have been ignored. Beginning with the 1840 race of William Henry Harrison, and continuing at least through the 1948 Henry Wallace campaign, songs were thought of as powerful political propaganda tools.[2] Harrison's campaign literature included a songbook called *Log Cabin and Hard Cider Melodies* which contained material such as "Van Buren":

> Who rules us with an iron rod—
> Who moves at Satan's beck and nod—
> Who heeds not man, who heeds not God—
> VAN BUREN![3]

The 1948 Progressive party relied heavily on campaign songs, even to the extent of making use of professional songwriters. "Yip" Harburg, librettest for "Finian's Rainbow" and composer of "Buddy, Can You Spare A Dime," wrote the lyrics for "I've Got A Ballot":

> The Republicans they grieve me
> The Democrats deceive me
> But I've a brand new party, believe me
> As we go rolling up the vote
> Roll it up FOR WALLACE
> Roll it up FOR TAYLOR. . . .[4]

Other kinds of movements are also studied by rhetoricians. The rhetoric of civil rights, or Black militancy, involves study of the speaking of Martin Luther King or Stokely Carmichael but neglects evaluation of "We Shall Overcome" or

---

[2]Irwin Silber, *Election Songs of the United States* (New York: Folkways Records and Service Corporation, 1960).   [3]Silber.   [4]Silber.

"We Shall Not Be Moved."[5] In a consideration of the labor movement the speeches of Sam Gompers and Clarence Darrow are examined while labor songs are forgotten. In order to understand the persuasive tactics of emerging labor, attention must be given to songs of the Industrial Workers of the World such as "Rebel Girl" and "Solidarity Forever":

> Is there aught we hold in common with the greedy parasite
> Who would lash us into serfdom and would crush us with his might?
> Is there anything left for us but to organize and fight?
> For the Union makes us strong.[6]

The CIO made use of professional singers in its recruiting drives. The Almanac singers used Woody Guthrie's "Union Maid" at CIO rallies:

> There was once a union maid
> She was never afraid
> Of goons and ginks and company finks
> And the deputy sheriffs that made the raids.[7]

The peace movement was, and still is, a singing movement noted for songs designed to persuade society to abandon warfare. Great popularity has been achieved by some of these songs such as "Where Have All The Flowers Gone?", and "Strangest Dream":

> I dreamed I saw a mighty room,
> The room was full of men,
> And the paper they were signing said,
> They'd never fight again.[8]

That song has been an integral part of many political and protest movements is easily shown; that these songs were rhetorical works designed to persuade is also readily demon-

basic questions for understanding protest song rhetoric

---

[5] An interesting collection of contemporary freedom songs used by the Student Non-Violent Coordinating Committee is Guy and Candie Carawan (eds.), *We Shall Overcome* (New York: Oak Publications, 1963).

[6] Ralph Chaplin, "Solidarity Forever," *Songs of the Workers* The Little Red Song Book (Chicago: Industrial Workers of the World, 1956), p. 10.

[7] Woody Guthrie, "Union Maid," Waldemar Hille (ed.), *The People's Song Book* (New York: Sing Out, 1960), p. 70.

[8] Ed McCurdy, "Strangest Dream," Pete Seegar (ed.), *American Favorite Ballads* (New York: Oak Publications, 1961), p. 32. Words and music by Ed McCurdy. TRO—ⓒ Copyright 1950, 1951, and 1955 by Almanack Music, Inc., New York, N.Y. Used by permission.

strated.[9] However, one needs to go further than mere demonstration to have comprehensive understanding of this rhetorical medium. One question that naturally arises is whether or not there is available evidence suggesting that protest songs can be persuasive. If songs do effect attitude change, how do they compare with speeches in persuasive intensity? Since protest songs are usually performed in conjunction with speeches, how does a song-speech combination compare with a solo song or speech in effectiveness? These questions form the basis for an experiment that was designed to test the following hypotheses:

(1) Protest songs will produce significant attitude change toward concepts in the direction advocated.

(2) Protest speeches, directly adapted from the experimental songs, will be more effective in producing change than the protest songs.

(3) The combination of protest songs and speeches will effect significantly more attitude change than either songs or speeches alone.

PROCEDURE

Ninety-seven undergraduate male and female students enrolled in the Fundamentals of Speech course at the University of Oregon were administered an attitude pretest on three concepts: Professional Boxing, Americans Fighting in Viet Nam, and the Eighteen Year-Old Vote. The questionnaire contained twelve evaluative seven-point, bipolar, adjectival scales for each concept.

experimental comparison between protest songs and speeches

One of the experimenters then composed three songs, the lyrics of which advocated in one case *against* Americans fighting in Viet Nam, in another *against* professional boxing, and *for* the eighteen year-old vote in the third. These protest songs were recorded by the composer to the accompaniment of a banjo only. The lyrics were then converted into brief speeches, thus constituting the independent variable.

same arguments in the same order

The validity of this experimental variable is, of course, dependent upon the experimenters' success in making the conversion without permitting any other variables to interfere.

[9] See Stephen Kosokoff (formerly Kaye), The Rhetoric of Song: Singing Persuasion in Social-Action Movements'' (Unpublished Ph.D. dissertation, Dept. of Speech, University of Oregon, 1966).

The only major varying factor should be the form of presentation. The same arguments were used, and in the same
order. The experimenters composed each speech sentence
by sentence from the song lyrics, attempting to maintain the
same meanings. Whenever word changes seemed desirable,
a synonym was carefully chosen. This aspect of the conversion process was sometimes necessary to avoid rhyming in
the speeches. The experimental comparison was between
protest songs and speeches, not between songs and poems.
A few minor adaptations were necessary, then, to make the
message appropriate to the form, and to insure believability
by the subjects who would be exposed to the song-speech
combination, but such changes were minimal and relatively
insignificant. A few samples might illustrate the kind and extent
of adaptation. The second verse of the Viet Nam song begins:

> The President says he is sorry.
> The Congress demands it be done
> The South Vietnamese need our army,
> Our planes and our tanks and our guns.

While the speech counterpart of these lyrics after conversion
read:

> The President answers that he is sorry. The Congress insists
> that what we are doing is necessary. They say that South Viet
> Nam needs American troops, planes, and guns.

Or, for another example, the first line of the song advocating
a lowering of the voting age was:

> We want a ballot
> A simple little ballot

and for the speech, was converted to:

> What are we asking for? A ballot—it's that simple.

While this procedure remains open to criticism, it should be
emphasized that the proposed experimental comparisons
could only be made with some message adaptation, but that
such changes were kept to a minimum and carefully thought
out in an attempt to keep meaning constant.

The subjects were divided into one control and three experimental groups. Three weeks following the protest, the
experimental subjects were exposed to the three manipulated

three experimental
conditions for groups

TABLE 1

Mean Changes In Attitude $\mp$

	Experimental Group			Control Group
Concept	Song	Speech	Combination	
Leave Viet Nam	+0.96	+2.1	+4.4*	−1.75
Ban Boxing	+1.07	+3.63*	+4.7*	−1.00
Lower Voting Age	+0.63	−1.8	+4.3*	−1.06

$\pm$ Positive Number Indicates Change in Advocated Direction.
* Significant at .05 Level.

conditions, each condition advocating attitude change toward a different topic. Each of the three groups heard a song on one of the topics, a speech on another, and both a song and a speech on the third; thus, the procedural design forms a Latin Square from the two within-subject variables; topics and song-speech combination conditions. Immediately following exposure to the experimental conditions, the subjects were administered the same attitude tests without exposure to the manipulated treatments.

The dependent variable in this experiment, subjects' attitude change toward the three concepts, was obtained by subtracting the post-test from the pretest scores on the attitude tests. A Lindquist Type II Mixed Factorial Analysis of Variance design was appropriate for statistical analyses of the data.[10]

RESULTS

speech-song combination: significant attitude change for all concepts

As can be seen in Table 1, all conditions except one (speech on lowering the voting age) resulted in attitude change in the direction advocated by the songs and speeches. The Lindquist Type II design yielded a significant F-ratio of 3.21 (at the .05 level of confidence) for the tri-factor independent variable. Then, t-tests were applied to determine precisely on which levels the differences occurred. On both the Viet Nam and boxing issues the results show that the speeches alone brought greater change than did song alone, and, further, speech-song combination shows greater change than either

[10] E. F. Lindquist, *Design and Analysis of Experiments in Psychology and Education* (Boston: Houghton Mifflin, 1953), pp. 273–281.

speech or song. However, not all of these differences were statistically significant. Comparisons between the experimental and control group means reveal that Hypothesis I was not confirmed; none of the song-only conditions resulted in attitude change that was statistically significant. Hypothesis II was not confirmed with the Viet Nam or voting age speeches, but only with the boxing speech. The third hypothesis was confirmed, however, as the speech-song combination resulted in significant attitude change for all three concepts.

DISCUSSION

The most striking aspect of this study concerns the significant attitude change seen as a result of the speech-song combination condition. In every case there was significant attitude change after exposure to the combined media, even when the song or speech alone did not produce such change. In fact, even when the speech on voting proved to be a complete rhetorical failure (resulting in opposite change), the song-speech combination on the same concept was quite effective. In an examination of the use of song in social-action movements it is found that songs rarely, if ever, are sung alone for persuasive purposes. Protest meetings or political rallies usually have songs and speeches mixed in no particular order. This experiment, then, did show that songs can add to the attitude change resulting from a speech of social action. In fact, in the case of the voting-age concept, it appears that a poor speech was saved when it was combined with a song that, by itself, had also failed to produce statistically significant attitude change.

combined media most effective

Further experimentation is needed in order to determine how persuasive protest songs are under varying conditions. First, songs of social action are not always sung by skilled entertainers. The more usual practice is for the entire membership to join in the singing. In fact, many of the songs mentioned previously were successful because they were quite singable. The comparison of the rhetorical effect of songs heard with that of songs sung would be useful. Second, this study was done in a controlled laboratory situation. Most of the elements present in a real protest or political meeting were absent. Many of these elements pertain to songs or singers. Further field work, at the scene where the songs are sung, is needed. Then, and third, replications of the present study with strategic design improvements would be in order.

songs of social action
are rhetorical

There is some evidence, then, that in certain situations social-action-type songs can be persuasive. Songs of social action not only were a part of the rhetoric of the movements in which they were used, but either were, or had the potential for becoming, rhetorical vehicles in themselves. Thus, it can be stated, with a limited degree of certainty, that songs of social action are rhetorical.

SUGGESTED FURTHER READING

Anderson, Walt, ed., *The Age of Protest.* Pacific Palisades, California: Goodyear Publishing Company, Inc., 1969.

Bryant, Donald C., *The Rhetorical Idiom.* Ithaca, N.Y.: Syracuse University Press (1958), See pp. 145–159.

Fabrizio, Roy and Edith Karas and Ruth Menmuir, eds., *The Rhetoric of No.* New York: Holt, Rinehart and Winston, Inc., 1970. (An anthology of examples.)

Giffin, Leland, "The Rhetorical Structure of the New Left Movement: Part I," *Quarterly Journal of Speech,* L (April, 1964), 113–135.

Lippman, Monro, "An Analysis of the Protest Play," *Southern Speech Journal,* XXI (Winter, 1955), 127–132.

Lomas, Charles, *The Agitator in American Society.* Englewood Cliffs, New Jersey: Prentice Hall, Inc., 1968.

Toch, Hans, *The Social Psychology of Social Movements.* Indianapolis: Bobbs-Merrill Co., 1965.

Trent, Judith S., "The National Rifle Association: Credibility In a Propaganda Campaign," *Journal of the American Forensic Association,* VII (Winter, 1971), 216–223.

ACTIVITIES

1. Attend a formal speaking situation such as a convocation, a political meeting or a campus rally in which at least one speech is presented. Write a short commentary on the speaker's purpose (as you see it) and on the speaker's effectiveness in joining his purpose with the attitudes and preconceptions of his audience. Remember the concepts you learned in Part Two as you write your commentary.

2. Select three class speeches (during one class period) and on 3 x 5 cards record (a) the central idea of the speech and (b) strategies such as value orientation, credibility, ordering effects, and evidence which you thought the speakers used effectively to communicate their ideas.

3. Using two protest speeches that the entire class has read or heard, attempt as a class to compile some general lines of argument or rhetorical strategies which may be generalizable to all protest speaking.

4. Suggest in a brief paper some of the ways in which critics of American public address may have contributed to existing rhetorical or communication theory by their studies of individual speakers, protest campaigns or movements. Perhaps you can use the essays by Kosokoff and Carmichael, Trent and Trent, and Rosenfield as starting points.

5. On the basis of your reading of the essays by Ericson, Hilbruner, and McGuckin, try your own skills as a rhetorical critic. Select a speech and discuss in some detail the way you would approach the following aspects of the rhetorical event:
   a) reconstruction of the social setting
   b) the status of the speaker with his audience
   c) the various strategies employed by the speaker as he attempted to relate his message to his audience
   d) the style of the address
   e) the measurement of the effectiveness of the speech in terms of its intentions

Part 4.

Concepts of Interpersonal Communication

4.

Introduction (by Jimmie D. Trent). The process of communication involves a speaker's formulation and a listener's reformulation of a message. The speaker acts and the listener reacts, so that both speaker and listener are affected by participation in this process. Audience reactions can be studied in order to determine the most effective ways to achieve the speaker's goals, and that approach has been followed with the speaker-message orientation of the preceding sections.

The emphasis of a speaker-message orientation is upon factors which influence the decisions listeners make. Thus you have studied ordering effects, the meaning of style, source credibility, and the situations which require evidence to gain acceptance. The reactions of audiences to messages have been examined in terms of whether the speaker's purpose was achieved. And from that examination, variables have been stated which should help you as potential message source to plan methods of gaining belief or action according to your goals.

Now we turn our attention to interpersonal communication. In its simplest form, the difference between interpersonal communication study and speaker-message study is our attitude toward the people involved. The listener is considered to be a person who is expected to make his own decision on the basis of understanding. The speaker is not emphasized as a decision-maker who seeks acceptance of his beliefs. Instead, he is viewed as a participant in the communication process who is interested in the effects he and his message will have on the receiver's ability to formulate messages and make his own decisions.

Interpersonal communication involves two-way communication. Where we examined the speaker-message orientation with the view that we were the source, interpersonal communication study requires that we assume both speaker and listener roles.

And where we emphasized the ability to influence receivers while we were taking a speaker-message orientation, we now turn to studying the effects of attitudes and acts on us in our dual roles of source and receiver. We are interested in developing our own ability to receive as much as we are to improve our ability to gain accurate reformulation of our ideas by other receivers.

None of this is to say that people do not try to influence in two-way communication situations. Obviously interviews and negotiations involve attempts to influence with each participant alternating as speaker and listener. But with a focus on interpersonal communication, the primary emphasis of study is not on attempts to influence; the primary emphasis is on breaking down barriers to understanding. If agreement in belief or mutual understanding follows, it comes as a natural consequence of two people submitting their perceptions of reality to each other and finding a basis for consensus in areas mutually agreed.

The effect of communication on people is emphasized in "An Interpersonal Ethic for Communication" by Professors Paul W. Keller and Charles T. Brown. Their ethic is premised on the concept that conditions should be created and maintained in which the potential of the individual is best realized. The proposed ethic calls for maximizing the opportunity for individual growth through creating psychological freedom. Their ethic is based on receiver development, in contrast with the receiver-influence ethic implied in the speaker-message orientation.

Professor Charles M. Kelly argues in "Empathic Listening" that receivers frequently do not achieve understanding because they listen incorrectly. His research indicated that the tendency to listen critically may actually inhibit our ability to comprehend. Kelly argues that some of the principles of listening behavior which have been commonly advocated may actually be counterproductive.

The first two articles in this section discuss concepts applying to interpersonal communication in general. The last four articles discuss specific elements and their effects on deriving meaning.

Professor Jack R. Gibb's classic article on "Defensive Communication" describes the destructive effects which occur "when an individual perceives threat or anticipates threat in the group." Specific suggestions are given for reducing the need for defensive reactions.

"Interpersonal Trust in Small Group Communication" by Professor Kim Giffin summarizes the results of experimental literature relevant to the effects of trust or the lack thereof on meaning derivation. He derives a theory which hypothesizes that interpersonal variables and personality factors combine to produce trust which, in turn, increases certain types of interpersonal behavior.

We have all observed the destructive effects of intense emotion on the process of communication. The late Professor Irving Lee explains an attitude and method for handling anger in his "When Angry Look Again." Lee tells us that emotion is always present in communication and that anger should be treated as a signal of a problem calling for solution.

The final selection is "The Black Bag", a review of a series of incidents which occurred when an unidentified student wore a bag to class for a whole term. Professor John Keltner's report is not really about the "bag" so much as it is about the reactions of people to the unknown. The reactions were not really unique; the elements of distrust, defensiveness, anger, and critical "listening" to nonverbal symbols are all present. The uniqueness of the situation highlights these and many other elements of more typical communication situations.

Interpersonal Communication and Public Speaking. This book begins by contrasting a traditional view of speech with the current emphasis of speech-communication. Nowhere is the difference between the two approaches more apparent than in the contrasting of approaches to public speaking and interpersonal communication. At the same time, there ought to be good possibilities for drawing from both approaches to derive principles which will help us to become more effective as communicators and people.

Keller and Brown's proposal for a receiver development ethic should provide a conscience for those who feel it is necessary to make decisions for others. In those circumstances, the least we can hope for is restraint.

Kelly points to empathic listening as an area of emphasis which is required by our natural tendencies to premature judgment. There is no reason to limit his suggestions to two-way communication situations. His research applies equally well to interpersonal or public speaking situations.

Gibb, Giffin, and Lee report conclusions from research on interpersonal situations with listeners who are building barriers to understanding. Traditional textbooks on public speaking have always included sections on talking to hostile audiences. A hostile audience was one which did not trust or respect a speaker or one which disagreed with the speaker's point of view. Methods were suggested for reducing the hostility to speaker and subject. The work of Gibb, Giffin, and Lee should give us new insight in methods to reduce or prevent hostility.

The "Black Bag" incidents occurred in an interpersonal situation, but the reactions are not unknown in public speaking. The fear of the unknown, defensiveness and anger are not unique. Similar, though perhaps not so pronounced, reactions can be observed in public speaking situations when an audience is faced with an unknown.

The results of speech-communication research are not restricted to specific types of communication activities. We can learn about public speaking by studying individual reactions in interpersonal communications, and we can learn of people's reactions to people by studying public speaking situations. The key to both is studying the audience, whether that means studying one or many. When we apply our findings, the important variables are specific to audiences rather than specific to the type of speech activity which is occurring. By considering audience reactions, we can learn to adapt both our speaker roles and our listener roles in ways which will increase our ability to communicate in any situation according to variables which are present.

An Interpersonal Ethic
for Communication

Paul W. Keller and Charles T. Brown

Abstract. A modern rhetoric has developed concerning itself with considerably more dimensions of speech than was the case with traditional rhetoric's concentration on persuasion and public address. Indeed, this modern rhetoric has expanded its domain to include the whole range of types of oral communication. But while this very basic kind of evolution has been taking place, it appears that a corresponding ethic (an interpersonal one) has not emerged. The authors make bold to try to stimulate that study.

The interpersonal ethic proposed in the article can be stated as follows: A's communication is ethical to the extent that it accepts B's responses; it is unethical to the extent to which it develops hostility toward B's responses, or in some way tries to subjugate B. The ethic can be observed best, the authors believe, when A discovers that B rejects the message A is sending.

Such an ethic springs from the following assumptions: (1) By virtue of the very nature of the communicative act, the two parties to a communication exercise control over each other. Both the listener and the speaker are, in part, at the other's mercy. (2) One of the highest values in a democratic culture is that conditions be created and maintained in which the potential of the individual is best realized. (3) The individual will be able to realize his potential to the extent that psychological freedom can be increased for him.

An interpersonal ethic, the article suggests, may have more to do with the attitude of the speaker and listener toward each

Note: [When this article first appeared in the *Journal of Communication* in March, 1968,] Paul W. Keller [had] been chairman of the Department of Speech at Manchester College since 1950. His Ph.D. was earned at Northwestern University. He [has been] a member of a number of professional organizations in the speech area and has been a contributor to journals in this area for many years. He is well known to readers of this *Journal* as the author of several articles in recent years. He [has been] a visiting professor at Western Michigan University.

Charles T. Brown [had] been with the Speech Department at Western Michigan University since 1948 and [was] chairman of that department. His contributions to professional journals have been unusually extensive. His latest book, *Speech and Man,* was published in 1966. He [has been] one of the associate editors of this *Journal.*

other than with elements of the message (as in the more traditional rhetoric). It may concern itself more with loyalty to the person with whom one is in communication than to rationality or cosmic truth.

At one of the many philosophical climaxes in *The Brothers Karamazov,* Dostoevsky has Ivan, the intellectual, engaging in an agonizing effort to convince his younger brother Alyosha, the cleric, of the soundness of his life view. In the midst of the effort Ivan states, with classic sharpness, the problem that lies at the very heart of his own system of ethics. He says to Alyosha,

> "Imagine that you are creating a fabric of human destiny with the object of making men happy in the end, giving them peace and rest at last, but that it was essential and inevitable to torture to death only one tiny creature . . . and to found that edifice on its unavenged tears, would you consent to be the architect on those conditions? Tell me, and tell the truth."
> "No, I wouldn't consent," says Alyosha softly.

There is implied commitment to a set of values in Ivan's question. There is revealed commitment to a different set of values in Alyosha's answer. What remains to be said about either or both of those views, enticing as it may be, is not the business of this study. We use the scene rather as an analog to the kind of question we would like to pose concerning communication:

> Imagine that you have the welfare of another at heart, and that you are convinced that you know what would be good for him in a given situation. Suppose that you recommend to him the "right" course of action, explaining your reasons fully, developing the empirical foundations for your proposition patiently. And suppose that when you are finished—perhaps after repeated dialogues—he rejects your proposal. Would you accept his response without rancor, without an undercover resolution to set him right—in short, would you accept his response as the *bona fide* reaction of a free individual?

The answer to that question may seem infinitely easier than the one Dostoevsky requires for his. But the question points to what we think may be the central problem in the ethics of persuasion.

the central problem in
the ethics of persuasion
Man has wrestled long with the ethics of persuasion. In the course of his struggle tests for measuring whether the influence of the spoken word was for "good" or for "evil" have

been set up [See References 13, 12, 7, 4, 8, 1]; values upon which an ethic could be built have been specified [9, 6, 7]; warnings have been issued against allowing ourselves to drift, unknowingly, into valuelessness [5]; and the case has been made for a "culturally relative" view of the ethics of persuasion [10].

But in spite of the rich, and burgeoning, literature on the subject, we have emerged, it seems, into a modern rhetoric that has reached beyond public address and propaganda to include the whole range of oral communication, without sufficient consideration for what the corresponding new ethic might look like. On the ground that it is a healthy thing to keep the fountain of conjecture and theory bubbling, we venture to describe one of the shapes a "new" (interpersonal) ethic might take.

modern rhetoric lacks a new ethic to fit all communication

A NEW INTERPERSONAL ETHIC

We begin with the assertion that any unit of communication, by virtue of its psychological nature, involves mutual control (if the negative connotations were not so strong in the phrase we would prefer to use "mutual manipulation" since it implies something more dynamic than does "control"). We take this to be self-evident: when an oral message is sent, the speaker intrudes himself into the life-span of the listener and, to the extent that anything is communicated, determines that the listener shall hear, think, perceive one thing rather than another; at the same time, the listener to such a message inescapably influences the speaker by virtue of the way he either rewards him or withholds rewards from him. There is reason to believe that our communicative habits, as speakers, are molded and shaped by the responses we get from listeners. [11] To put it another way, we are strongly conditioned by the reward systems of our listeners.

communicative habits of speakers are molded by listener responses

If it can be admitted that this two-way control system is constantly at work in communication, and that its influence on both the sender and receiver of messages is profound, then the values the parties regard as important become a matter of urgency, for both the speaker and the listener are, in part, at the other's mercy. The value frequently placed highest in a democratic culture, and we think rightly so, is that *conditions be created and maintained in which the potential of the individual is best realized.* Contributing to this value is the complementary notion that the individual will be able to realize his

values and psychological freedom are important

potential to the extent that psychological freedom can be increased for him.

The logical next step in such an analysis would be to recognize any effort to persuade as an infringement of freedom and to postulate a way of dealing with the dilemma created by our propositions. The key, we think, rests in the distinction between *immediacy* and *ultimacy.* The mutual control, characteristic of communication, is inescapable in the moment of communication. Indeed, unless that control is *mutual,* contact is likely not being made. But the exercise of that kind of control need not be extended to ultimate choices. Thoreau could not have foregone the control he exercised over Emerson when he engaged him in conversation on the topic of civil disobedience, but he could (and likely did) forego the attempt to exercise control of the ultimate choice Emerson made in the matter.

the ethical concern is how the speaker reacts to the listener's reaction

What we are suggesting is that, in the very nature of things, the mutual impact of two or more people in communication is inevitable, and the impact on each is shaped by both. Moreover, we feel that the ethical problem, as traditionally framed, builds a better foundation for the critic to stand on than it does for the man who must decide and act. Who is to say what argument, evidence, or conclusion is valid? What is the truth and who knows when he knows it? How can we be responsible for what we believe? Let us make the point more crucial. Even a deliberate lie, or the withholding of what is believed, may be justified by the most careful exercise of conscience. Deliberate distortion is surely dangerous, but who has not painfully chosen, as the lesser of two evils, to skirt the facts? And unconscious distortion is involved in every communication, perhaps. How else can we explain the uniqueness of each man's perceptions? "It's a wise cove as knows wot's wot," says one of Stevenson's pirates. Here, then, is the heart of the argument: the ethics of communication may have more to do with signs concerning the attitude of the speaker and the listener toward each other than with elements of the message or channel involved. It may be that the central question in ethics does not concern so much one's loyalty to rationality, or cosmic truth, as it does loyalty to the person with whom one is in communication. The crucial question may be: *How does the speaker react to the listener's reaction?* (And how does the listener react to the speaker?) If the listener does not respond in a way that satisfies the speaker's goal, is the speaker angered? Is he despondent, and thus tempted to play for sympathy? Does he "wash his hands" of the listener? Does he, in short, refuse to accept the responses of the listener as those of a free individual? In terms of the test we are proposing, A's communication is ethical to the extent that it accepts (in the sense of implicit psychological acceptance) B's responses; it is unethical to the extent it develops hostility toward B's responses, or in some way tries to subjugate B. This is another way of saying that behavior which enhances the basic freedom of response in the individual is more ethical; behavior which either overtly or covertly attacks it is less ethical.

The idea is not new. Others have hinted at it, as we propose to point out in a moment. We try to give it emphasis because 1) if it is valid it opens some new avenues for inquiry among students of communication, and 2) it is conceivable that a communicator could meet all of the other ethical tests and violate this one. Take out lying, distortion, deliberate omission of evidence (items the authors certainly do not choose to advocate). Take out the use of devices that render a listener suggestible. Imagine a communicator dedicated to what Bronowski [2] sees as the ultimate value of science—truth. It remains true that unless there is in him a sensitivity to the importance of freedom of choice for the listener (and a consciousness of the damage possible through a denial of that freedom) his communicating is likely to be unethical. The speaker who speaks truth, but who resents another's rejection of his conclusions, falls short of our ethical standard. He passes the tests involving "devices." He fails the test involving his attitude toward the other.

the ethical communicator: sensitive to freedom of choice for listeners

We have said the idea is not a new one. So let us piece together the thinking from which it springs. A number of years ago Thomas Nilsen [9] set forth what he regarded as the paramount values of a democracy. They were: "A belief in the intrinsic worth of the human personality; a belief in reason as an instrument of individual and social development; self-determination as the means to individual fulfillment; man's fulfillment of his potentialities as a positive good." The values he mentions, interestingly enough, could be translated, almost completely, into Erich Fromm's "humanistic values." [6] They seem to us to represent an extraordinarily cogent statement of a value system on which an ethical rhetoric could be established.

Particularly important in Nilsen's list is the belief in "self-determination as the means to individual fulfillment." It is this kind of implied freedom for which we have been arguing in our proposed test of the ethics of communication. We proceed

self-determination: the means to individual fulfillment

on the assumption that to discourage a listener from the conviction that he has powers for choice-making is to downgrade his humanity. As Fromm puts it, freedom can be thought of as "the ability to preserve one's integrity against power." Moreover, he says,

> . . . freedom is the necessary condition of happiness as well as of virtue; freedom, not in the sense of the ability to make arbitrary choices and not freedom from necessity, but freedom to realize that which one potentially is, to fulfill the true nature of man according to the laws of his existence. [6]

ethical test for communicators: accepting rebellion with equanimity

It is easy enough to pay lip service to such a concept of freedom, but the readiness to employ it in communicative behavior is by no means automatic. There is something in the very effort to persuade that seduces us into an authoritarian ethic. Fromm's analysis of the way this works is worth quoting at length:

> Unless the authority wanted to exploit the subject, it would not need to rule by virtue of awe and emotional submissiveness; it could encourage rational judgment and criticism—thus taking the risk of being found incompetent. But because its own interests are at stake the authority ordains *obedience* to be the main virtue and disobedience to be the main sin. The unforgiveable sin in authoritarian ethics is rebellion, the questioning of the authority's right to establish norms and of its axiom that the norms established by the authority are in the best interests of the subjects. [6]

Put in Fromm's terms, then, the ethical test we have been proposing is a matter of measuring one's willingness to accept rebellion with equanimity.

There is, however, an implication that goes beyond simply the question whether one is granted freedom or is inhibited from exercising that freedom in a given instance. It has to do with the *cumulative effect* of having another person react with hostility, or reserve, or vindictiveness, when one makes a choice that is not consistent with the desires of the persuader. Learning theory suggests that if an individual is rewarded in an interpersonal situation for making his own decisions, he is likely to habituate that kind of independence in decision-making—that is, he learns to take responsibility in expressing his own potential. If he is not rewarded, he is likely to learn dependence on others for his decision-making, and comes, thereby, to live at a level below his potential as a person. Nilsen has expressed it this way:

> When being persuaded a man is not only influenced directly
> or indirectly in his choice of a course of action, he is influenced
> in his method of making the choice. The problem of ethics
> enters when what we do affects the lives of others. How we
> influence others to make choices about things of importance
> to them is obviously affecting their lives in a significant way.
> [9]

All of this emphasizes the common threat to "self-determination as the means to individual fulfillment" and shows that our temptation to use that threat is the core of the ethical problem in persuasion.

Does this point of view present us with an impossible problem in human relations? It does not seem so to us. To the contrary, it more carefully defines the nature of communication and highlights its role in the human experience. It footnotes Burke's insistence that "identification" is the ethical and practical answer to the "division" among men. [3]

Communication is, in its best sense, communion. It involves what Wieman and Walter [13] have called "mutual appreciative understanding." And even though this sort of mutuality leads, as these authors saw, to mutual control, the mutual control is of a sort built on a positive ethic: to bring to their finest fulfillment the purposes of each party to the communicative act. Identity, to return to Burke's term, implies "union with." It is quite right, therefore, to develop around it, as Burke has done, a rhetoric of courtship. But not a courtship that makes the suitor the slave of the courted, or the converse. The relationship we speak of is a mutuality which leaves those in communication mutually bound, yet mutually free.

a mutual relationship, leaving participants mutually bound, yet mutually free

A NEW DIMENSION IN COMMUNICATION

We have surveyed a variety of tests of the ethics of persuasion and have advanced a suggestion for an "ethic of communication." The suggestion shares a great deal with the traditional tests, but attempts to add a new interpersonal dimension to our thinking about ethical problems in communication. It is predicated on the belief that those things which allow an individual to realize his potential with a minimum of influence and control from others are best. The test may be stated as follows: *How does the speaker react to the listener's reactions?* (And how does the listener react to the speaker?) *If he reacts in such a way as to enhance the self-determination forces within the other, his communication can be considered more ethical.*

If he reacts in such a way as to inhibit the self-determination forces within the other, his communication can be considered less ethical, regardless of the purity of the devices used in the communicative effort. This adds to the tests of one's ethics of persuasion the question of his attitude toward the person who rejects his view.

It may be asserted that the signs of an individual's unwillingness to grant another ultimate freedom of choice are too slippery and uncertain to be detected with confidence. The same objection can be levelled at any of the ethical tests we have traditionally applied. Indeed, our own experience leads us to believe we can learn to know our attitudes toward others with considerably more certitude than we can know that what we know is true or rational.

It is encouraging that we are developing, as in psychiatry, increased reliability in certain kinds of diagnosis regarding feelings and attitudes. But the problem of measurement is, in a way, beside the point. What is important, if we are not to admit to a nihilism in our view of communication, is to determine those values we regard as paramount and to construct our theory of communication upon them. Looked at in that light, the ethic we envision is one which will not only make communicative intercourse practically effective, but will enrich the participants in the process.

Finally, it may be argued that the ethical test we have proposed here is nothing more than words; that an ego is an ego, and therefore the desire to dominate and control another will rage unabated no matter what the persuader tells himself. The idea that one can (or even that one *should*) change feelings of resentment toward a listener who rejects his view may be held to be pure poppycock. In the face of such arguments we can only offer as hypotheses: (1) There is an observable difference between the degree to which the people one meets are willing to grant the function of "self-determination" to those with whom they communicate, and (2) The tendency for the speaker to want to reject the person who doesn't accept his message is close to universal in human experience.

Our faith is that man is not in the clutches of hapless forces—that he is endlessly fascinated by the search for more humane communication.

REFERENCES

1. Brembreck, Winston L., and William S. Howell. *Persuasion.* New York: Prentice-Hall, 1952, ch. 24.

2. Bronowski, Jacob. *Science and Human Values.* New York: Harper, 1959.

3. Burke, Kenneth. *A Rhetoric of Motives.* New York: Prentice-Hall, 1950, p. 22.

4. Cooper, Lane. *The Rhetoric of Aristotle.* New York: Appleton, 1932.

5. Eubanks, Ralph T., and Virgil L. Baker. "Toward an Axiology of Rhetoric." *Quarterly Journal of Speech* 48:157–68, 1962.

6. Fromm, Erich. *Man for Himself.* New York: Rinehart, 1947.

7. Haiman, Franklyn S. "A Re-examination of the Ethics of Persuasion." *The Central States Speech Journal* 3:5–10, 1952.

8. Minnick, Wayne C. *The Art of Persuasion.* Boston: Houghton Mifflin, 1957, p. 284–85.

9. Nilsen, Thomas R. "Free Speech, Persuasion, and the Democratic Process." *Quarterly Journal of Speech* 44:235–43, 1958.

10. Rogge, Edward. "Evaluating the Ethics of a Speaker in a Democracy." *Quarterly Journal of Speech* 45:419–25, 1959.

11. Verplanck, William. "The Control of the Content of Conversation: Reinforcement of Statements of Opinion." *Journal of Abnormal and Social Psychology* 51:668–76, 1955.

12. Wallace, Karl. "An Ethical Basis of Communication." *The Speech Teacher* 4:1–9, 1955.

13. Wieman, Henry Nelson, and Otis M. Walter. "Toward an Analysis of Ethics for Rhetoric." *Quarterly Journal of Speech* 43:266–70, 1957.

SUGGESTED FURTHER READING

Anderson, Kenneth E., *Persuasion Theory and Practice.* Boston, Mass.: Allyn and Bacon, Inc., 1971.

Bronowski, Jacob, *Science and Human Values.* (See reference 2 above.)

Burke, Kenneth, *A Rhetoric of Motives.* (See reference 3 above.)

Eubanks, Ralph T. and Virgil L. Baker, "Toward an Axiology of Rhetoric." (See reference 5 above.)

Fromm, Erich, *Man for Himself.* (See reference 6 above.)

Haiman, Franklyn S., "A Re-examination of the Ethics of Persuasion." (See reference 7 above.)

Nilsen, Thomas R., "Free Speech, Persuasion, and the Democratic Process." (See reference 9 above.)

Rogge, Edward, "Evaluating the Ethics of a Speaker in a Democracy." (See reference 10 above.)

Verplanck, William, "The Control of the Content of Conversation: Reinforcement of Statements of Opinion." (See reference 11 above.)

Wallace, Karl, "An Ethical Basis of Communication." (See reference 12 above.)

Wieman, Henry Nelson and Otis M. Walter, "Toward an Analysis of Ethics for Rhetoric." (See reference 13 above.)

Empathic Listening

Charles M. Kelly

In a research project exploring listening behavior, industrial supervisors gave the following reasons for communication problems in large management-level meetings and conferences: "things discussed here are often side issues that don't interest everyone," "I think about my job upstairs," "they get off the subject," and "a lot of people like to hear themselves talk." A content analysis was made of these and other responses dealing with the perceived deficiencies of meetings and discussions. Results indicated that most of the dissatisfaction centered around the general feeling that many different issues were discussed at a typical meeting, and that usually some of these issues were not directly related to all of the participants.[1]

Complaints such as the above are not unusual, and frequently are justified. Every text of discussion and conference methodology deals with the problems of keeping the discussion on relevant and significant issues, and of motivating the participants. However, most of the emphasis in the past has dealt with the obligations of the discussants (both leaders and participants) as *speakers,* rather than as *listeners.* This unbalanced emphasis, especially as it actually affects persons in real discussions, could be an important *cause* of the problems that speaking is supposed to cure: e.g., the reason a discussion leader may have difficulty clarifying the comments of another, may be that he did not listen carefully to begin with; when one is overly concerned about what *he* is *going* to say, he really can't devote his full attention to what *is* being said by others. If a person in a group preoccupies himself by privately bemoaning the irrelevancies that inevitably occur in discussion, he may be less able to get the group back on the

[1] Charles M. Kelly, "Actual Listening Behavior of Industrial Supervisors as Related to Listening Ability, General Mental Ability, Selected Personality Factors and Supervisory Effectiveness," Unpublished Ph.D. Dissertation, Purdue University, 1962, 129.

track; he misses opportunities for constructive action because he lacks an *accurate* analysis of the flow of ideas, even the irrelevant ones.

deliberative listening and empathic listening

Of course, listening is a multi-faceted activity and it can be considered from different viewpoints, but at least two ways of categorizing listening seem especially fruitful for theoretical analysis: *deliberative listening* and *empathic listening.* Most recent writers have treated listening as a unitary skill, i.e., as a rather definite and "deliberative" ability to hear information, to analyze it, to recall it at a later time, and to draw conclusions from it. Commercially-published listening tests and most listening training programs are based on this, the deliberative listening, viewpoint. On the other hand, empathic listening occurs when the person participates in the spirit or feeling of his environment as a communication *receiver.* This does not suggest that the listener is uncritical or always in agreement with what is communicated, but rather, that his primary interest is to become fully and accurately aware of what is going on. (See Figure 1.)

empathic listening: participation in the spirit of an environment as receiver

It should be observed that the terms "deliberative listening" and "empathic listening" are not mutually exclusive or exhaustive. Their main purpose is to differentiate between two basic ways of viewing the same listening activity. The desired result of both deliberative and empathic listening is identical: accurate understanding of oral communication. However, this understanding is achieved by different routes. The deliberative listener *first* has the desire to critically analyze what a speaker has said, and secondarily tries to understand the speaker (this can be the result of personal inclination or of training which emphasizes procedure at the expense of listening). The empathic listener has the desire to understand the speaker first, and, as a result, tries to take the appropriate action.

deliberative listener first analyzes; empathic listener first understands

The former kind of listening is characteristic of the discussant who is predisposed to be disagreeable, or to summarize, or to clarify—even when there is little that is significant to disagree with, when there is no need to summarize, or when further clarification is a waste of the group's time. The latter kind of listening is characteristic of the person who is able to adapt quickly to the real needs of a situation because he has a presence of mind and a greater confidence in the accuracy of his awareness—he does not handicap himself by deciding in advance that he does not have to listen to a particular person who is poorly dressed, or that he must be sure to expose all faulty reasoning if he is to demonstrate his competence.

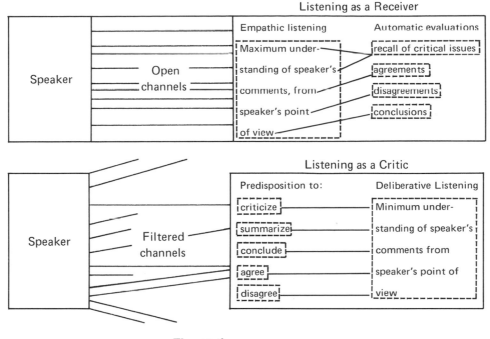

Figure 1.

The differences between empathic listening and deliberative listening are primarily motivational. Both listeners seek the same objective: accurate understanding of the communication from another. The model suggests that the motivation to receive information is superior to the motivation to use critical skills. The emphatic listener lets his understanding of the speaker determine his modes of evaluation, which are automatic; the deliberative listener's understanding of the speaker is filtered through his predetermined modes of selective listening, and actually spends less time as a communication receiver. The empathic listener is more apt to be a consistent listener, and is less prone to his own or other distractions. This theory is correct, only if the assumption is true that persons can and do think critically without deliberate effort—*while listening.* (Of course, if persons do not make the effort to listen *per se,* little or no understanding will occur.)

This is not to say that various skills in critical thinking are less important than emphatic listening. Without critical analysis, listening in a problem-solving discussion would be useless. The point is, however, that a person uses quite naturally whatever critical skills he has already acquired, as long as he is interested and actively listening; to the extent that he is not listening, critical skills will be of little value. Actually, a case can be made that "deliberative listening" is a self-contradiction and a misnomer—and that "empathic listening" is a redundancy. To the extent that one is deliberating (mentally criticizing, summarizing, concluding, preparing reports, etc.) he is *not listening,* but formulating his own ideas. And listen-

messages heard are understood only if their meaning, spirit is shared

TABLE 1

Correlations (Pearson r) Among the "Surprise" Listening Test, the Brown-Carlsen Listening Test, the Step Listening Test, and the Otis Test of General Mental Ability[a]

	Brown-Carlsen	STEP	Otis
Surprise Listening test	.79	.78	.70[bc]
Brown-Carlsen		.82	.85[b]
STEP			.85[c]

[a] All correlations are significant at the .01 level.
[b] The difference between the two correlations so designated is significant at the .05 level, t = 2.205.
[c] The difference between the two correlations so designated is significant at the .05 level, t = 2.162.

ing, by its very nature, *has* to be empathic; a person understands what he has heard, only to the extent that he can share in the meaning, spirit, or feeling of what the communicator has said.

There is some evidence that this line of reasoning is correct. In one experiment,[2] a researcher presented a 30-minute talk dealing with "The Supervisor and Communication" to 28 supervisors at a regularly scheduled business meeting. The supervisors were in no way led to believe that they were in an experiment or that their listening performance would be tested. Following the presentation, they were given a 30-item multiple-choice "surprise" listening test. During the following two weeks, the supervisors were given the Brown-Carlsen Listening Comprehension Test, the STEP Listening Test, the Otis Quick-Scoring Mental Ability Test, and the Cattell 16 Personality Factor Questionnaire. (Because of the nature of the Brown-Carlsen and Step listening tests, subjects have to know in advance that their listening ability is being tested.)

results show listening ability indistinguishable from general mental ability

The results (Table 1) indicated that the supervisors' "listening ability" (as measured by the Brown-Carlsen and the STEP) was indistinguishable from general mental ability (as measured by the Otis) when they knew in advance that their listening was being tested. In fact, the listening tests correlated *lower* with each other, than each did with the test of mental ability. In other words, when the supervisors had the extra motivation of a test, or were constantly listening, they made full use of their general mental ability, and the listening

[2] This study is reported in detail: Charles M. Kelly, "Mental Ability and Personality Factors in Listening," *Quarterly Journal of Speech,* XLIX, (April, 1963), 152–156.

TABLE 2

Statistical Significance of Differences (Chi Square with Yates' Correction) Between "High" and "Low" Criterion Groups (as Determined by Scores on Each of Four Tests) on the Cattell 16 PF Scales

Cattell Scale *Low Score vs. High Scores*	*Surprise Listening Test*	*Brown-Carlsen*[b]	*STEP*[c]	*Otis*[d]
Aloof vs. Outgoing	.14	.00**	.14	.00
Dull vs. Bright (intelligence factor)	.57	5.16	2.29	2.29
Emotional vs. Mature	3.57***	1.28	3.57***	1.28
Submissive vs. Dominant	.14	.00	.00	.15
Glum vs. Enthusiastic	.14	.00	.00	.00
Casual vs. Conscientious	.00	.00	.00	.00
Timid vs. Adventurous	9.19*	.57	2.29	.57
Tough vs. Sensitive	.00	.00	.00	.57[a]
Trustful vs. Suspecting	.57[a]	.00	.00	.00
Conventional vs. Eccentric	.00	.00	.00	.00
Simple vs. Sophisticated	3.65***	1.31	1.31	1.31
Confident vs. Insecure	.00	.57[a]	.00	.00
Conservative vs. Experimenting	.00	.59[a]	.00	.00
Dependent vs. Self-sufficient	.00	.00	.00	.00
Lax vs. Controlled	2.29	.00	.00	.00
Stable vs. Tense	7.00*[a]	.14[a]	1.31[a]	2.29[a]

* X^2 of 6.64 = 1% level.   ** X^2 of 3.84 = 5% level.   *** X^2 of 2.71 = 10% level.
[a] High scorers on the test scored low on the Cattell personality scale.

Using the sign test for statistical significance, the following differences were observed between tests, on the basis of personality scales (intelligence scale, "Dull vs. Bright," was not included):

[b] difference between tests so designated was significant at p = .03
[c] p = .008   [d] p = .055

tests became orally-presented tests of general mental ability, rather than of "listening." On the other hand, when the supervisors did not know their listening was being tested, their listening performance was significantly less related to general mental ability.

Further insight can be gained by analyzing the results in terms of personality variables (Table 2). Again, the Brown-Carlsen and STEP listening tests are indistinguishable from the Otis, when compared on the basis of personality variables; the same personality factors appear about equally important (as expressed in chi square values) in the test of general mental ability as in the tests of listening ability. However, the "surprise" listening test showed significantly more substantial

personality differences exist between good and bad listeners personality differences between good and poor listeners than did the other three tests.

The most significant differences between good and poor listeners, when they had no unusual motivation to listen because of test awareness, were that good listeners were more adventurous (receptive to new ideas), (emotionally) stable, mature, and sophisticated. Although the other six differences in Table 2 (under "surprise listening test") were not statistically significant, it is interesting to note that all were in the same direction, with the good listeners being more emotionally mature: outgoing, bright, dominant, enthusiastic, trustful and controlled (will control). The opposite ends of the personality scales, describing the poor listeners in the surprise listening test, were: aloof, dull, emotional, submissive, glum, timid, suspecting, simple, lax, and tense.

This and other studies[3] strongly indicate that when persons know that their listening comprehension is being tested, differences between individuals are primarily matters of general mental ability; when they do not know their listening performance is being tested, differences are due to personality differences (including motivation to listen), as well as general mental ability. Of these two kinds of research situations, the latter is more representative of realistic listening events.

communication problems result from inattention or mental inability

It is likely that most communication problems arise either because of participant inattention (poor motivation), or because of a lack of general mental ability—not because of anything that can be called "listening ability." Do teachers in a faculty meeting miss the details of registration because of a lack of listening ability, or because of a lack of motivation? Does an engineer fail to understand an explanation of a new process because he lacks listening ability, or because he simply has not yet been able to visualize unfamiliar relationships? In the rare cases when a discussion is vitally important to everyone and motivation is high (as in a listening test), there is little chance of an important point (or its significance) being missed, unless the listener simply lacked the mental ability to understand or appreciate it to begin with. But in most of the everyday discussions that deal with the nagging problems of industrial production, proposed new school construction, traffic safety, curriculum changes, etc., motivation to participate (and, hence, listen) is moderate at best and is not evenly distributed among the discussants—and with some persons,

problems of inattention, no motivation to listen

inattention seems to be habitual.

[3] For a detailed analysis of this issue, see: Charles M. Kelly, "Listening: Complex of Activities—and a Unitary Skill?" *Speech Monographs,* XXXIV, (November, 1967), 455–466.

In terms of *listening* theory, it is far more important to stress empathic, rather than deliberative, listening in discussion. This observation in no way depreciates the need for education and practical experience in critical analysis, debate, general semantics—or in any of the various mental skills brought into play *while* listening. But it is a mistake to consider these skills *as* listening, since this viewpoint suggests that the listener's analysis is part of the receiving process.

The degree to which one is able to listen, and to perform other mental acts at the same time is an open question; research into the exact nature of listening, as it relates to other general mental abilities, is unclear at best. However, because of the obvious difficulties that occur in discussion when listener motivation is poor or nonexistent, and in view of the probability that problems in discussion are due to factors other than listening *ability* when participant motivation is high, the following suggestions seem warranted:

Remember the characteristics of the poor listener. It is easy to sit back in your chair and complain to yourself that the discussion is boring or unimportant. However, the description of the kind of person who habitually does this is not very flattering, and should serve as an incentive to better listening; research suggests that the poor listener is less intelligent, and less emotionally mature than the good listener. Obviously, there are times when a person may be just as well off *not* listening, but the poor listener tends to make this a crutch for the easy way out of difficult listening events.

suggestions for better participation

Make a firm initial commitment to listen. Listening is hard work and it takes energy. If you have had difficulty listening in the past, and now decide merely to *try* to listen and to participate in the spirit of the discussion as long as you can, you will soon fall into old habits. Above all, don't make an initial decision *not* to listen; if discussions in the past have proved deficient, according to your standards, accurate listening will better enable you to correct them in the future.

Get physically and mentally ready to listen. Sit up, and get rid of distractions; put away paper you were reading, books, pencils, papers, etc., unless you plan to use them. Try to dismiss personal worries, fears, or pleasant reverie until a later time. Will these kinds of thoughts be more productive of personal gain than your participation in this discussion?

Concentrate on the other person as a communicator. View the others in a discussion as sources of ideas and information, not as personalities. If you are reacting to another as being dishonest, unethical, stupid, tedious—or as a college professor, or Republican, or student rioter, or disgruntled parent—it will be difficult for you to accurately perceive what he is trying to say. There is little to fear in such an open approach. Shoddy thinking or speaking needs no label to be recognized, and fewer good ideas will be discarded because they were never really listened to. Of course, it goes without saying that persons communicate with gestures as well as with their voices, and the listener is concerned with perceiving the total communication environment as accurately as possible.

Give the other person a full hearing. Avoid interrupting another person unless you are sure you understand him fully, and that it is necessary. If you feel that you aren't sure you understand him, a well phrased question is usually more appropriate than an attempt by you to clarify his position. Impatience with others can lead to false understanding or agreement, and eventually leads to greater difficulties.

empathic listening: full attention to total communication environment

Use analytical skills as supplements to, not instead of, listening. To the degree that successful participation in discussion requires your understanding of others, rather than your speaking contributions, it is important not to be distracted by our own note taking, mental review of main points, critical analysis, or preparation for argumentative "comeback." An especially dubious recommendation frequently found in articles on listening is that, since listeners can listen faster than speakers can talk, the extra time should be used to review main points, "read between the lines," etc. Whether this conscious effort is exerted between words, sentences, or major ideas is never made clear. However, interviews with subjects following "surprise" listening tests have indicated that one of the major causes of listener distraction was a speaker's previous point: "I suddenly realized that I didn't know what he was talking about, because I was still thinking about what he had said before."

Omitted from this list are the many sound suggestions that have been made by other writers about: analyzing the speaker's intent, figuring out what he is going to say or what he has not said, note-taking, mental reorganization of a speaker's comments, etc. These, and others, are perfectly valid tools to be used in an oral communication setting, but their success is due to factors other than listening. For example, a discussion leader may wisely decide to mentally review the progress of a discussion while "listening" to a certain person unnecessarily repeating himself—but the wisdom of his action is due to his prior analysis, not to "listening ability." While listening to a specific individual, he may briefly jot down the person's main ideas for future reference; if he has developed an efficient note-taking skill, he may not miss anything significant—but he is effective because he is able to take notes with very little or no conscious effort, not because note-taking is a *listening* activity. Other less talented persons may never be able to take notes without distracting them from what is truly listening.

Conclusion

Many factors make up a discussion, and listening is only one of them; however, it is an extremely important factor, and it has been diluted in the past by a shift of its meaning from one of reception to one of critical analysis.

Empathic listening cannot of itself make a good speaker out of a poor one, a clear thinker out of a dull thinker, or a good discussion out of a bad discussion. But to the extent that problems result from a lack of participant reception and understanding of the discussion interaction, empathic listening appears to be the best answer.

SUGGESTED FURTHER READING

Barbara, Dominick A., *The Art of Listening.* Springfield, Illinois: Charles C. Thomas, Inc., 1958.

————, "Listening with a Modest Ear," *Today's Speech,* IX (February, 1961), 1–3.

Drake, Francis E., "How Do You Teach Listening?," *Southern States Journal,* XVI (May, 1951), 268–271.

Johnson, Wendell, *Your Most Enchanted Listener.* New York: Harper and Brothers, 1956.

Kelly, Charles M., "Mental Ability and Personality Factors in Listening," *Quarterly Journal of Speech,* XLIX (April, 1963), 152–156. (See footnote 2 above.)

————, "Listening: Complex of Activities—and a Unitary Skill?" *Speech Monographs,* XXXIV (November, 1967), 455–466. (See footnote 3 above.)

Lieb, Barbara, "How to be influenced Discriminatingly," *Today's Speech,* VIII (April, 1960), 24–26.

Nichols, Ralph G., "Listening: Questions and Problems," *Quarterly Journal of Speech,* XXXIII (February, 1947), 83–86.

————, "Do We Know How to Listen? Practical Helps in a Modern Age," *The Speech Teacher,* X (March, 1961), 118–124.

Nichols, Ralph G., and Leonard A. Stevens, *Are You Listening?* New York: McGraw-Hill Company, 1957.

Defensive Communication

Jack R. Gibb

One way to understand communication is to view it as a people process rather than as a language process. If one is to make fundamental improvement in communication, he must make changes in interpersonal relationships. One possible type of alteration—and the one with which this paper is concerned—is that of reducing the degree of defensiveness.

DEFINITION AND SIGNIFICANCE

Defensive behavior is defined as that behavior which occurs when an individual perceives threat or anticipates threat in the group. The person who behaves defensively, even though he also gives some attention to the common task, devotes an appreciable portion of his energy to defending himself. Besides talking about the topic, he thinks about how he appears to others, how he may be seen more favorably, how he may win, dominate, impress, or escape punishment and/or how he may avoid or mitigate a perceived or an anticipated attack.

> defensive behavior from perceived or anticipated threat in the group

   Such inner feelings and outward acts tend to create similarly defensive postures in others; and, if unchecked, the ensuing circular response becomes increasingly destructive. Defensive behavior, in short, engenders defensive listening, and this in turn produces postural, facial, and verbal cues which raise the defense level of the original communicator.

   Defense arousal prevents the listener from concentrating upon the message. Not only do defensive communicators send off multiple value, motive, and affect cues, but also defensive recipients distort what they receive. As a person becomes more and more defensive, he becomes less and less able to perceive accurately the motives, the values, and the emotions of the sender. The writer's analyses of tape recorded discussions revealed that increases in defensive behavior

> defensive group climate makes greater distortion; supportive climate, less distortion

TABLE 1

Categories of Behavior Characteristic of Supportive and Defensive Climates in Small Groups

Defensive Climates	Supportive Climates
1. Evaluation	1. Description
2. Control	2. Problem orientation
3. Strategy	3. Spontaneity
4. Neutrality	4. Empathy
5. Superiority	5. Equality
6. Certainty	6. Provisionalism

were correlated positively with losses in efficiency in communication.[1] Specifically, distortions became greater when defensive states existed in the groups.

The converse, moreover, also is true. The more "supportive" or defense reductive the climate the less the receiver reads into the communication distorted loadings which arise from projections of his own anxieties, motives, and concerns. As defenses are reduced, the receivers become better able to concentrate upon the structure, the content, and the cognitive meanings of the message.

CATEGORIES OF DEFENSIVE AND SUPPORTIVE COMMUNICATION

In working over an eight-year period with recordings of discussions occurring in varied settings, the writer developed the six pairs of defensive and supportive categories presented in Table 1. Behavior which a listener perceives as possessing any of the characteristics listed in the left-hand column arouses defensiveness, whereas that which he interprets as having any of the qualities designated as supportive reduces defensive feelings. The degree to which these reactions occur depends upon the personal level of defensiveness and upon the general climate in the group at the time.[2]

[1] J. R. Gibb, "Defense Level and Influence Potential in Small Groups," in L. Petrullo and B. M. Bass (eds.), *Leadership and Interpersonal Behavior* (New York: Holt, Rinehart and Winston, Inc., 1961), pp. 66–81.

[2] J. R. Gibb, "Sociopsychological Processes of Group Instruction," in N. B. Henry (ed.), *The Dynamics of Instructional Groups* (Fifty-ninth Yearbook of the National Society for the Study of Education, Part II, 1960), pp. 115–135.

EVALUATION AND DESCRIPTION

Speech or other behavior which appears evaluative increases defensiveness. If by expression, manner of speech, tone of voice, or verbal content the sender seems to be evaluating or judging the listener, then the receiver goes on guard. Of course, other factors may inhibit the reaction. If the listener thought that the speaker regarded him as an equal and was being open and spontaneous, for example, the evaluativeness in a message would be neutralized and perhaps not even perceived. This same principle applies equally to the other five categories of potentially defense-producing climates. The six sets are interactive.

speech which appears evaluative increases defensiveness

Because our attitudes toward other persons are frequently, and often necessarily, evaluative, expressions which the defensive person will regard as nonjudgmental are hard to frame. Even the simplest question usually conveys the answer that the sender wishes or implies the response that would fit into his value system. A mother, for example, immediately following an earth tremor that shook the house, sought for her small son with the question: "Bobby, where are you?" The timid and plaintive "Mommy, I didn't do it" indicated how Bobby's chronic mild defensiveness predisposed him to react with a projection of his own guilt and in the context of his chronic assumption that questions are full of accusation.

Anyone who has attempted to train professionals to use information-seeking speech with neutral affect appreciates how difficult it is to teach a person to say even the simple "who did that?" without being seen as accusing. Speech is so frequently judgmental that there is a reality base for the defensive interpretations which are so common.

When insecure, group members are particularly likely to place blame, to see others as fitting into categories of good or bad, to make moral judgments of their colleagues, and to question the value, motive, and affect loadings of the speech which they hear. Since value loadings imply a judgment of others, a belief that the standards of the speaker differ from his own causes the listener to become defensive.

Descriptive speech, in contrast to that which is evaluative, tends to arouse a minimum of uneasiness. Speech acts which the listener perceives as genuine requests for information or as material with neutral loadings is descriptive. Specifically, presentations of feelings, events, perceptions, or processes which do not ask or imply that the receiver change behavior or attitude are minimally defense producing. The difficulty in

speech which appears descriptive arouses minimum defensiveness

avoiding overtone is illustrated by the problems of news reporters in writing stories about unions, communists, Negroes, and religious activities without tipping off the "party" line of the newspaper. One can often tell from the opening words in a news article which side the newspaper's editorial policy favors.

CONTROL AND PROBLEM ORIENTATION

speech to control or influence evokes resistance

Speech which is used to control the listener evokes resistance. In most of our social intercourse someone is trying to do something to someone else—to change an attitude, to influence behavior, or to restrict the field of activity. The degree to which attempts to control produce defensiveness depends upon the openness of the effort, for a suspicion that hidden motives exist heightens resistance. For this reason attempts of nondirective therapists and progressive educators to refrain from imposing a set of values, a point of view, or a problem solution upon the receivers meet with many barriers. Since the norm is control, noncontrollers must earn the perceptions that their efforts have no hidden motives. A bombardment of persuasive "messages" in the fields of politics, education, special causes, advertising, religion, medicine, industrial relations and guidance has bred cynical and paranoidal responses in listeners.

Implicit in all attempts to alter another person is the assumption by the change agent that the person to be altered is inadequate. That the speaker secretly views the listener as ignorant, unable to make his own decisions, uninformed, immature, unwise, or possessed of wrong or inadequate attitudes is a subconscious perception which gives the latter a valid base for defensive reactions.

Methods of control are many and varied. Legalistic insistence on detail, restrictive regulations and policies, conformity norms, and all laws are among the methods. Gestures, facial expressions, other forms of nonverbal communication, and even such simple acts as holding a door open in a particular manner are means of imposing one's will upon another and hence are potential sources of resistance.

problem oriented communication evokes less resistance

Problem orientation, on the other hand, is the antithesis of persuasion. When the sender communicates a desire to collaborate in defining a mutual problem and in seeking its solution, he tends to create the same problem orientation in the listener; and, of greater importance, he implies that he has no predetermined solution, attitude, or method to impose. Such behavior is permissive in that it allows the receiver to set his own goals, make his own decisions, and evaluate his own progress—or to share with the sender in doing so. The exact methods of attaining permissiveness are not known, but they must involve a constellation of cues and they certainly go beyond mere verbal assurances that the communicator has no hidden desires to exercise control.

STRATEGY AND SPONTANEITY

When the sender is perceived as engaged in a stratagem involving ambiguous and multiple motivations, the receiver becomes defensive. No one wishes to be a guinea pig, a role player, or an impressed actor, and no one likes to be the victim of some hidden motivation. That which is concealed, also, may appear larger than it really is with the degree of defensiveness of the listener determining the perceived size of the suppressed element. The intense reaction of the reading audience to the material in the *Hidden Persuaders* indicates the prevalence of defensive reactions to multiple motivations behind strategy. Group members who are seen as "taking a role," as feigning emotion, as toying with their colleagues, as withholding information, or as having special sources of data are especially resented. One participant once complained that another was "using a listening technique" on him!

ambiguous or concealed motives, gimmicks, all forms of deceit produce defensiveness

A large part of the adverse reaction to much of the so-called human relations training is a feeling against what are perceived as gimmicks and tricks to fool or to "involve" people, to make a person think he is making his own decision, or to make the listener feel that the sender is genuinely interested in him as a person. Particularly violent reactions occur when it appears that someone is trying to make a stratagem appear spontaneous. One person has reported a boss who incurred resentment by habitually using the gimmick of "spontaneously" looking at his watch and saying, "My gosh, look at the time—I must run to an appointment." The belief was that the boss would create less irritation by honestly asking to be excused.

Similarly, the deliberate assumption of guilelessness and natural simplicity is especially resented. Monitoring the tapes of feedback and evaluation sessions in training groups indicates the surprising extent to which members perceive the strategies of their colleagues. This perceptual clarity may be quite shocking to the strategist, who usually feels that he has cleverly hidden the motivational aura around the "gimmick."

This aversion to deceit may account for one's resistance to politicians who are suspected of behind-the-scenes planning to get his vote, to psychologists whose listening apparently is motivated by more than the manifest or content-level interest in his behavior, or to the sophisticated, smooth, or clever person whose "oneupmanship" is marked with guile. In training groups the role-flexible person frequently is resented because his changes in behavior are perceived as strategic maneuvers.

spontaneous behavior arouses minimal defensiveness

In contrast, behavior which appears to be spontaneous and free of deception is defense reductive. If the communicator is seen as having a clean id, as having uncomplicated motivations, as being straightforward and honest, and as behaving spontaneously in response to the situation, he is likely to arouse minimal defense.

NEUTRALITY AND EMPATHY

neutrality arouses defenses

When neutrality in speech appears to the listener to indicate a lack of concern for his welfare, he becomes defensive. Group members usually desire to be perceived as valued persons, as individuals of special worth, and as objects of concern and affection. The clinical, detached, person-as-an-object-of-study attitude on the part of many psychologist-trainers is resented by group members. Speech with low affect that communicates little warmth or caring is in such contrast with the affect-laden speech in social situations that it sometimes communicates rejection.

empathy reduces defenses

Communication that conveys empathy for the feelings and respect for the worth of the listener, however, is particularly supportive and defense reductive. Reassurance results when a message indicates that the speaker identifies himself with the listener's problems, shares his feelings, and accepts his emotional reactions at face value. Abortive efforts to deny the legitimacy of the receiver's emotions by assuring the receiver that he need not feel bad, that he should not feel rejected, or that he is overly anxious, though often intended as support giving, may impress the listener as lack of acceptance. The combination of understanding and empathizing with the other person's emotions with no accompanying effort to change him apparently is supportive at a high level.

The importance of gestural behavioral cues in communicating empathy should be mentioned. Apparently spontaneous facial and bodily evidences of concern are often interpreted as especially valid evidence of deep-level acceptance.

SUPERIORITY AND EQUALITY

When a person communicates to another that he feels superior in position, power, wealth, intellectual ability, physical characteristics, or other ways he arouses defensiveness. Here as with the other sources of disturbance whatever arouses feelings of inadequacy causes the listener to center upon the affect loading of the statement rather than upon the cognitive elements. The receiver then reacts by not hearing the message, by forgetting it, by competing with the sender, or by becoming jealous of him.

superiority arouses defensiveness

The person who is perceived as feeling superior communicates that he is not willing to enter into a shared problem-solving relationship, that he probably does not desire feedback, that he does not require help, and/or that he will be likely to try to reduce the power, the status, or the worth of the receiver.

Many ways exist for creating the atmosphere that the sender feels himself equal to the listener. Defenses are reduced when one perceives the sender as being willing to enter into participative planning with the mutual trust and respect. Differences in talent, ability, worth, appearance, status, and power often exist, but the low defense communicator seems to attach little importance to these distinctions.

equality reduces defensiveness

CERTAINTY AND PROVISIONALISM

The effects of dogmatism in producing defensiveness are well known. Those who seem to know the answers, to require no additional data, and to regard themselves as teachers rather than as co-workers tend to put others on guard. Moreover, in the writer's experiment, listeners often perceived manifest expressions of certainty as connoting inward feelings of inferiority. They saw the dogmatic individual as needing to be right, as wanting to win an argument rather than solve a problem, and as seeing his ideas as truths to be defended. This kind of behavior often was associated with acts which others regarded as attempts to exercise control. People who were

the need to be right (certainty) produces defensiveness

right seemed to have low tolerance for members who were "wrong"—i.e., who did not agree with the sender.

provisionalism (investigating, exploring) reduces defensiveness

One reduces the defensiveness of the listener when he communicates that he is willing to experiment with his own behavior, attitudes, and ideas. The person who appears to be taking provisional attitudes, to be investigating issues rather than taking sides on them, to be problem solving rather than debating, and to be willing to experiment and explore tends to communicate that the listener may have some control over the shared quest or the investigation of the ideas. If a person is genuinely searching for information and data, he does not resent help or company along the way.

CONCLUSION

The implications of the above material for the parent, the teacher, the manager, the administrator, or the therapist are fairly obvious. Arousing defensiveness interferes with communication and thus makes it difficult—and sometimes impossible—for anyone to convey ideas clearly and to move effectively toward the solution of therapeutic, educational, or managerial problems.

SUGGESTED FURTHER READING

Barker, Larry L., *Listening Behavior.* Englewood Cliffs, New Jersey: Prentice-Hall, Inc., 1971.

Brooks, William D., *Speech Communication.* Dubuque, Iowa: William C. Brown Company Publishers, 1971.

Gibb, J. R., "Defense Level and Influence Potential in Small Groups," in L. Petrullo and B. M. Bass, eds., *Leadership and Interpersonal Behavior.* New York: Holt, Rinehart & Winston, 1961. (See footnote 1 above.)

Giffin, Kim and Bobby R. Patton, *Fundamentals of Interpersonal Communication.* New York: Harper & Row Publishers, 1971.

Keltner, John W., *Interpersonal Speech-Communication.* Belmont, California: Wadsworth Publishing Company, Inc., 1970.

Wheeler, Ladd, *Interpersonal Influence.* Boston: Allyn and Bacon, Inc., 1970.

Wiseman, Gordon and Larry Barker, *Speech-Interpersonal Communication.* San Francisco, California: Chandler Publishing Company, 1967.

Interpersonal Trust in
Small Group Communication

Kim Giffin

INTRODUCTION

Traditionally trust has been viewed as a somewhat mystical and intangible factor, probably defying careful definition. Dictionary definitions include such abstract terms as "confidence," "reliance," "expectation," and "hope." People have talked about trust and have recognized its existence, but until recently this has been the extent of scientific interest in the concept.

In his pioneering research on trust in 1958, Morton Deutsch[1] noted its importance to an understanding of social life and personality development, and indicated his view of the current state of research: ". . . an examination of a half-dozen or more of the leading textbooks in social psychology (*e.g.,* texts by Cartwright and Zander, Homans, Krech and Crutchfield, Lewin, Lindzey, Newcomb) reveals that the word 'trust' does not appear in any of their indexes. So far as we know, the research summarized in this paper represents the first attempt to investigate experimentally the phenomena of trust."[2]

Deutsch struggled with the problem of defining trust; he noted that it involved more than predictability, although expectation was involved; he also noted that risk or "motivational relevance" (something invested) is requisite, and that "when trust is not fulfilled, the trusting individual will suffer an un-

Note: Mr. Giffin is Director of the Communication Research Center, University of Kansas.

[1] Morton Deutsch, "Trust and Suspicion," *Journal of Conflict Resolution,* II (December 1958), 265–279.

[2] *Ibid.,* 265.

pleasant consequence."[3] He defined trust in such a way that it captured some of the connotations of everyday usage and also permitted experimental research: "An individual may be said to have trust in the occurrence of an event if he expects its occurrence and his expectation leads to behavior which he perceives to have greater negative motivational consequences if the expectation is not confirmed than positive motivational consequences if it is confirmed."[4]

It appears that the following elements are essential to describing the behavior of a trusting person:

(1) A person is *relying* upon something.

(2) This *something relied upon* may be an object, an event, or a person.

(3) Something is *risked* by the trusting person.

(4) The trusting person *hopes to achieve some goal* by taking this risk.

(5) The desired goal is *not perceived as certain.*

(6) The trusting person has some degree of confidence in the object of his trust.

In view of these essential elements this writer has adopted this formal definition of interpersonal trust in the communication process: *reliance upon the communication behavior of another person in order to achieve a desired but uncertain objective in a risky situation.*

definition of interpersonal trust

In an analysis of the communication process that has become a classic reference in modern times, Newcomb described the relationship between a person and the object or concept about which he is communicating as an "orientation."[5] He defined "orientation" as "equivalent to 'attitude' in its more inclusive sense of referring to both cathectic and cognitive tendencies." In this writer's conceptualization of trust the relationship between a trusting person and the trusted person is viewed similarly as an orientation, and thus as an attitude in the broad meaning of the term. Both cathectic and cognitive behavior appear to be involved in the phenomenon of personal trust.

[3] *Ibid.*

[4] *Ibid.,* 266.

[5] Theodore M. Newcomb, "An Approach to the Study of Communicative Acts," *Psychological Review,* LX (May 1953), 393–404.

TRUST AND COOPERATION IN SMALL GROUPS

In his experiments Deutsch used a two-person non-zero-sum game, a variation of the "prisoner's dilemma" which Luce and Raiffa describe:

> Two suspects are taken into custody and separated. The district attorney . . . points out to each that he has two alternatives: to confess to the crime the police are sure they have done or not to confess. If they both do not confess then the district attorney states that he will book them on some trumped-up charge . . . ; if they both confess, they will be prosecuted, but he will recommend less than the most severe sentence; but if one confesses and the other does not, then the confessor will receive lenient treatment for turning state's evidence, whereas the latter will get the 'book' slapped at him.[6]

As illustrated below, in the design used by Deutsch, Person I has to choose between rows X and Y, and Person II has to choose between columns A and B:

		Person II	
		A	B
Person I	X	(+9, +9)	(−10, +10)
	Y	(+10, −10)	(−9, −9)

Person I's payoffs are the first numbers in the parentheses and Person II's are the second. The amount of money won or lost by each is a function of the combination of the choices made by each of the two persons. For example, if Person I chooses row Y (in an attempt to win $10), and Person II chooses column B (in an attempt to win $10), they both lose $9. Examination of the possibilities of choice for Person I shows that he can win most and lose least by choosing Y, as Person II can do by choosing B. But if Person I chooses Y and Person II chooses B they both lose $9. Both can win only in the AX box.

Throughout his various published accounts of his use of this game Deutsch has emphasized the principle noted in his 1958 paper: "The essential psychological feature of the game is that there is no possibility for 'rational' behavior in it unless . . . mutual trust exists."[7] He went on to generalize that there

---

[6]R. D. Luce and H. Raiffa, *Games and Decisions: Introduction and Critical Survey* (New York, 1957).

[7]Deutsch, "Trust and Suspicion," 270.

are many social situations that are not rational unless mutual trust exists—for example, buyer-seller transactions, husband-wife relations, pedestrian-driver interactions, and a crowd in a theater when there is a fire.

Using this basic experimental situation Deutsch and his associates conducted a series of studies. His results suggest that when communication is absent and one has to choose without knowledge of the other person's choices, a cooperative orientation will tend to produce trusting and trustworthy behavior. On the other hand, a competitive orientation will tend to result in suspecting rather than trusting behavior, even when situational factors such as communication possibilities are encouraging. In contrast to both the cooperative and competitive orientations, which are not influenced by situational factors to any great extent, the subject led to have an individualistic orientation is influenced greatly by interpersonal conditions.[8]

cooperative orientations produce trusting behavior: competitive produce suspecting behavior

Studies of some of the social conditions under which mutual trust would arise between subjects who originally have an individualistic orientation were conducted by students of Deutsch. They focused upon the influence of communication, the influence of social power, and the influence of a third party.

individualistic orientations influenced by interpersonal conditions

For the study of the influence of communication Loomis employed a game matrix similar to the one described above.[9] About two hundred college students each played five trials where Player II was always the confederate of the experimenter. The subjects were all individualistically oriented. Ten experimental groups were selected, half of the members "note-senders" and the other half "note-receivers." A control group without such communication was also employed. The notes were standardized forms which expressed four message variables: *expectation, intention, retaliation,* and *absolution.*

Communication produced a higher degree of trust, both in the senders and the receivers. About one-tenth of the non-communicating subjects demonstrated trust in the other person, whereas two-thirds of the communicating subjects did. The percentage of trust increased as communication increased. In essence, the research by Loomis indicated that communication is likely to be effective to the extent that the basic features of a cooperative interrelationship are mani-

communication influences trust

[8] *Ibid.,* 271.

[9] James L. Loomis, "Communication, The Development of Trust, and Cooperative Behavior," *Human Relations,* XII (November 1959), 305–315.

fested in the communication; these basic features are as follows:

(1) Expression of one's intentions.

(2) Expression of one's expectations.

(3) Expression of one's planned reaction to violation of one's expectation.

(4) Expression of a means of restoring cooperation after a violation of one's expectation.

power relationships, motivational strategies influence trust

Solomon, another of Deutsch's students, conducted research on the influence of certain types of power relationships and motivational strategies upon the development of trust. Game matrices for four power conditions were set up in the experiment. One member of the dyad was a subject (S) while the other (O) was a confederate of the experimenter. O interacted with S in one of three conditions of relative power—O in absolute power, partial power and equal power. O employed one of three types of game strategies in each power condition—conditional cooperation, unconditional cooperation, and non-cooperation. Solomon's findings supported the following conclusions:

(1) A subject is more likely to engage in trusting behavior as the amount of power he has over the trusted person is increased.

(2) Under conditions of equal power, a subject tends to respond to unconditional cooperation by another person with exploitative game behavior, whereas he tends to cooperate more with a conditionally cooperative other person.[10]

Deutsch noted that the results of this study indicate that an individual is more likely to trust another if he believes the other person has nothing to gain from untrustworthy behavior and if he perceives that he is able to exert some control over the other.[11]

third parties influence trust

As to the influence of a third party, the research by Farr, another of Deutsch's students, was designed to determine if

[10] Leonard Solomon, "The Influence of Some Types of Power Relationships and Game Strategies upon the Development of Interpersonal Trust," *Journal of Abnormal and Social Psychology,* LXI (May 1960), 223–230.

[11] Deutsch, "Trust and Suspicion," 277.

two individualistic-oriented players in the game situation would trust each other more if they each knew that they both disliked a third player. The results were that the introduction of a disliked third person increased the tendency to make trusting choices.[12]

In a later study, Deutsch reported an investigation of trust, trustworthiness, and the F scale.[13] Deutsch has his subjects play an interpersonal game in which they were required, in one situation, to choose between trusting and suspecting another person; in the second situation subjects were required to choose between acting in a trustworthy manner and in an untrustworthy manner. Subjects who were more trusting were more likely to be more trustworthy. Subjects with low F scores tended to be trusting and trustworthy, whereas subjects with high F scores tended to be more suspicious and untrustworthy. The importance of these correlations is the demonstration of a relationship between trusting and untrusting behavior and a measurable personality dimension. Further work needs to be done, possibly with Rokeach's dogmatism scale.[14]

investigation of trust, trustworthiness, and the F scale

Evans reported the use of two-person non-zero-sum games in an experiment concerned with the effect of unilateral promise, enforceable or unenforceable, upon cooperation and trust. The results were that subjects receiving an enforceable promise showed more trusting behavior than subjects receiving no promise.[15]

unilateral promises influence trust

The theory of interpersonal trust and cooperation in small groups is at present still in its infancy. Deutsch's beginning has been very significant and beneficial in that he has maintained a high degree of scientific rigor. From his work and that of his students the following hypotheses can be formulated concerning personal trust in the communication process:

(1)   A cooperative (or non-cooperative) orientation on the part of the listener will influence his tendency to trust a speaker.

(2)   Communication between the speaker and listener will

---

[12] James N. Farr, "The Effects of a Disliked Third Person upon the Development of Mutual Trust," an unpublished paper presented to the American Psychological Association Annual Conference, New York, September, 1957.

[13] Morton Deutsch, "Trust, Trustworthiness, and the F Scale," *Journal of Abnormal and Social Psychology,* LXI (July 1960), 138–140.

[14] Milton Rokeach, *The Open and Closed Mind* (New York, 1960).

[15] Gary Evans, "Effect of Unilateral Promise and Value of Rewards upon Cooperation and Trust," *Journal of Abnormal and Social Psychology,* LXIX (November 1964), 587–590.

tend to increase the likelihood of interpersonal trust between them, especially if they express their intentions and expectations regarding interpersonal trust, and indicate their plan of reacting to violations of their expectations.

(3)   Increased social power over the communicator by the listener increases the likelihood of the listener's trusting the communicator.

(4)   A listener will tend to trust a speaker if he knows they both dislike a specified third person.

(5)   Trusting listeners probably have identifiable personality factors similar to those persons who produce high scores on the F scale.

INTERPERSONAL TRUST AND DEFENSIVE COMMUNICATION

defensive behavior influences trust

Starting a long-range research effort in 1953, Jack Gibb emphasized the reduction of defensive behavior in groups.[16] This defensive behavior seemed to be caused, in part, by distrust. In later work Gibb began to focus on trust and its development.[17] Still later Gibb associated trust with interpersonal acceptance.[18]

Gibb's approach, in comparison with that of Deutsch, follows developmental lines frequently associated with the clinic more than with the laboratory. In the main, Gibb (1964) has presented a very useful theoretical formulation of the relationships between trust and primary dimensions of group behavior.

close relationships between self-trust, self-awareness, self-acceptance

About a quarter of a century ago Carl Rogers began to report a movement toward a non-directive approach to psychotherapy, culminating in Rogers' client-centered therapy.[19] Relevant to this paper is Rogers' emphasis on the patient's need for personal trust in the therapist and his communication behavior. Rogers' concept of *acceptance* or *psychological safety* in psychotherapy groups was a forerunner of Gibb's

[16] Jack Gibb, "Factors Producing Defensive Behavior within Groups," *Final Technical Report, ONR Contract Nonr-3088 (00)* (Washington, D.C., National Training Laboratories, 1962).

[17] Jack Gibb, "Defensive Communication" *Journal of Communication,* XI (September 1961), 141–148. (See preceding article in this text.)

[18] Jack Gibb, "Climate for Trust Formation," in Leland P. Bradford, Jack Gibb and Kenneth D. Benne, eds., *T-Group Theory and Laboratory Method: Innovation in Re-Education* (New York, 1964), pp. 279–309.

[19] Carl Rogers, *Client-Centered Therapy* (Boston, 1951).

concept of *supportive climate* in the communication process. In a more recent work Rogers emphasizes a very close relationship between self-trust, self-awareness, and self-acceptance.[20]

In 1964 Gibb reported that his research on "a wide variety of groups in various life settings" indicated that people are concerned about four basic goals which are inevitably derived from all social interaction: *acceptance, information, goal-achievement,* and *social control.*[21]

The *acceptance* goal, according to Gibb, is related to the formation of trust of self and others.[22] Gibb's theory was derived from analysis of tape recordings of a large number of human relations training groups (T-Groups). This research approach does not allow the definitive assessment of complex hypotheses, but it can indicate cyclic changes, "with movement back and forth across dimensions," according to Gibb.[23] It allowed the identification of early, "persuasive" attempts on the part of group members. Fear and distrust were shown to produce in the group a reaction of cynicism and suspicion. At a later time, "participative" behavior, involving confidence and trust, produced reactions from the group identified as trust, diversity, and exploitation of opportunities to achieve group progress.

Gibb's work provides the basis for specific hypotheses regarding interpersonal trust in the communication process: interpersonal trust is facilitated by communication which is perceived as descriptive rather than evaluative, oriented toward problems instead of interpersonal control, spontaneous rather than strategic, empathic rather than neutral, indicative of an attitude of equality instead of superiority, and expressive of provisionally held viewpoints rather than dogmatic certainties.

behavior categories of supportive and defensive climates

GROUP CONFORMITY AND PERSONAL TRUST

In addition to the studies reviewed above there is a third series which focuses upon an individual's trust in the communication

conformity influences trust

[20]Carl Rogers, *On Becoming a Person* (New York, 1961), pp. 102–105 and 173–175; see also Carl Rogers, "A Theory of Therapy, Personality, and Interpersonal Relationships, as Developed in the Client-Centered Framework," in Sigmund Koch, ed., *Psychology: A Study of A Science,* Vol. 3 (New York, 1959), 184–256.

[21]Gibb, "Defensive Communication," 281.

[22]*Ibid.,* 280.

[23]*Ibid.,* 289.

of the other members of the group. These studies do not focus on the concept of trust, but they very clearly study attitude change as a result of interpersonal trust. They are known as the studies on conformity.

The Asch[24] study was a prototype for a large number of studies showing that an individual tends to trust the communication of the majority when he is in a group situation *in spite of contradictory evidence literally in front of the eyes of the subject.* This principle has been demonstrated experimentally many times in studies reported by Asch[25] and by Crutchfield.[26]

How can such apparent interpersonal trust be explained? What about source credibility, with its probable (logical) dimensions of expertness, reliability, and intentions of the source? Is it possible that an individual would rather believe what he is told by the majority of his associates in spite of evidence of their *lack* of expertness, reliability, or good intentions? Is conformity thus so attractive?

Familiarity with the conformity studies on the part of the reader may be assumed—they have been neatly summarized by Krech, Crutchfield, and Ballachey.[27] Our interest will be focused upon conditions which influence such extreme inter-

[24] Solomon E. Asch, "Effects of Group Pressure upon the Modification and Distortion of Judgment," in Harold Guetzkow, ed., *Groups, Leadership, and Men* (Pittsburgh, 1951), pp. 177–190.

[25] See: Solomon E. Asch, *Social Psychology* (Englewood Cliffs, 1952); Solomon E. Asch, "Studies of Independence and Conformity: A Minority of One Against a Unanimous Majority," *Psychological Monographs,* LXX (1956), No. 9 (Whole no. 416); and Solomon E. Asch, "Effects of Group Pressure upon the Modification and Distortion of Judgments," in Eleanor E. Maccoby, Theodore M. Newcomb, and E. L. Hartley, eds., *Readings in Social Psychology* (New York, 1958), pp. 174–183.

[26] See: Richard S. Crutchfield, "A New Technique for Measuring Individual Differences in Conformity to Group Judgment," *Procedures of the Invitational Conference on Testing Problems* (Princeton, Educational Testing Service, 1954), pp. 69–74; Richard S. Crutchfield, "The Measurement of Individual Conformity to Group Opinion among Officer Personnel," *Research Bulletin* (Berkeley, Institute of Personality Assessment and Research, University of California, 1954); Richard S. Crutchfield, "Conformity and Character," *American Psychologist,* X (May 1955), 191–198; Richard S. Crutchfield, "Conformity and Creative Thinking," a paper delivered at the Symposium on Creative Thinking, University of Colorado (Boulder, 1958); Richard S. Crutchfield, "Personal and Situational Factors in Conformity to Group Pressure," *Acta Psychologica,* XV (1959), 386–388; Richard S. Crutchfield, "The Effect on Individual Conformity of Authoritative Confirmation or Repudiation of Group Consensus," a paper delivered at the Annual Meeting of the Eastern Psychological Association, Atlantic City, New Jersey, 1959; and Richard S. Crutchfield, "Detrimental Effects of Conformity Pressures on Creative Thinking," *Psychologische Beiträge,* VI (January 1962), 463–471.

[27] David Frech, Richard S. Crutchfield, and Egerton L. Ballachey, *Individual in Society* (New York, 1962).

personal trust, and a theoretical explanation of the psychological forces involved.

The findings of the Asch studies indicated that a disturbance of the unanimous majority by the presence of a subject who gave true responses markedly increased the independence of the critical subjects. The withdrawal of this "true" partner by having him initially respond correctly and then switch to join the confederate majority produced a powerful and surprising reversal: it restored the majority effect to full force. The opposite condition, that is, the *late* switching of a "true" partner, reduced the level of yielding to about nine percent, but did not completely contravene the influence of the remaining confederates. With the confederate opposition reduced to one other person only, the erroneous influence all but disappeared; with the opposition (to one naïve subject) increased to two, it produced about thirteen percent errors; with the opposition increased to three, the conformity influence appeared in full force. Further increases in the number of confederate opponents did not significantly change the results. Crutchfield's findings may be summarized as follows:[28]

(1) Substantial amounts of yielding were produced despite the fact that bogus group consensus was manifestly wrong; for example, forty-six percent of fifty military officers agreed that a star, actually one-third *smaller* than a circle, was the *larger.*

(2) Many individuals could be pressured into yielding on an opinion item *which degraded them personally;* for example, thirty-seven percent of the military officers tested agreed that they probably were not good leaders.

(3) Yielding was far greater on difficult items than on easy ones.

(4) There were extremely large individual differences in amount of yielding, with some individuals giving way on almost all items, and some few yielding on none.

(5) When individuals were retested privately, a significant part of the yielding disappeared, but by no means all of it; for example, in a study of applicants to medical school, about fifty percent of the original group-pressure effect persisted.

[28] *Ibid.,* pp. 509–511.

<table>
<tr><td>

type of issue or
problem influences
trust and conformity

</td><td>

Coleman, Blake, and Mouton supported findings of Crutchfield that the type of issue or problem is related to interpersonal trust of other members of the group and subsequent conformity of opinion. They reported correlations of about 0.89 between degree of yielding and degree of difficulty of the item; they also found direct evidence that yielding on difficult items was related to the degree of certainty felt by the individual concerning his own judgment.[29] Supporting evidence was also found by Tuddenham.[30]

</td></tr>
</table>

type of issue or problem influences trust and conformity

Coleman, Blake, and Mouton supported findings of Crutchfield that the type of issue or problem is related to interpersonal trust of other members of the group and subsequent conformity of opinion. They reported correlations of about 0.89 between degree of yielding and degree of difficulty of the item; they also found direct evidence that yielding on difficult items was related to the degree of certainty felt by the individual concerning his own judgment.[29] Supporting evidence was also found by Tuddenham.[30]

extremity of majority opinion influences conformity

The extremity of the opinion presented by the majority is also an influential factor. Tuddenham found that when the distorted opinion lies well outside the range of ordinarily acceptable judgment, yielding occurs in fewer individuals, and to a much lesser degree.[31]

cohesiveness influences trust and subsequent conformity

If the naïve subject is a bona fide member of a group (in a psychological sense), the cohesiveness of the group is related to the degree of interpersonal trust and subsequent conformity. Cohesiveness has come to be defined in small group research, according to Golembiewski, as a combination of personal attractiveness of people in the group, attractiveness of the group's tasks or activities (including resultant rewards), and prestige associated with belonging to the group.[32]

Evidence of the influence of cohesiveness on conformity was found by Crutchfield: persons belonging to ethnic or racial minorities conformed highly when tested in groups where they were the only such minority member.[33] Further evidence of the influence of cohesiveness on conformity was reported by Gerard.[34] Harvey and Consalvi discovered that the *second* highest status member in a small group was more conforming than either the leader or those lower in status.[35]

[29] James F. Coleman, R. R. Blake, and J. S. Mouton, "Task Difficulty and Conformity Pressures," *Journal of Abnormal and Social Psychology,* LVII (1958), 120–122.

[30] Read D. Tuddenham, "The Influence upon Judgment of a Grossly Distorted Norm," *Technical Report No. 2, ONR Contract NR 170–159* (Berkeley, University of California, 1957).

[31] Read D. Tuddenham, "The Influence upon Judgment of the Apparent Discrepancy between Self and Others," *Journal of Social Psychology,* LIII (February 1961), 69–79.

[32] Robert T. Golembiewski, *The Small Group* (Chicago, 1962), p. 151.

[33] Crutchfield, "Personal and Situational Factors in Conformity to Group Pressure," 387–388.

[34] Harold B. Gerard, "The Anchorage of Opinions in Face-to-Face Groups," *Human Relations,* VII (August 1954), 313–315.

[35] O. J. Harvey and C. Consalvi, "Status and Conformity to Pressures in Informal Groups," *Journal of Abnormal and Social Psychology,* LX (March 1960), 182–187.

Jackson and Saltzstein demonstrated that the influence of cohesiveness upon conformity is dependent upon the person's position of status in the social structure of the group, and upon the nature of the group task.[36]

Personality factors influential in an individual's conforming to group opinion have been studied primarily by Crutchfield; these findings may be summarized as follows:[37]

personality factors
influence conformity

(1) Conformists are significantly less intelligent as measured on the Concept Mastery Test developed by Terman.[38]

(2) Conformists are clearly lower in "ego-strength" and in ability to work under stress as measured on the Manifest Anxiety Scale developed by Taylor.[39]

(3) Conformists are inclined toward pronounced feelings of personal inferiority and inadequacy as measured on the Adjective Check List developed by Gough.[40]

(4) Conformists exhibit intense preoccupation with other people, as contrasted with the more self-contained, autonomous interpersonal attitudes of the independent persons.

(5) The conformists express attitudes and values of a far more conventional and moralistic nature than do the independent subjects. Support for this point was provided by Nadler who found F-scale scores correlated 0.48 with conformity scores measured by the Asch technique.[41]

(3) Conformists are inclined toward pronounced feelings of personal inferiority and inadequacy as measured on the Adjective Check List developed by Gough.[40]

(4) Conformists exhibit intense preoccupation with other people, as contrasted with the more self-contained, autonomous interpersonal attitudes of the independent persons.

[36] Jay M. Jackson and H. D. Saltzstein, "The Effect of Person-Group Relationships on Conformity Processes," *Journal of Abnormal and Social Psychology,* LVII (February 1958), 17–24. For an explanation of the personal relationships involved in Jackson's concept of group structure, see: Jay Jackson, "A Space for Conceptualizing Person-Group Relationships," *Human Relations,* XII (February 1959), 3–15.

[37] *Individual in Society,* p. 526.

[38] Louis M. Terman, *Concept Mastery Test Manual* (New York, Psychological Corporation, 1956).

[39] Janet A. Taylor, "A Personality Scale of Manifest Anxiety," *Journal of Abnormal and Social Psychology,* XLVIII (April 1953), 285–290.

[40] H. G. Gough, "The Adjective Check List as a Personality Assessment Device," *Psychological Reports Monograph Supplement,* VI (1960), 107–122.

(5)   The conformists express attitudes and values of a far more conventional and moralistic nature than do the independent subjects. Support for this point was provided by Nadler who found F-scale scores correlated 0.48 with conformity scores measured by the Asch technique.[41]

perceptions of reality validated by checking with others

What explanation can be offered for the conformity behavior described above? Three explanations may be considered: (1) a need to validate one's perceptions of reality, (2) a need for social approval (to "belong" to a group), and (3) a need for the removal of cognitive dissonance.

In a classic essay of modern times Festinger set forth a theory of the need to validate one's understanding of reality (the world about us) by checking with other people.[42] He identified a continuum on which he placed at one end "physical reality" and on the other end "social reality." In a later paper Festinger further elaborated his theory of social comparison processes.[43] Physical reality was said to involve such things as surfaces or objects, the perception of which an individual can validate with his physiological senses. Social reality was said to involve perceptions of such things as appropriate social behavior, judgments of a moral or ethical nature, those elements of "reality" which we usually associate with attitudes, opinions or beliefs. An opinion, attitude, or belief was said to be perceived by the individual as valid to the extent it was anchored in (or reflected by) an approved reference group.

The theory of a need to validate one's opinions may account, in part, for some of the experimentally derived conformity behavior, but it does not account for all of it very well. The Asch technique, with judgment of the length of lines drawn on cardboard, is not in the category usually identified as "social" reality.

man needs social approval

A second theoretical explanation is the theory of man's need for social approval, a need to "belong" to a group. There is a vast literature on this theory, and there is some evidence of its appropriateness to explain the conformity behavior in Asch's reports of interviews with his subjects, in which they

[41] E. B. Nadler, "Yielding, Authoritarianism, and Authoritarian Ideology Regarding Groups," *Journal of Abnormal and Social Psychology,* LVIII (July 1959), 408–410.

[42] Leon Festinger, "Informal Social Communication," *Psychological Review,* LVII (September 1950), 271–282.

[43] Leon Festinger, "A Theory of Social Comparison Processes," *Human Relations,* VII (May 1954), 117–140.

indicated that they "longed" to agree with the majority and missed the feeling of being "at one" with the group.[44]

A third theoretical explanation lies in the cognitive consistency theories. In fact, in the long run, the balance theory of Heider,[45] as well as the congruity theory of Osgood,[46] the cognitive dissonance theory of Festinger,[47] and especially Newcomb's discussion of the communicative significance of cognitive consistency,[48] may go far toward explaining behavior involving interpersonal trust in the communication process, at least much further than is currently reflected in the studies of ethos or source credibility.

cognitive consistency theories aid in explaining trust

All three consistency theories are somewhat different, but they have this in common: they assert that the normal condition of a person's attitudes is that of internal consistency between components perceived as related, and that attitude change is the consequence of the reduction of inconsistency which has been generated by new communications about, or new perceptions of, an attitude object. The recent summary of these theories by Roger Brown brings out this principle.[49]

Heider's cognitive balance theory asserts that unbalanced cognitive systems tend to shift toward a state of balance. He presents a detailed account of a cognitive system made up of three elements: a person (P), his perception of another person (O), and an object (X). There is balance if P likes O, and O is perceived as liking X, and P likes X. Balance theory suggests that the cognitive process strives to achieve balanced cognitive structures. With Heider's work should be grouped Cartwright and Harary's mathematical restatement,[50] and Newcomb's later extension of it to the development of attitudinal consensus through communicative processes.[51]

cognitive balance theory

[44] Solomon E. Asch, "Opinions and Social Pressure," *Scientific American,* CXCIII (1955), 31–35.

[45] Fritz Heider, "Attitudes and Cognitive Organization," *Journal of Psychology,* XXI (January 1946), 107–112. Also see Fritz Heider, *The Psychology of Interpersonal Relations* (New York, 1958).

[46] Charles E. Osgood, George J. Suci, and Percy H. Tannenbaum, *The Measurement of Meaning* (Urbana, Illinois, 1957).

[47] Leon Festinger, *A Theory of Cognitive Dissonance* (Evanston, Illinois, 1957).

[48] Theodore M. Newcomb, "Individual Systems of Orientation," in Sigmund Koch, ed., *Psychology: A Study of A Science, Vol. 3* (New York, 1959), 384–422.

[49] Roger Brown, "Models of Attitude Change," in Roger Brown, E. Galanter, E. Hess, and G. Mandler, eds., *New Directions in Psychology* (New York, 1962).

[50] Dorwin Cartwright and Frank Harary, "Structural Balance: A Generalization of Heider's Theory," *Psychological Review,* LXIII (September 1956), 277–293.

[51] Newcomb, "Individual Systems of Orientation," 384–422.

congruity theory

Osgood, Suci, and Tannenbaum presented a congruity theory which reflected their primary interest in the meaning of signs. It has been extended through additional work on attitudes as measured by semantic differential scales. Thus, whenever two concepts are related by an assertion, a person's attitude toward the two shifts toward congruence. The magnitude of the shift is inversely proportional to the intensity of the original attitudes toward the two concepts.

cognitive dissonance

Festinger's theory of cognitive dissonance holds that two cognitions are in dissonant relation if, considering these two alone, the obverse of one would follow from the other. The theory further holds that such dissonance, being psychologically uncomfortable, will motivate the individual to try to reduce dissonance and achieve consonance.

These three approaches by Heider, Osgood, and Festinger, together with the elaborations by Newcomb and by Cartwright and Harary, may be identified as theories of cognitive consistency. They appear to provide a most reasonable explanation of conformity behavior. With some slight adjustments, at least Festinger's theory can be made to include the theory of a need for belonging; lack of acceptance, or partial acceptance, can produce cognitive dissonance. Festinger, in his experimental applications of his theory, in large part focuses upon the influence of what one does upon how one thinks. This brings out the dark yet compelling notion that what one is influenced to do (particularly if the influencing force is veiled or disguised) determines what one internally becomes. (Anticipated by William James, this concept is not new.)[52] But the idea, as developed by Festinger and his associates in their documented studies, and as reviewed by Rosenberg,[53] has produced an instrument which resonates something of the temper of our times: that we do not make our acts, but that they make us; and that we do not exercise as much free will as we once thought. The dissonance group, with penetrating insight and forceful laboratory demonstrations, have not only come upon something of significance, but have led us into deep philosophical waters. However, the nature of their thinking and the actual conformity behavior of experimental subjects seem to fit together.

Meanwhile, further studies of conformity are in progress. A recent report by Willis indicates continuing work on re-

[52]William James, *Psychology, Briefer Course* (New York, 1892), pp. 448–449.

[53]Milton J. Rosenberg, "An Evaluation of Models for Attitude Change," a paper delivered as part of the Division 9 Symposium on Attitude Change at the Annual Meeting of the American Psychological Association, 1963.

sponse modes in social influence situations.[54] Revised conceptualizations of the nature of conforming responses are being formulated; experimental evaluation of them by Willis is in progress.

TOWARD A THEORY OF INTERPERSONAL TRUST IN GROUP COMMUNICATION

The word "theory" is here used to refer to thoughtful guesses about the ways in which factors in a system are related. In this sense a "good theory" should be based upon available information and should also suggest fruitful areas for further investigation. Thus, a theorist may employ hypothetical constructs for possible, but as yet unmeasurable, variables; also, he may posit relationships which appear to be present, but are more hypothetical than certain, and for which little evidence is currently available.

It appears that personal trust is *influenced by* certain variables, and that it in turn *influences* certain variables. Thus, trust is viewed by this writer as a mediating variable, produced by behavior which can be changed (somewhat), and functionally related to desirable behavior in groups.

Factors which Tend to Produce Interpersonal Trust

It appears that trust is influenced both by *interpersonal* variables and by *personality* factors. *Interpersonal* variables which tend to influence a person (p) to trust another person (o) appear to be the following:

factors producing trust

1. A cooperative interpersonal relationship wherein p expects cooperation from o, and p believes he is expected to give cooperation in return.

2. Communication from o which indicates to p an intention on the part of o to reciprocate trust when offered by p.

3. Communication from o which indicates to p an expectation by o of trusting behavior on the part of p.

4. Communication from o to p which indicates o's plan of reaction to a violation by p of o's trust in p.

[54] Richard H. Willis, "Social Influence, Information Processing, and Net Conformity in Dyads," *Technical Report, ONR Contract Nonr-916(12)* (St. Louis, Department of Psychology, Washington University, 1964).

5. Communication from o which indicates a way of restoring o's cooperation when o's trust has been violated by p.

6. A condition in which p has a high degree of power (control) over o.

7. Behavior by o which is interpreted by p as conditional trust of p.

8. Behavior on the part of o which indicates to p that o has nothing to gain by untrustworthy behavior.

9. A situation into which is introduced a third person who is disliked by both o and p.

10. An enforceable promise to p from o.

11. Communication from o perceived by p as:
    (a) descriptive rather than evaluative;
    (b) problem-oriented rather than oriented toward social control;
    (c) spontaneous rather than strategic;
    (d) empathic rather than neutral;
    (e) between equals rather than between persons of unequal status;
    (f) provisional rather than certain.

12. The presence of a strong majority opinion on the part of the others present; this influence toward trust will be strengthened when:
    (a) there are at least three others unified on the majority opinion;
    (b) all others present are unanimous in their opinion;
    (c) when the issue involved requires a decision believed by p to be difficult to make;
    (d) when the majority opinion is not outside the range of ordinarily acceptable judgment;
    (e) when p has psychological membership in a reference group presenting a majority opinion;
    (f) when p is accepted as a member of a goal-oriented group of interdependent persons working on a group task.

Personality factors which tend to influence a person to trust others in general appear to be the following:

1. High flexibility on the part of p; that is, low scores on the F Scale (less authoritarianism) or on Rokeach's Dogmatism Scale.

2.   Low intelligence of p.

3.   Low "ego-strength" of p and poor ability to work under stress, as measured on the Taylor Manifest Anxiety Scale.

4.   Pronounced feelings of personal inferiority and inadequacy as measured by Gough's Adjective Check List.

Conditions of Group Interaction Influenced by Interpersonal Trust

It appears that the following dimensions of *interpersonal* behavior tend to increase when interpersonal trust is increased:

conditions influencing trust

1.   Acceptance of legitimate influence by others.

2.   Acceptance of perceived motives of others.

3.   Acceptance of diverse (deviant) behavior of others.

4.   Acceptance of distrust by others.

5.   Seeking of control over process rather than over people.

6.   Nonconformity to group opinion.

7.   Tentative offers of trust of others.

8.   Increased communication with others.

9.   Increased communication of one's personal opinions (value judgments).

10.   Increased positive affect (liking) for others.

The following *personality* dimensions appear to increase as a person increases his trust of other people:

1.   Feelings of personal adequacy as measured by Gough's Adjective Check List.

2.   Ability to work under stress as measured by the Taylor Manifest Anxiety Scale.

3.   Flexibility (less authoritarianism) as measured by the F Scale or by Rokeach's Dogmatism Scale.

It should be understood that in no sense does the writer view the "educated guesses" listed above as proven principles; they are suggested as bases for further research by all interested scholars.

SUGGESTED FURTHER READING

Brown, Roger, "Models of Attitude Change," in Roger Brown, E. Galanter, E. Hess, and G. Mandler, eds., *News Directions in Psychology.* New York: Holt, Rinehart Co., 1962.

Deutsch, Morton, "Trust and Suspicion," *Journal of Conflict Resolution,* II (December, 1958), 265–279. (See footnotes 1–4, 7, 8, 11.)

Egan, Gerard, *Encounter: Group Processes for Interpersonal Growth.* Belmont, California: Brooks/Cole Publishing Company, 1970.

Loomis, James L., "Communication, the Development of Trust and Cooperative Behavior," *Human Relations,* XII (November, 1959), 305–315. (See footnote 9.)

Newcomb, Theodore M., "An Approach to the Study of Communicative Acts," *Psychological Review,* LX (May, 1953), 393–404. (See footnote 5.)

Rogers, Carl R., *Client-Centered Therapy.* Boston: Houghton Mifflin, 1951. (See footnote 19.)

————, *On Becoming A Person.* Boston: Houghton Mifflin Company, 1961. (See footnote 20.)

Rokeach, Milton, *The Open and Closed Mind.* New York: Basic Books, 1960. (See footnote 14.)

When Angry Look Again!

Irving Lee

A lawn, a rabbit hutch, a much-loved rabbit hopping about free in the sun. Its owner, a little girl, has heard a noise that fills her with dismay. She rushes out to find that the terrier from next door has escaped into her garden . . . loud barkings, a horrifying scuffle. The inevitable is happening . . . she flings herself to the ground, for she cannot see that dreadful end.

Minutes pass, blackness, abysmal horror, when faintly a voice reaches her. "It's all right, Jennifer, the rabbit's safe." The child uncovers her face; slowly she approaches the hutch; no cry of joy; she turns away in contemplation. Five minutes later she is heard saying to herself . . .

"I must remember, always have a good look before you cry."—Innes H. Pease and Lucy H. Crocker, *The Peckham Experiment,* George Allen and Unwin, Ltd., 1943, p. 8.

"Make people a little less emotional, and you'll solve your discussion problems."

"Give me a group of men who won't let their emotions run away with them and we'll work anything out."

emotional behavior is expressed in many ways

"There's nothing to this human relations but emotion. When you lick man's emotions, you'll lick his communication difficulties, too."

These are the more extreme examples of views expressed over and over by both leaders and participants. They were unsolicited diagnoses of *the* cause and cure of the discussion problem.

I tried on twenty-six occasions to pin them down. What do you mean by emotion or emotional response? What does a man do when he is emotional? In general, they had two things in mind: (1) behavior that was excited, agitated, or vehement, and (2) expressions of outrage, anger, irritation, or resentment.

I was struck, however, by something else in these interviews. These people talked about the emotion factor with overtones of gloom and defeat. Several threw up their hands in the traditional "what's the use?" gesture. "People are going to give way to their emotions and that's that." "When a man is in the grip of his emotions it's impossible to reason with him." "If a man gets emotional, and he's bound to if the subject is important and if his interests are involved, what good is it to try to persuade him to become problem-centered?"

This was the voice of futility. It was also the suggestion of an impossible objective. We were being forced to think about a phenomenon which was defined in terms which made dealing with it a waste of time. Our informants seemed to say that emotionality was inevitable and impossible to cope with, on the one hand, and then, on the other, that it had to be corrected if group operations were to be made efficient.

Is there a way out of this impasse?

symptoms of anger

We had some rough conclusions to start with. Excited talking was a sign of interest in what was happening. A direct attempt to make a man quiet down was not always successful. He often became angry at that. Is there any indirect way of persuading or forcing a man to soft-pedal or stop his expression of anger? We could not find one. We saw that an angry man disrupts a group. He refuses to listen. He makes others angry. People think about his anger rather than about the problem. Occasionally, we saw a man kid another out of his irritation. Sometimes irritation could be softened by another's expression of friendship. But most of the time an angry man was not to be side-tracked. He usually had his say, and his way, too.

We were almost ready to give up when once again we saw Jon Stone in action. It is ironical, but he helped us find a way out of our impasse.

His group was considering the draft of a statement of company policy. He was his usual antagonistic, arrogant self. As the clock ticked off the minutes he became even more so. But this time we thought he had a point. The rest of the members seemed unable to concentrate on the paper before them. They kept drifting off to other topics. His irritation mounted every time he tried to bring them back to the statement. And then we had it! We had been missing the point. It wasn't the anger, as such, we had to deal with but the reason for the anger. Jon Stone's anger made sense. If there was justification for it why try to get rid of it? We had been looking at symptoms. Was there some infection behind the fever? The theoretical issue was now in the open. We had to deal not with every

dealing with reasons
for anger or emotion

show of anger but only with those which were unjustified. Could those be dissolved?

A POINT OF VIEW

What should a leader know about a man's emotionality and what should he do about it? A point of view which seemed to square with our understanding of the practical problem was worked out around the argument which follows.

Let us admit that a man is emotional. Let us also see that emotion is not something which merely comes and goes, but something that occurs whenever he is awake. He does more than feel, however. Alexis Carrel's insight is still a good one: "The man who thinks, observes and reasons, is, at the same time, happy or unhappy, disturbed or secure, stimulated or depressed by his appetites, his aversions, and his desires. The world, therefore, assumes a different visage, according to the affective and physiological states which are the moving background of consciousness during intellectual activity."[1] Feeling, in short, is not some occasional manifestation. It is there all the time. So is thinking.

We will not try to dodge Francis Bacon's assertion: "Numberless, in short, are the ways, and sometimes, imperceptible, in which the affections color and infect the understanding." An angry or frightened man will think differently from one who is amicable and secure.

a way of feeling goes with a way of thinking

Of course, emotions make a difference. But—have you ever wondered how the emotions come to be and when and why they become noticeable?

Consider this theory: A way of feeling goes with a way of thinking.

If you think something damaging is going to happen to you or those you love, and if you think you may not have the resources to ward off the damage, won't you feel fear and apprehension?

If you think that your well-being will continue or that danger is remote, and that your sources of strength are great enough to cope with danger if it should come nearer, won't you feel safe and confident?

If you think that what you are doing is important and useful and also appreciated, recognized, and adequately rewarded won't you feel interested, alert, enthusiastic?

If you think that someone is holding you up to ridicule, or is slighting or insulting you, or is making you "lose face," won't you feel angry, irritated, annoyed? (Such an analysis could be made of all the other patterns of thinking that go

[1] *Man, the Unknown,* Harper & Brothers, 1935, pp. 126–127.

with other patterns of feeling. Interested readers might well see how Aristotle analyzed the classic emotions in Book II of his *Rhetoric*.)

Feeling, in short, accompanies thinking. No thinking, no feeling. A certain mode of thinking, a certain mode of feeling. A kind of feeling, a kind of thinking.

> Suddenly I encounter my old enemy. Anger surges up in me; I strike out at him murderously; he raises his right hand— and then I see that it has all its fingers. My enemy had two missing. Because my mind can go through a process of thought, . . . I realize that here is a case of mistaken identity. My desire to kill drops from me and becomes instead a desire to make amends, to help. The change in the direction of emotion has been brought about by thought. . . .[2]

Angell thought something. He then felt anger. He thought anew. He then felt apologetic.

attempting to stop anger is not the answer

What are we trying to do in discussion? Would we stop men from feeling angry, afraid, confident, interested? Not at all. We want only to have them look at "the man's hand." How many fingers does it have?

This is by no means easy, because an angry man is far more likely to look to his anger than to the situation which set him off. He doesn't do this because it is instinctive or natural but, we think, because he has rarely been told to do anything else. So we tell him to do something else. "Stay angry—but look again at what you are responding to."

situations that set off anger must be examined

In our training classes we make a game of this. We deliberately try to persuade participants not to repress their anger but to add to it one thing more: *another look* at what they are angry at. "Stay angry," we say, "but look again, please, at the situation, the remark, the person. See if you are justified in being as angry as you are. Maybe the man has all his fingers."

This tactic is not designed to eliminate the anger, but to get the angry man to see if he has a sound basis for being so. If A purposefully insults B and B knows that it was done on purpose, B's anger makes sense. But if B merely surmises something in A's behavior, another look might change the direction of his thinking and his angry feeling.

anger often results from false assumptions about the situation

The most interesting result of this point of view is that we now believe that three times out of four a man becomes angry because he thinks he knows his enemy when in fact he doesn't. So often the presumed enemy has all his fingers. In

[2] Norman Angell, *The Steep Places,* Harper & Brothers, 1947, p. 111.

twenty-seven discussion interchanges in which one of the participants seemed angry, follow-up interviews with both revealed that nineteen contained elements in which someone became angry at his believing that he knew something that wasn't so. He was in those cases making assumptions about the situation. He was acting as if he knew when in fact he did not know. His anger was grounded on a guess.

The instruction was considered successful when a leader (and others) could be moved to say, "Now, B, before you really get going, how about looking to see if he has all his fingers."

leader and participants help emotional people examine facts in the situation

When they grew weary of the Angell anecdote we told them one about Blackie:

> Quick-tempered John Stuart Blackie, the celebrated Scottish professor, was unusually irritable at the opening of a college term.
>
> "Show your paper!" he commanded as the applicants for admission lined up at his desk. One lad held his a mite awkwardly and Prof. Blackie bellowed: "You little chap there, hold your paper properly. Not in your left hand, you loon, in your right!"
>
> The boy muttered something, but did not shift his paper.
>
> "The right hand, you loon!"
>
> Trembling and pale, the boy lifted his right arm, revealing a burned stump.
>
> The other students in the line howled and hissed at the irascible teacher, but Blackie had already jumped down from the platform to fling a strong arm about the boy's shoulder.
>
> "Eh, laddie, forgive me," said the gruff professor, fighting back tears of remorse. "I did not know, laddie."
>
> He turned a suffering face on the other boys. "I thank God He has given me gentlemen to teach—who call me to account when I go astray," he said.
>
> Three dozen boys grasped his hand. It was the most successful year in the great teacher's entire life.[3]

[3] The Rev. Philip Jerome Cleveland, "A Man of Class." Reprinted from October, 1947, *Coronet,* p. 45. Copyright, 1947, by Esquire, Inc.

SUGGESTED FURTHER READING

Lee, Irving J., *How to Talk with People.* New York: Harper and Brothers, Publishers, 1952.

————, "Making Phrases at Each Other," *Central States Speech Journal,* III (December, 1951), 11–14.

————, "Leadership Without Imposition," *Speech Teacher,* III (September, 1955), 3–5.

————, "General Semantics and Public Speaking," *Quarterly Journal of Speech,* XXVI (December, *1940*), *594.*

————, "General Semantics 1952," *Quarterly Journal of Speech,* XXXVIII (February, 1952), 1–12.

————, "Some Conceptions of Emotional Appeal in Rhetorical Theory," *Speech Monographs,* VI (1939), 66–86.

————, *Language Habits in Human Affairs.* New York: Harper and Brothers Co., 1941.

"The Black Bag"

John Keltner

On the first day of the Elements of Persuasion class in the spring quarter of 1967 at Oregon State University an event took place which was to change the lives of several people.* At that first session, a male student appeared in the class completely encased from head to feet in a black cloth bag, commonly known as a stone bag. This extraordinary event had not been planned as part of the course. After talking with the instructor about the course during registration, the student had decided to try an experiment with his fellow class members to see how they would react when he appeared in the black stone bag which he had received as a gift. The instructor agreed and explained later, "I'm enough of a nut to try anything once." The experience turned out to be more than a casual incident.

Now, how do you think a class would react to the presence of such a figure—a black bag with a human being inside it? According to reports, the members of the class for almost four weeks of the eleven-week term outwardly *ignored* the Black Bag. However, the instructor noted "strange looks" being exchanged between students and directed toward the Black Bag. He also noted that there were always at least two seats between the Black Bag and anyone else. Inside the bag, the young man became more and more irritated and "up tight" in response to the manner in which he was being treated, so one day he sat next to a young man about twice his weight. The husky young man reacted by poking the Black Bag with an umbrella saying "What do you want? I didn't do anything to you." When the Black Bag did not answer, hostility and defensive behavior increased; and with an angry "Get away from me!" his adversary got up and moved to another part

---

*This brief résumé of a series of events that took place in the classroom of Dr. Charles S. Goetzinger at Oregon State University in the spring of 1967 was reviewed by Dr. Goetzinger and is published here with his approval.

of the room. (Keep in mind that no one other than the instructor and the student inside the bag knew the identity of the person inside.)

Finally an assigned speech was due. Everyone in the class had spoken but the Black Bag. He rose in his place and stood mute for three minutes. Hostility became intense. Students reported later that they felt he had not met the norms of the class.

Tension mounted and reactions became explosive, even though the students in the class refused to discuss the Black Bag inside the classroom. The instructor gave leads for discussing the situation; and he noted later, "They [the students in the class] just absolutely refused to even consider that there was anything going on in the class. . . . They just weren't about to even concede he was there."

A drastic change occurred when one of the class members gave a speech in which he said, "I don't know what your problem is; the Black Bag isn't bothering *me.*" He then spent eight minutes pointing out how the Black Bag *was* disturbing him. In the process, he revealed that he and a friend had been following the Black Bag in an attempt to discover more about him. In fact, he had collected quite a record of things he had observed. This broke the log jam, the subject was finally out in the open, and the class began to examine its own behavior and feelings.

More people started to follow the Black Bag, and he naturally became more of a celebrity on campus. The general tone of the class discussions, according to the instructor, was one of wishing the Black Bag had never appeared and not knowing what to do about him since he had. "We found out later that the biggest frustration was trying to explain to the outside world what was going on," the instructor said.

Once the log jam of noncommunication about the situation was broken, the class began to work out its problem of its Black Bag. Subsequent speech assignments brought the Black Bag to the front where he tried to explain what he was doing and, of great importance, how he felt about the way people responded to him. He responded to questions of his classmates, and an intense and significant dialog began. His classmates went from hating him to loving him to partially accepting him.

Led by the instructor, the class examined why it had responded to the Black Bag as it had. This analysis opened up many avenues of the effect of norms and attitudes upon people as individuals and groups. Here was an unknown. The characteristic behavior of most groups toward the unknown is fear. Fear is expressed by such behaviors as hostility and avoidance. The class began to see how it had followed these patterns quite unconsciously.

The class developed a protective attitude toward the Black Bag as a result of the curiosity of the society that existed outside the classroom. Naturally, such a bizarre event commands some attention. Once the press became aware of the matter, newspapers, television, and radio were full of the situation. At one very critical time, members of the press approached the instructor for permission to attend the class while the Black Bag was there. The instructor referred the matter to the class to make the decision. After some discussion, the class decided it didn't want any intruder in the classroom but agreed to publication of a story about the situation. A well-written story did appear. Then another newspaper published a sarcastic editorial to which a class member responded with a biting letter in defense of the Black Bag. Soon national syndicates became interested. Due to pressures by people outside the classroom, it seemed almost necessary to allow the press in. And so, after another request, the class decided that on a given day the press would be allowed into the classroom provided that the regular class activity would not be disturbed.

On the scheduled day, the press arrived early in the morning for the class, which was to begin at eleven o'clock. Other classes scheduled for that room during the earlier parts of the morning were moved so that the press could have time to set up recording, camera, and lighting equipment. The scene, when the class began to assemble shortly before eleven o'clock, was very much like the mob scenes at a national event or after a boxing match. The small room was filled with high-intensity lights, three or four tripods with large cameras on them were placed at points in the room. Eight or nine cameramen with hand cameras were milling around taking pictures of anything, everything, and everyone. Microphones were taped on the tables in front of each chair. Amplifiers and large recorders were set up in the back of the room. In the hall outside the classroom, nearly a hundred students and faculty gathered to see what was going on. Through this screen and into this arena the members of the class sifted. Students coming late to class had to crawl under cables, tables, and tripods to get to their seats. A copy of a San Francisco paper with big black headlines about the Black Bag was shoved into a student's hands by a reporter, and the student was ordered to be reading it while cameras rolled and clicked. One student was forcibly directed to crawl under a tripod in order to get to his regular seat.

Obviously, the reality of press coverage was not what the class had expected or what the press had promised. Everyone in the class was uncomfortable and angry, even the instructor. One member of the class said that he was ready to go on with the regular class work for the day, which was to give a five-sentence speech that would get some specific action from an audience. The instructor agreed, and the student stood up in the glare of the hot lights and began to speak. The essence of his comments was that he felt the press would not report the situation fairly or honestly, that it viewed the whole situation as a joke which it definitely was not, that he did not like the intrusion of the press into the classroom, and he was *leaving.* Whereupon he forced his way out of the room. This caused some scurrying of the assembled onlookers, during which time a girl student rose to her feet. When the noise subsided, she gave her speech in much the same vein. At that point, the instructor scratched his head, slowly arose from his chair, picked up his books and papers and also left. Whereupon all but three or four of the class followed after.

The three or four students who stayed attempted to answer questions for their classmates. Downstairs in the professor's office, the rest of the class gathered with serious, disturbed intensity. Here the Black Bag was finally accepted as a human entity in the same crisis as they. He was not separate from them then. The students were mad, the instructor was mad, the press was mad. The students and the instructor felt that the media had violated every principle of professional ethics by violating the agreements made with the class and the instructor, and because of this feeling they wanted nothing more to do with any media. The husky young man who had jabbed the Black Bag with an umbrella was one of those who stayed behind to defend him to the press.

With deep concern, the group in the instructor's office began to examine what had happened to them and why they had retreated in such panic. The discussion was serious, intense, probing, and each student there began to discover things about himself and his fellow human beings that he had never known before. A few of the press representatives were allowed to eavesdrop on this discussion, and they were shocked and sobered by the depth and intensity of the students' discussion. The seriousness of the situation to the students so concerned one member of the national press that he arranged to stay several days to talk with the students and to get the feel of the actual situation. The result was a quite sympathetic article in a national magazine.

The following weeks were filled with stories about the Black Bag. But none of them came from the class or its members. After the incident with the press, the classroom door was closed to outsiders with the full support of the department chairman. Nevertheless, as the Black Bag continued to come to class, hordes of students gathered daily outside the building and in the lobby to watch his coming and going. Significant was the fact that the campus student community, in part, after its first reaction of hostility and laughter and after the national press had covered the event so widely, began to refer to the Black Bag as "*Our* Black Bag." Even one of the local barbers commented several times to his customers about "Our Black Bag," while shaking his head in puzzlement.

Anticipation rose high as the end of the quarter approached. Would the man in the Black Bag reveal himself? Attempts by the press to find out who he was even went so far as to try to get copies of the official class roll from the chairman of the department. When the class heard of this, it tightened its own security measures. Many times, the Black Bag was asked if he would reveal himself, and each time he answered honestly that he really didn't know.

The executive director of a very popular national network TV show tried to negotiate with the Black Bag to reveal his identity on that show. Although the network offered an astounding reward to the Black Bag to reveal himself, he turned down the offer. (Earlier he had received $50 from a regional radio station for a telephone interview which he had immediately donated to the library to purchase books of poetry.)

The day of the final exam arrived. Again the press was very much in evidence, although the classroom itself was protected and was not invaded. Again cameras and microphones were hooked up in the lobby outside the classroom. Outside the building between 500 and 1,000 students and townspeople gathered to view the event. The Black Bag entered the classroom, the door was closed, and the exam period passed. When the final bell rang, the door opened and the Black Bag came out and was whisked away by bodyguards provided by the department and class members. He never did reveal himself to any other than the instructor, a few friends, and a few of the department officials, who were sworn to secrecy. To this day few people know who was in that bag and many of those who were directly involved—such as class members, reporters, teachers—have said they would just as soon *not* know.

The incident of the Black Bag is a real one. The class, the press, the university community, the local community, and other groups exhibited behavior that tells a great deal about the way people alone, in audiences, in mobs, and in societies behave. The characteristic reactions of a group under pressure—retreat, fear, hostility, protective and defensive behaviors; the significance of feedback by nonverbal means; the manner in which the class and surrounding community cultures moved from rejection to eventual acceptance of the Black Bag—are patterns of interaction that emerged with unexpected impact.

ACTIVITIES

1. Observe a brief communication interaction between two people. Discuss the purpose of each communicator (as you see it). Was each achieving his purpose? Can you explain the successes and failures in terms of the principles stated by Gibb, Giffin, Kelly, or Lee?

2. Team up with someone and role play for your class the communication event you observed. Ask other members of the class to suggest changes which would have improved the chances for communication.

3. Consider the Keller and Brown concept of an interpersonal ethic. Do you accept it as one that you can live by? Try to be conscious of all of your communication interaction for 48 hours. To what extent were you accepting of other's rights to disagree? Reformulate your own ethical concept into a statement that you can accept for a basis of communicative interaction.

4. In his essay, "Defensive Communication," Gibb maintains that defensive behavior reduces efficiency in communication. Try a two-day experiment with one person who is not a member of your class and with whom you have had little, if any, interaction. On the first day, involve your subject in a conversation in which you insert the types of behavior that Gibb said would create a defensive climate. On the second day, exhibit the types of behavior which Gibb said would create a supportive climate. Which conversation was more fruitful in terms of communication efficiency? In which conversation was there more trust? To what extent did defensive reactions created the first day carry over to the second conversation?

5. Using Kelly's suggestions for improved listening, test your own listening ability. Select a day in class when speeches are presented and without taking any notes during the speeches, attempt to reconstruct the central and supporting ideas of each speech after the class is over. How often did you find it difficult to listen empathically? Was empathic listening more difficult on some types of messages than on others?

EPILOGUE

Summary of Key Speech Communication Concepts

Rhetoric is the rationale of informative and suasory spoken or written discourse.—Bryant

Rhetorical function is the function of adjusting ideas to people and of people to ideas.—Bryant

Communication is a word that describes the process of creating a meaning.—Barnlund

The aim of communication is to increase the number and consistency of our meanings within the limits set by patterns of evaluation that have proven successful in the past, our emerging needs and drives, and the demands of the physical and social setting of the moment.—Barnlund

Communication is a circular, irreversible and unrepeatable, complex process involving the total personality.—Barnlund

Communication is the process through which one person formulates a meaning and induces a second person to formulate approximately the same meaning.—Trent and Trent (Process)

Meaning does not exist distinct from people; people create meanings according to the way they perceive reality.—Trent and Trent (Process)

Words, like other signals, have no meaning; meanings are assigned to signals by people and communication depends upon the source and receiver approaching agreement on the meaning.—Trent and Trent (Process)

Intrapersonal communication can ultimately have a significant effect on an individual because of the future commitments it may make for him, the choices it may close to him, and the image it portrays to which he must adjust.—Trent and Trent (Process)

People are not capable of being completely rational, but tolerance for the views of others is encouraged by accepting that man is rational to the extent of his capabilities.—Scott

The basic materials of discourse are (1) ethical and moral values and (2) information relevant to these.—Wallace

Whether something is considered desirable depends upon one's motives, goals, or ends.—Wallace

Things that are morally obligatory and acts that are praiseworthy seem to acquire their meaning and force in the regard that others have for us.—Wallace

The language of practical discourse bears meanings that testify to man's attempts to identify and solve problems.—Wallace

Rhetoric is the art of finding and effectively presenting good reasons.—Wallace

A speaker who wants understanding or acceptance of his ideas must learn to construct messages in terms of his audience's value system.—Trent (Values)

It is the listener who judges what is good and it is the listener to whom the effective speaker adapts.—Trent (Values)

Values are the factor which will determine the choice an individual will make when he must choose between courses of action. His selection of a course of action will reflect his judgment of the situation and an application of his values.—Trent (Values)

The values of listeners, whether as individuals or as individuals in a group, are revealed in their acts. And if we study their acts we can determine the operational value system which controls behavior.—Trent (Values)

Values are the key to human behavior. We decide what actions we will take on the basis of what we believe will create good results. As we examine alternatives, we attempt to determine results of each. Then, according to our individual value systems, we decide whether those results are good or bad. If our value system labels the results as bad, we try to avoid them.—Trent (Values)

As a principle of language behavior, style is evinced when a grammatical statement departs from the lexical or syntactical norms for the conception being phrased.—Carpenter

Style is personal and reflective of a man's singular condition.—Carpenter

The notion of style presumes a relative independence of matter from manner. That is, any manipulation which changes the meaning intended by the utterance is an alteration of content rather than form and is not in the realm of style.—Carpenter

In matters of arranging materials in primacy order or in recency order, there is little evidence to support the existence of a general law of primacy or recency. Rather primacy and/or recency effects appear to depend on other variables in the communication setting.—Anderson

Nonsalient, controversial topics, interesting subject matter and highly familiar issues tend toward primacy. Salient topics, uninteresting subject matter and moderately unfamiliar issues tend to yield recency.—Anderson

The impact of a one or two sided message appears to be influenced by the audience's prior attitude, education, familiarity with the topic, awareness of the persuader's intent, and the likelihood that they will be exposed to competing persuasive appeals.—Anderson

It is inappropriate and misleading to speak of *ethos* as we speak of logic and emotion—as a basic element of the communicative interaction—until such time as an "ethical" physiological base can be established.—Rosenthal

There is a real difference between the phenomenon denoted by the broad concept of *ethos* and the casually used classification, "ethical appeal."—Rosenthal

Ethos is an end product of the combined logical and emotional responses—that is, a specific type of persuasion, *in toto.*—Rosenthal

Persuasion may be classified either as personal or nonpersonal, depending upon whether the speaker's personality or his message becomes the primary object of value response. If the reaction to the content is direct (if the message itself activates the dominant value response) the process may be designated nonpersonal persuasion, regardless of the source. However, if the message functions primarily as a medium by which the speaker's personality activates the dominant value response, the process may be categorized as personal persuasion.—Rosenthal

Whether persuasion is personal or nonpersonal is determined by the configuration of the communication: the relationship between the listener and (1) the speaker, (2) the environment, and (3) the message, at a given period of time and in a given place.—Rosenthal

The impact of evidence on decision making depends on variables in the speech situation, on the nature of the evidence, on the relation of the evidence and the assertion it supports to the listener, and how much faith the listener has in the speaker.—Dresser

Including good evidence has little, if any, impact on immediate audience attitude change or source credibility if the source of the message is initially perceived to be high-credible.—McCroskey

Including good evidence has little, if any, impact on immediate audience attitude change if the message is delivered poorly.—McCroskey

Including good evidence has little, if any, impact on immediate audience attitude change or source credibility if the audience is familiar with the evidence prior to exposure to the source's message.—McCroskey

Including good evidence may significantly increase immediate audience attitude change and source credibility when the source is initially perceived to be moderate-to-low-credible, when the message is well delivered, and when the audience has little or no prior familiarity with the evidence included or similar evidence.—McCroskey

Including good evidence may significantly increase sustained audience attitude change regardless of the course's initial credibility, the quality of the delivery of the message, or the medium by which the message is transmitted.—McCroskey

The medium of transmission of a message has little, if any, effect on the functioning of evidence in persuasive communication.—McCroskey

The role of the speech critic is to observe, analyze, describe, evaluate, and then use his results to formulate new principles or to confirm or revise existing theory.—Erickson

The most useful form of critical analysis may be whatever happens to be most useful.—Erickson

The role of the speech critic is to help form the ideas, habits, and values of society by criticizing the speeches of those who actively participate in the formulations.—Hillbruner

The speech critic's commitment to an interdisciplinary approach will make him more useful to American civilization.—Hillbruner

Traditional critics and experimentalists must be willing to work together using all available methodologies in charting the rhetorical process in the human condition.—McGuckin

Experimental research provides a useful supplement to the critic's traditional methodology but not a replacement. An eclectic approach is needed for obtaining maximum insight.—Trent and Trent (Nixon)

We can hypothesize that the characteristics of broadcast apologia rhetoric are 1) a short, intense, decisive clash of views, 2) the speaker will not limit himself to defensive remarks and may use some form of invective,

3) evidence may be used in only the middle third of the speech, and 4) no new arguments will be assembled.—Rosenfield

Songs of social action not only are a part of the rhetoric of the movements in which they are used, but either were, or have the potential for becoming rhetorical vehicles in themselves.—Kosokoff and Carmichael

We have emerged into a modern rhetoric that has reached beyond public address and propaganda to include the whole range of oral communication without sufficient consideration for what the corresponding new ethic might look like.—Keller and Brown

A's communication is ethical to the extent that it accepts B's responses; it is unethical to the extent to which it develops hostility toward B's responses, or in some way tries to subjugate B.—Keller and Brown

An interpersonal ethic may have more to do with the attitude of the speaker and listener toward each other than with the elements of the message. It may concern itself more with loyalty to the person with whom one is in communication than to rationality or cosmic truth.—Keller and Brown

Emphatic listening occurs when the person participates in the spirit or feeling of his environment as a communication receiver. His primary interest is to become fully and accurately aware of what is going on.—Kelly

The differences between empathic and deliberative listening are primarily motivational. Both listeners seek the same objective: accurate understanding of the communication from another. The deliberative listener first critically analyzes and then tries to understand. The empathic listener first tries to understand and then analyzes.—Kelly

Studies indicate that when persons know that their listening comprehension is being tested, differences between individuals are primarily matters of general mental ability; when they do not know their listening performance is being tested, differences are due to personality differences (including motivation to listen) as well as general mental ability.—Kelly

Most communication problems arise either because of participant inattention (poor motivation), or because of general mental inabilities—not because of anything that can by itself be called "listening ability."—Kelly

In terms of listening theory, it is far more important to stress empathic, rather than deliberative, listening in discussion. This observation in no way depreciates the need for education and practical experience in critical analysis, debate, general semantics—or in any of the various mental skills brought into play while listening. But it is a mistake to consider these skills in themselves as listening, since this viewpoint suggests that the listener's analysis is only one part of the total receiving process.—Kelly

Successful participation in discussion requires your understanding of others, more than your speaking contributions. It is important not to be distracted 'by your own note taking, mental review of main points, or critical argumentative "comeback."—Kelly

If we are to make fundamental improvements in communication, we must make changes in interpersonal relationships. One type of alteration is reducing degree of defensiveness.—Gibb

The defensive behavior of one person tends to create similarly defensive postures in others; and, if unchecked, the ensuing circular response becomes increasingly destructive.—Gibb

As a person becomes more and more defensive, he becomes less and less able to perceive accurately the motives, the values, and the emotions of a message source.—Gibb

The more "supportive" or defense-reductive the climate is, the more the receiver is able to concentrate upon the structure, content, and the cognitive meanings of the message.—Gibb

Trust in the communication process can be defined as reliance upon the communication behavior of another person in order to achieve a desired but uncertain objective in a risky situation.—Giffin

Personal trust is influenced by certain variables, and trust in turn influences certain variables. Thus trust is a mediating variable, produced by behavior which can be changed somewhat, and functionally related to desirable behavior in groups.—Giffin

Feeling accompanies thinking. No thinking, no feeling. A certain mode of thinking will accompany a certain mode of feeling; a kind of feeling will also accompany a kind of thinking.—Lee

It is not useful to stop an individual's anger, but rather to re-channel the anger to the facts of the situation that touched off the emotion.—Lee